# GCSE ISLAM–
## The
## Do-It-Yourself
## Guide

*Also by Ruqaiyyah Waris Maqsood*

Living Islam: Treading the Prophet of Ideal

The Beautiful Commands of Allah

The Muslim Prayer Encyclopaedia

The Beautiful Promises of Allah

The Muslim Marriage Guide

A Basic Dictionary of Islam

Muslim Travel Guide

After Death, Life!

# GCSE ISLAM–
## The Do-It-Yourself Guide

Ruqaiyyah Waris Maqsood

First published 2002
© Goodword Books 2002

GOODWORD BOOKS
1, Nizamuddin West Market
New Delhi 110 013
Tel. 435 1128, 435 5454, 435 6666
Fax: 435 7333, 435 7980
e-mail: info@goodwordbooks.com
www.goodwordbooks.com

Printed in India

قَالَ رَبِّ اشْرَحْ لِي صَدْرِيٓ ۙ
وَيَسِّرْ لِيٓ أَمْرِيٓ ۙ

*'O Lord,*
*expand my knowledge,*
*and make my task easy for me:*

Qur'an 20:25-26

# *Preface*

The motivation for writing this Work-book partly arose from the distance-learning courses in GCSE*, A and AS Level Religious Studies (Islam) started by the Association of Muslim Researchers (AMR) in 1996. These excellent courses provide Course-Tutors to guide and provide support to students through the course eg. by telephone contact, written feedback on assignments etc. The GCSE syllabus used in the AMR distance-learning course is exactly the same as that used in this book i.e. the EdExcel, formerly the University of London (ULEAC) syllabus leading to nationally recognised qualifications. Students on the AMR GCSE distance-learning course pay a small fee for the engagement of a Course Tutor and are quite likely to be recommended to purchase this Work-book for the course. For more information, AMR can be contacted at the following address : AMR, PO Box 8715, London SE23 3ZB, UK. Tel: +44 (0) 181 699 1887. E-mail: amr@amrnet.demon.co.uk

However, any student wishing to study for home without paying for a tutor will find that this course-book, together with the set books by Sr. Ruqaiyyah (i.e. 'World Religions', Islam-Heinemann Press and 'Dictionary of Islam' — Stanley Thornes or 'The Basic Dictionary of Islam' — Goodword Press) covers adequately and gives all the information you need to know to Do-it-Yourself, either for the EdExcel Syllabus or any other UK syllabus in Islam.

---

*GCSE means the 'General Certificate of Secondary Education.

# Contents

# Letter From Sr. Ruqaiyyah

Asalaam aleikum wa rahmatullah, wa barakatuh.

Welcome, thrice welcome!

So, you wish to take a GCSE in Islam? Good for you. This exam is of just the same credit in the eyes of the State as all the other GCSEs you could take, and if you happen to be a Muslim already, it may be a particularly useful and valid qualification open to you.

Nobody thinks it odd that English people do GCSEs in English, or that Christians do GCSEs in Christianity (in their RE exams). Up until now, it has been possible to study Islam on its own for half a GCSE, but now, at last, with the Edexcel 1478/9 Syllabus, we have a GCSE that is based on Islam alone, and does not require knowledge of any other religion. It is a GCSE that any Muslim could do. Of course, it is open to non-Muslims as well, but a practising Muslim might for once just get the edge.

However, you may not be able to do it at school - there may be nobody there qualified to teach it, or no room available on the timetable. Up until Syllabus 1478 it was very difficult for people outside school to do any GCSE as an 'external student', because coursework was required to be handed in for official marking throughout the study. This is still the case for every other Syllabus I know of, including Edexcel Syllabus 1479 which tests exactly the same subjects as Syllabus 1478. So, if you prefer this system, it is still available.

The beauty of Syllabus 1478 is that it requires no coursework to be handed in separately; the full 100% of marks are available on the day, through the exam. Therefore, anyone can have a go - not only you, but your Mum, even your Grandad if he wants to! GCSE students do not have to be teenagers - there is no age limit. People drawing their Old Age pensions sit GCSEs sometimes, just out of interest and for personal satisfaction. Any folks who have a reasonable knowledge of Islam, and can express themselves well in English could have a go.

This exam is not for those who cannot write and speak English adequately, however. And it would come as a shock to those not used to the notion of testing your ability to think for yourself and argue different points of view. You don't score many marks if you just put down 'because Allah ordered it' for every answer!

If you think about it - there is no reason why every able student attending a madrassah should not have a go at this, if they want to—they would probably pass well. I would be thrilled to see every madrassah entering students for this exam, and giving youngsters a chance to gain a GCSE as well as their mosque Islamic studies certificates. Incidentally, there is no reason why students should not also have a go at GCSEs in Arabic, Urdu, Turkish or Sylhetti, or any other language they can already speak, if it is available. Just think of that ––two extra GCSEs in subjects you may not have realized were available. At my school, I had one lad who put in for Arabic, without ever attending one lesson (there was no teacher). He passed with an 'A' grade, a distinction. How come? He came from Egypt.

I've tried, through my books and this course, to give you the chance to see how it is done, and have a go. All you need to find out is where there is a centre that can enter you, and get your application in at the appropriate time. If you can't find out from your local school, write to Edexcel for information. It may even be possible for your own mosque to qualify as a centre - again, Edexcel will explain the rules. For my own students in Hull, Yorkshire, one of the local schools that has some Muslim pupils has made itself available for all 'sitters' to go and take the exam together there - even though some of the students are in their forties, and only three of them actually go to that school as pupils. If you ask, you will surely find.

What have you got to lose? Nothing except the cost of the books and the exam entry fee. The three books together will cost you around £20, and exam entry fee at school is usually around £16; at a sixth-form college it can be around £40. Pupils at the school generally get free entry.

Supposing you fail? Never mind - you will have had good experience and practice, and you can try again as many times as you wish.

This workbook, along with my two coursebooks, covers everything you will need for Syllabus 1478/9. As far as I know, there is no other book that offers this guide. I am looking forward to the day when thousands of Muslims try for this GCSE. It might even make the authorities find time in the State schools for study, who knows?

God bless you, and bring you to every success,
Your friend and sister,

**Ruqaiyyah**

PS: If you do go to school, and you are attending the compulsory RE lessons on your timetable, it might be possible for you to do this study in that time, if your teacher agrees. It could be worth asking!

PPS: If you are doing any other syllabus that involves Islam, this course will cover everything you need to know for that too, and more.

*Section One*

# PRELIMINARIES

# *Preliminaries*

## 1. THE SYLLABUS

If you are about to take on the challenge of studying for the GCSE in Islam, the one most important thing to do is to make a close examination of the SYLLABUS.

This is not the exam paper, but it gives the full outline of all the subjects and topics from which the questions in your examination will be taken.

The exam questions you will have to answer are kept a careful secret until you actually enter the exam room. The examiner may ask you anything he/she likes, so long as it has been included on the syllabus. If you spend time studying any aspect of Islam (and there are many more, of course) that are not on this syllabus, you will have gained knowledge (and all credit to you); but it will NOT HELP YOU TO PASS THIS EXAM, because no questions will be asked about those topics. If the examiner asks about any topic NOT on the syllabus, they can be challenged for unfair conduct.

You will find the full Syllabus, followed by a close analysis of it, starting on p. 218.

If you want any other information on the rationale, aims and explanations of how the course is marked may be obtained from the publications department of Edexcel Foundation, Stewart House, 32, Russell Square, London, WCIB 5DN. (Customer Care Tel. No.0171 383 4500).

If you successfully work through all the units presented in the study section of this book, you will have covered every aspect mentioned on that Syllabus.

This workbook is specially intended to fit Edexcel Syllabus 1478, (or 1479 - the Option including coursework during the year); but any student studying for any other exam in Islam will find the work covers their syllabus too.

You will find specimen exam papers for Syllabus 1478 starting on p. 236.

Specimens of a few other exams, for comparison, start on p. 248.

## 2. THE COURSE BOOKS

The worksheets in this study-book are based on the following two GCSE books, plus the relevant passages in the Qur'an:

Examining Religions: Islam by Ruqaiyyah Waris Maqsood

Islam: A Dictionary by Ruqaiyyah Waris Maqsood

'Examining Religions: Islam', Ruqaiyyah Waris Maqsood, Heinemann Educational Press, ISBN 0.435.30319.8

'Islam: a Dictionary', Ruqaiyyah Waris Maqsood, Stanley Thornes, ISBN 0.7487.2560.1

You do not need to speak or read Arabic for this course.

(There is no reason, of course, why you should not study for your GCSE in Islam from other books. There are many to choose from. However, the worksheets given in this book refer to specific pages and details in the two course-books named above, and are meaningless without those two books).

## 3. HIGHLY RECOMMENDED FOR EXTRA READING

One of the main difficulties for Muslim students studying in English is that there are few books on the market in English that cover the moral and ethical topics demanded by the Syllabus 1478/9 that have been written by Muslim authors.

However, there are many good books on the market that deal with these issues written for the 'People of the Book' (ie Jews and Christians). Some of these are very useful. They give general background knowledge of all the topics, which you can compare to the Islamic point of view. You may totally agree with their points, or you may find it gives good ammunition for an argument.

Highly recommended are the Heinemann books:

'Contemporary Moral Issues', Joe Jenkins, Heinemann, ISBN 0.435.30311.2

'Moral Issues in Six Religions" six authors, Heinemann, ISBN 0.435.30299.x

These books can be ordered from any bookshop.

## 4. THINGS TO BE SORTED OUT

### (i) The Time-Span

Be ruthlessly realistic. Consult a calendar and work out how long you've got, and think through all the other things you have to do in the same space of time.

Year 11 at school may not be the best time; you may already have seven or more subjects to worry about.

Remember that the clever, motivated students who intend to gain academic success think nothing of doing at least two hours homework every day. Some do more.

### (ii) Things Happen

You will not be able to work every day, or even every week. Plans go wrong. People get ill, relatives and friends die. People move house. Parents get divorced. Visitors arrive. Don't panic. Just keep on chugging along, and if you get a 'good flow', go with it. Do as much as is comfortable for you. Remember, once a section is done, it's done and you don't have to do it again.

### (iii) The Vital Dates

Your official entry for the GCSE MUST be done in January.

Sometimes a late entry is allowed, but you have to pay extra.

If you are doing the early course-work option 1479, your work must be marked by your tutor and sent away to the examiner at the start of May. You should have finished it by April, and handed it in.

The exam will be in June.

You will get the results in August.

You can try again - until you are 100 years old or more if you wish. There's no age limit.

## (iv) The Official Necessities

You have to book in at a special centre, one that has students sitting London Board examinations. With a bit of luck, this could be your own school. The first thing to do is ask, and check this out.

If your school does this Board, they will either pay for your entry, if you are lucky, or charge you a fee as an 'external entry' student, or 'private candidate'.

If your school does NOT do this Board, they may have the addresses of local schools or colleges that do. The person to ask is the teacher in charge of exams in your school. If they don't know, they should 'know a person who does'. Otherwise, telephone the London Board direct to find your nearest centre - 0171 383 4500.

A sixth form college will charge a higher exam entrance fee than a school. You have to make sure your entry goes in. This is your responsibility. If your entry has not gone in, you can't just turn up and sit the exam. You will be given a number.

## (v) Making Your Own Work Time-Table

This course is divided into 76 units, following the 76 units in the GCSE text-book on Islam published by Heinemann. The units are not all of the same length.

If you worked at the rate of one unit each week, it would obviously take you 76 weeks to complete.

There are only 52 weeks in a year.

If you decide to work only in school term time, you usually have around 14 weeks in the Autumn term, and around 10-12 in the Spring term. By the summer term, you are virtually into the exams - they start around halfway through May.

WORK OUT YOUR
OWN TIME-TABLE
CAREFULLY.

If you do two units a week, it will take you 38 weeks. You can, of course, start on this course at any time that suits you, and work much faster than that. Many might like to start it just after they finish their school summer exams, and get the bulk of it completed during the summer vacation.

How much you do, and when, and the speed at which you work - is up to you.

## 5. SNAGS

### (i) You Don't Speak or Write good English

This will make a big difference. Only you can do something about this. If you are going to live and work in an English-speaking society and want to be well educated, you MUST become as fluent as possible in English. Remember, many people with parents who can't speak English at all well end up even better than English people at their own language!

### (ii) You are over-confident

You think you know it all already. Be a bit more humble. This is an academic test, and not just vague 'general knowledge'. The cleverest people know that they know very little, and keep on studying and finding things out all their lives. And even if you

DO know everything, you do not necessarily have good essay-writing ability, or self-expression.

### (iii) You are too religious

It's worth repeating - this is an academic test and not a judgement on your personal life, standards, morals, prayer practice, or anything else. It's very annoying, but sometimes the most naughty and non-believing people can score very highly on tests of religious knowledge and understanding!

Don't forget, until very recently nearly all the students in the UK who did a GCSE in Islam were not even Muslims. We're trying to change that - but it is not an issue that will make any difference to you.

Sometimes very saintly, religious people fall into the trap of only repeating 'formulas' or answers they have learned 'parrot-fashion' - things they think will please Allah, please the Imam, or please their families. Remember that neither Allah, nor the Imam, nor your families will be marking your answers.

Your answers are confidential - your own teacher, Imam or family may not see them, except in highly special circumstances. Allah may well know what you have written, but He is not marking the paper.

Nearly all questions on GCSE papers require a student to outline more than one point of view and then argue a case. If your answer to a question 'Why?' is a blunt 'Because Allah forbade it', you may well be right, but you will not score more than one point, and will throw away the other points available. You have to THINK.

Some Muslims have a 'chip on their shoulder' against the 'Evil West', and despise their dear teachers and examiners who are trying to help them, who will no doubt have all sorts of faults and weaknesses. Be more generous, and grateful for their help.

Be warned - THIS IS NOT A TEST OF YOUR OWN GOODNESS or LIFE, but of your KNOWLEDGE and UNDER-STANDING and ABILITY TO REASON AND EVALUATE.

### (iv) You always waffle and write too much

Remember the GOLDEN RULE - answer the question, the whole question, and nothing but the question. The paper tells you what the marks are for. There are no marks available for anything not asked for.

## (v) You never write enough

Try harder. Write more.

## (vi) You have no time to study

If you want to do this GCSE, you have to make time; and, as the Prophet recommended, let your practice be regular. If you have good general knowledge of Islam and are clever, it is possible to just walk in and sit the exam without all the study - but the more study you do, the higher your marks will probably be. It doesn't usually pay to be over-confident.

## (vii) You have no place to study in

You may need to train your parents, or get your family organised. If your parents were not academics in their time, they will probably have no idea of what you will be going through. They may be supportive, if you are lucky, or they may not understand at all.

The biggest problems are parents interrupting you (usually for jobs), and other children interrupting you. Be fair to your parents - try to get your jobs done too, and don't let them down. It is not really fair for a mother to pick up a whole load of extra work simply because you wish to achieve something. You should not be achieving it at her expense!

If you really cannot work at home, try staying on after school, try the public library, or find a quiet friend or relative.

## (viii) You keep losing things

Get organised. Your work is worth more than gold. Hopefully you will have got for yourself all the paper and equipment suggested to make the best presentation of your work. Value it. At least, keep it all in a special file, or a cardboard box properly labelled.

Hide it from marauding toddlers, pets seeking a cosy resting-place, or mothers who clear up too much. (Under the bed or on top of a cupboard are good places). Do not let greasy fingers get near it. Don't risk putting a cup of tea or other liquid near it - someone is bound to tip it over.

## 6. PRACTICAL ADVICE, AND 'ON-GOING' IDEAS

This section gives suggestions and encouragement for practical ideas to build up your knowledge and achievement as you go along.

It suggests several things to start now, which will gradually build up into collections that will add to your Knowledge and Understanding, and help you gain more marks.

- Instant revision tests
- collection of key texts
- press-file
- fashion boutique
- artifact collection.

(i) When you do the 'fact' questions, if you take the trouble to divide your paper down the middle and write out the questions on one side and your answers on the other side of the paper, it gives you a ready-made series of tests to help you revise. You could get someone to

ask you the questions, or you could cover the answers and test yourself. Don't write all the questions out first, though, some of the answers need more than one line.

Don't forget - if you can get a 'volunteer' to help you, it will help that person to learn too, and may spur them on to have a go at the exam themselves.

(ii) Some of the work involves copying out key verses or sayings. You could do this just as part of your normal work on your normal paper, or you could make something of it. You could make a lovely set of index cards or postcards with these texts on. Some could even be framed, and go up on a wall. An 'Id gift for Auntie?

(iii) Always put headings to your work sections; write them very clearly, and underline them, or make sure they stand out in some way or another. This helps a great deal when revising.

(iv) Keep a press-file. Cut out and collect any press-cuttings or magazine articles that crop up concerning Islam, mosques, Islamic politics, moral issues, general articles that give food for thought on such issues as abortion, surrogacy, euthanasia, the death penalty, drug issues, Muslim issues such as the provision for halal food or cemeteries, ecological disasters and the reasons for them - floods, famines, wars, etc.

These will all help to give you ideas for your essays, and broaden your mind. (You will also begin to take note of biased reporting, and the differences between the various newspapers!).

(v) Build up a 'fashion boutique' - a collection of photos or drawings showing different styles of Muslim costume in various parts of the world. You could try to get a male and female example for, say, ten Muslim societies.

(vi) Artifact collection - collect various Muslim artifacts for displaying in your folder - 'Id cards, stick-on cards with Qur'an or hadith phrases (easily obtainable from Islamic bookshops), postcards of famous mosques, photographs - family feasts, khitan, weddings, funerals, your Imam, your madrassah 'at work', places you have visited, hajj photos, etc.

# 7. FINAL EXAM TIPS

## (i) General Tips

**Turn up.** The exams are held at special times and in special places, because there are all sorts of regulations to prevent cheating. Nobody is allowed to see the questions in advance. It is your duty to turn up at the right place at the right time. If you miss it, that's too bad - you'll have to wait until the next summer to re-sit.

**Read the whole paper through before you start.** Where you have a choice of questions, pick the ones you think you can score the most points for. This is a POINT-SCORING 'GAME'.

**Decide on the order you will do your answers.** Please notice that in some exam papers (like the NEAB short course) the most points are scored on the answers for the difficult questions. Some people like to do this section first, while they are still fresh and not tired, but it's up to you. Others like to do the paper in the order set, because they can get the feel of it, and score lots of small points in the early sections. Whichever way you choose to do it - remember that when you eventually arrive at the final sections with big marks, it may feel like just another question, but it is a very big section. Don't skimp it.

**Check how many points are on offer before you answer.** Always look to see how many points are awarded for each bit before you commence your answer. If the answer only carries one or two points, a one-sentence answer is usually quite sufficient. If the answer carries six to eight points, then you must make sure you say at least six to eight things, in order to score those points. Judge the 'size' of your answer from the number of points allotted.

**Never waste time writing about things which are not asked for.** There are no points, available for these extra things. Don't waste your valuable time. Always check that your answer fits the points available.

**The Golden Rule : Answer the question, the whole question, and nothing but the question.**

**Don't leave out the obvious.** Many of the marks are for very obvious facts, and you may feel that this is too simple. It isn't. Just pretend that the examiner is either one of your sharp non-Muslim teenage friends (always critical) who wants to know everything, especially 'Why?'; or a really senile and sad decrepit old examiner who can't seem to understand anything. That way, you will not make yourself sound like a pompous idiot, or forget to put down the obvious things. If you knew an answer, but didn't put it down, you have simply dustbinned those marks.

**Things you don't know** - The exam you actually sit will ask different questions from those on the specimen papers, but they will all be based on the syllabus given

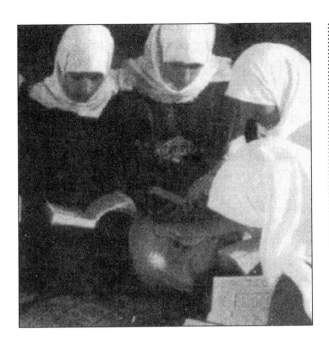

here. It is highly unlikely that you will know everything, but don't panic. Do what you can.

**Predicting topics** - In future years, a student will be able to look back on past papers, and see what sort of questions are favourites. If a really important topic was not on the previous year's paper, it is quite likely to be on the next paper. However, there is no rule which states that the examiner cannot set the same, or very similar questions in consecutive years. You can't rely on prediction. All you can rely on is that no question should be set on something which was not included in the syllabus.

**Your handwriting - Can we read it?** If the examiner cannot read your writing, you will fail. This is the first rule of the exam. Make sure you write very clearly. Use either a black or dark blue biro or ink pen. Do not take into the exam room bottles of ink that could spill. Do not use brilliant blue, green, purple or red ink, as that gives exam markers eye-strain and irritates them.

**Your handwriting - is it the right size?** The best size is at around six to eight words on each line. If you write very large, only three or four words per line, you may be kidding yourself you've done a big answer, when you haven't at all. It never fools the examiner, who is just looking for points. Write smaller. If your writing is very small and cramped, over twelve words per line, it not only becomes difficult to read, but you are in danger of it looking as if you have not said as much as those with more normal writing. I know the examiners are just looking for points, but they are only human - they get eyestrain and get irritated, and could miss something. Write bigger.

**You can't spell.** If you can't spell a word - don't use it. Put your answer into words you can spell. Many people try to show off by using long words, but it gains nothing extra, and sometimes they get them wrong and look silly. Just be clear.

**Style.** A very good tip is to look back over your answers after you have written them. Hopefully, there will be time at the end for this. Imagine you are reading them aloud to someone, perhaps your worst enemy. If your answer sounds awkward, babyish, stupid, embarrassing, or creepy-crawly, then it probably is. (It is an excellent idea to practice reading your work aloud to others while you are still studying. It starts a good habit of being aware of style).

**Wittering and waffle.** You do get credit for your ability to express yourself clearly, especially in those questions where you are asked for your opinion, to evaluate something. But remember, there are no marks for wittering and waffle.

## (ii) How the GCSE Marks are Scored

Don't panic about your answers. Always do your best. People who only write a few lines on the subjects with lots of points still may not fail - but they cannot expect to score high grades. This is one of the ways in which the examiner works out what level you are. Someone who writes only two or three lines on each high-point-scoring section, will probably only end up with level F/G, even if the answer is basically right. Sometimes the answer book has the space for the answer ruled out for you. This gives you a good clue on how much is expected.

When you have done everything required, the markers will analyse your score. It goes like this:

If you scored around 25 - 30%, you will get grade G or F, a basic pass.

If you scored around 50 - 55%, you will get grade C. (This is the level where your certificate has real value).

If you scored over 70%, you will get grade A, a distinction!

In other words, you can get nearly three-quarters of it wrong and still pass. So don't let worry or nerves or vaguely feeling ill, or a 'bad hair day' get the better of you. Don't get depressed. If you are already a practising Muslim, and you've looked at the specimen papers, you may find you could get at least half of it right already. Don't forget this paper will be attempted by a large number of students who are not Muslim at all, who will have none of your background.

Indications of what sort of things the markers were looking for in the specimen papers are included in this booklet for your guidance.

If you fail. You may re-sit exams as many times as you like. If you fail the first time, don't despair. You have still had very valuable experience in finding out what to do and what is required. Don't get depressed - BETTER LUCK NEXT TIME!

### (iii) The Exam Day Arrives

- Get a good sleep the night before, after reading through your notes. DO NOT sit up late in a state of panic.

- Have all your necessary equipment ready the night before.
- Get out of bed earlier than usual - avoid rush and panic.
- Expect to feel nervous.
- Allow yourself more time than usual to make the journey to the exam room.
- Get to the exam room at least fifteen minutes before the exam is due to start.
- Make provision for emergencies - take an extra pen and pencil. Take your ruler.
- Take a watch - time is vital. The exam room may not have an easily visible clock.
- Avoid nerves by keeping busy - read your notes again.

Don't be afraid of feeling vaguely ill - this is normal. The chances of your being seriously ill that day are extremely small. Minor niggling things will fade away once you start writing your answers. Feelings that you want to vomit, urinate or have diarrhoea will soon go away. Even if you really do have some of those symptoms, but you were not significantly ill yesterday, ignore them. If they get so bad you can't cope after the exam has started, you will be excused. But the chances really are that the feelings are just down to 'nerves' and will go away. Don't let headaches, sore throats, period pains, or hay fever put you off. Take what you usually take, and get on with it. You will only have to suffer a couple of hours, and you can leave if you get really bad, but you'll have to wait a full year to have another go.

### (iv) Doing the Exam

Make sure you check the instructions. They are usually just the same as they were the previous year, but you never know! Check.

Make a sound start. Spot something you feel confident about, and get into it. It will calm down your nerves.

Never waste any of your time. Never finish and leave an exam early - that is a sure waste of marks you might have got. Use every second, even if it is only checking. NEVER LEAVE THE EXAM EARLY.

If you get stuck on a major problem, leave it and go on to something else. The chances are that when you come back to the problem, you will see what to do straight away. Even if not, you haven't wasted time fretting or panicking.

If you have time left over, after checking, see if you can add a bit more to something you thought you had finished.

Always check when you think you have finished, that you really have finished. Are you sure you have answered all the things you were supposed to? Have you done enough questions? Did you forget to turn over a page? Did you have a go at all the 'bits' of a question? Don't leave blank spaces. If you have a guess, it could be right - but there are no marks for a blank. Check, and check again.

Check that you really did write about the correct things; for example, did you write all about abortion when you were really asked about birth control? Check, and check again. There are no marks allocated for the wrong answers.

## (v) Post-Mortems

Be warned - these are often disappointing and upsetting; you will think you have made mistakes which you may not have made; if you have made a serious mistake, there is nothing you can do about it now anyway.

Post-mortems always reveal some mistakes, or things someone else put in which you didn't.

Nobody ever gets 100%, so you are

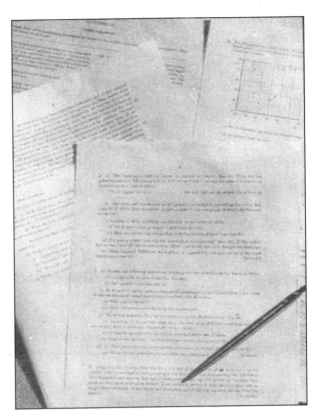

bound to discover mistakes. Forget it. You have seen from the grading analysis how you can get 75% wrong, and still pass!

If you are not sure that you have passed, then you probably have. Only a small percentage of students fail, and your chances of passing are much greater than of failing, especially if you've done all this work. If you made a reasonable attempt, and finished, YOU'VE PASSED.

Huge numbers of students think they've failed, when they've actually passed well. Good students are usually the sensitive worrying kinds - their own severest critics.

If you did fail - never mind. You can have another go again next year, and you've lost nothing. The knowledge you retain is yours for ever.

If you have passed - well done! Be proud, and be grateful for any help you received. It is always good manners to give thanks and appreciation where it is due.

So, my dear brothers and sisters
God bless you, and good luck!

Sister Ruqaiyyah

Some comments made by the Prophet :

*"The search for knowledge is a duty for every Muslim male and female."*

*"Seek knowledge from the cradle to the grave."*

*"Seek knowledge even if you have to go as far as China."*

*"One learned person is harder on the devil than a thousand ignorant worshippers."*

*"Knowledge is the stray camel of the believer. Let him seize it wherever he finds it."*

# 8. HERE WE GO

## (i) How to proceed

There are two ways of doing this course:

The first is the 'Anorak Way'. Just do it as it comes, no frills, no fuss. That's cool - and perfectly acceptable, but the second way will give you more fun and more feeling of achievement.

The second is to do it in this suggested format:

(a) The short fact questions - divide your page into two halves. Write out the questions on one side of your page and leave the other side for your answers. Do not write all the questions out first, as some of the answers are longer than others and may need more than one line.

If you do it like this, you will have some ready-made tests to use when you do your revision; someone will be able to help by asking you the questions while you can't see the answers!

(b) Do all the work sections called Things to Do, For Your Folders, For Discussion, Art Work, or Dictionary Work on different sheets of paper from the fact questions. These sections test your Understanding and train your ability to form your own values (called evaluation). This ability carries a lot of marks in the exam - more than just the knowledge part of it.

(c) The special texts: you could either do these as set pieces of art work, perhaps on plain paper; or you could do them on plain or coloured card, and keep them as a set.

(d) The 'High Flier Files'. These contain extra information to help give you ideas. These files are specially useful for any high-flier students going for top grades.

The best way to use these is to look them up and read the material when you get to the appropriate place in your work units.

It will always tell you if there is a special file.

## (ii) Differentation

Not everyone is an 'A',
Some of us are 'D's.

This course is designed for the most brilliant student 'going for gold,' and also for the rest of us who find it hard enough to run for a bus.

If you are a 'high-flier'-go for it! The more work you do, the better, and there are files with extra things to think about included after the worksheets.

BUT:

If you can only cope with the BASIC MINIMUM, don't despair :

- always do the short questions
- always do the Dictionary Work
- but only have a go at one of the Things to do, For Discussion or For Your Folder questions. Not one of each, just one.

## (iii) Art Work

If you don't want to do it — leave it out.

It does not matter if you are not good at drawing. No matter how bad you are, it will always look better if you keep the Rule of the Three Bs:

- Make it Big
- Make it Bold
- Make it Bordered

(Useful tip - draw in pencil first, with rubber handy, then ink it in with your fine-point black felt-tip. Do the border last).

## (iv) The Shopping List

Don't be a sad student - keep it neat!

(It's a good idea to get this lot before

you start - what a wonderful opportunity for Auntie or Gran to buy you a nice present!)

**The Two Course Books** - Islam, and the Dictionary

**A4 folder** - to keep your work in (many shops sell beautiful folders these days)

**A4 paper** - the best to use is ruled FM (feint and margin). It has wide lines, and is ready ruled margins.

**plain paper** - for art work

**plain index cards** - for special text collection

**pen** - black biro is smart, fine point is really smart

**red or green pen** - to underline headings in a different colour

**pencil** - 2B is best for art work

**black felt-tip pen, fine-point** - good for outlining art work and doing borders

**giant size black felt-tip pen** - for shading, but be warned, put a paper underneath as it often marks through

**rubber** - get a good big one

**ruler** - for underlining those headings and doing 'frames' for pictures

**colours** - your choice, of coloured pencil crayons or some felt tip colours, or even water-colour paints

**glue stick** - for mounting art work done separately

**white-out** - for covering up mistakes

**scissors**

**a plastic folder** for your press-cuttings

## (v) So Now, The Hard Work

Think of a nice big pile of building blocks.

You have to build the Taj Mahal, or the Ka'bah (Page 27 and 28).

How?

One block at a time.

The biggest problem is starting.

Once you get going, you just keep on going. The pile of blocks in place gets bigger as the building gets built.

No-one will take away what you've done, or learnt.

The knowledge is yours forever, insha'Allah.

This particular task has an end - and when you've finished it, you've finished it.

Good luck,

and

God Bless you

and Bring you

to success.

# BUILDING UP YOUR TAJ MAHAL

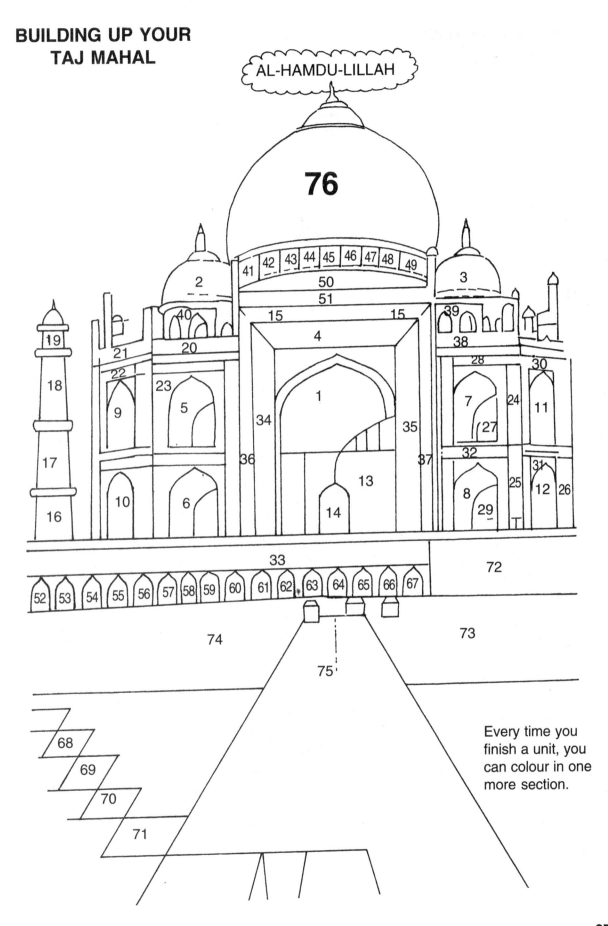

AL-HAMDU-LILLAH

Every time you finish a unit, you can colour in one more section.

## BUILDING UP YOUR KA'BAH

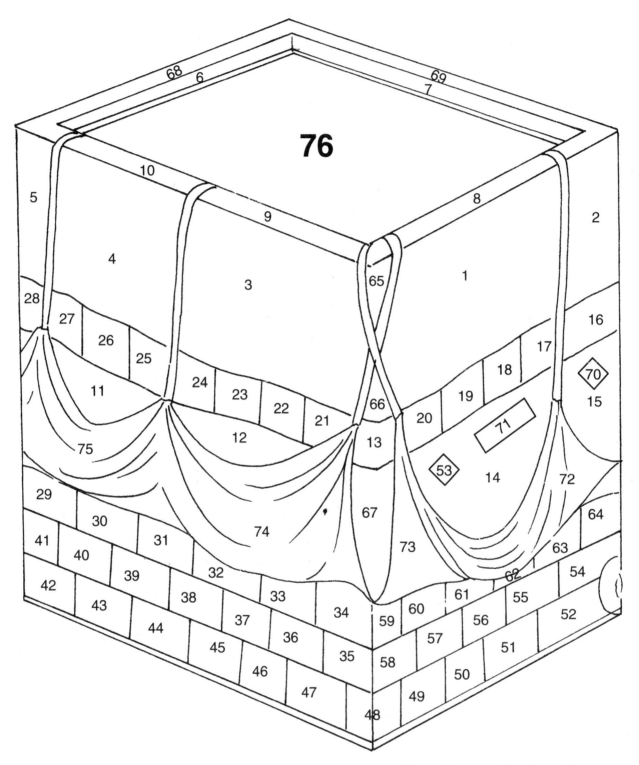

Every time you finish a unit, you can colour in one more section. *Al-hamdu-lillah!*

## *Section Two*

# THE GCSE COURSE WORKSHEETS

---

*In each case, the number of the given unit corresponds to the unit in the text-book 'Examining Religions: Islam' - Heinemann Press. Even if you can answer the questions without referring to the information in this book, it is wise just to check.*

*The instructions for the understanding and evaluation work are only given very briefly in these worksheets. They are given in full in the Heinemann textbook, and are very vital practice. Do not ignore them. They carry for more marks then the short factual questions.*

*The Dictionary Work questions refer to 'Islam: a Dictionary' - Stanley Thornes.*

# The Life of the Prophet Muhammad

## 1. INTRODUCTION

### Fact Questions

1. Give four meanings of the word 'Islam'.
2. What are the followers of Islam called?
3. What do Muslims do their best to obey?
4. Where do they find out about this?
5. Give the English words for 'iman' and 'amal'.
6. What is the Muslim name for God?
7. Name the special prophet of Islam.
8. In which month do Muslims fast?
9. What is a hadith?
10. Are Muslims always Arab or Asian people?
11. Where was the Prophet born?
12. What is the Ka'bah?
13. What was in the Ka'bah at the time of the Prophet?
14. Name three of the pagan Arab goddesses.
15. Which Arab tribe controlled the Ka'bah?
16. How did they make a profit?
17. What was a hanif?
18. List three things that hanifs believed.
19. Name one famous hanif.
20. State why he was famous.

Copy out the last paragraph.

### Understanding

Work through the suggestions in 'For Your Folders' and 'For Discussion'.

Why do you think so many people in the West dislike or are suspicious of Islam?

Explain what the hadith given on p.4 means.

### Art Work

Turn to either p.5 or p.26 in your dictionary, and draw the Ka'bah.

(Note: Remember, all pictures look better if you make them follow the rule of the 'Three Bs' - Big, Bold, and Bordered. Even if you are not good at art, if you make your picture a good size, perhaps ink it in with black felt tip, and put a border round it, it will look good).

### Dictionary Work

Look up IMAN: If you have iman, how does it affect your character?

The Ka'bah, Makkah.

Look up AMAL: When is faith worthless? What is meant by a hypocrite?

Look up HADITH: Copy out the second sentence.

Look up KA'BAH: How is this shrine traditionally connected with Adam?

## 2. THE PROPHET'S EARLY LIFE

### Fact Questions

1. Name the Prophet's mother.
2. What is a Bedouin?
3. Why did Bedouin ladies often take town babies into the desert?
4. Who was the Prophet's milk-mother?
5. How old was the Prophet when his real mother died?
6. Who looked after him next?
7. Who finally raised the Prophet to manhood?
8. Why was the Prophet called 'al-Amin'?
9. Who did the Prophet marry?
10. What was unusual about this marriage?
11. Name their six children.
12. How many other wives did the Prophet marry in his first wife's lifetime?
13. What happened to the Prophet's little sons?
14. Which two boys did the Prophet raise with his own little girls?

### Understanding

Do the work set in 'Talking Points' No.2.

### Special Texts

Copy out the three hadiths given here in neat, beautiful writing. make a decorated border around each.

(If you like, you could do these on special cards, or art paper, and keep them as a special collection. By the end of the course, you will have collected up a selection

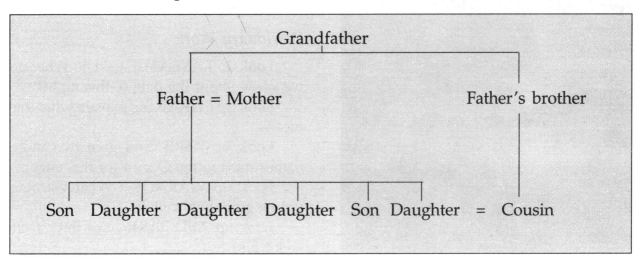

Grandfather

Father = Mother          Father's brother

Son  Daughter  Daughter  Daughter  Son  Daughter  =  Cousin

of some of the most beautiful and important sayings from the Qur'an and the Prophet's own teaching).

### Dictionary Work

Look up these people, and give one fact about each:

Aminah   Abu Talib   Khadijah   Ali

### Art Work

You should now be able to create the Prophet's family tree. Use the 'framework' given, but fill in the actual names. (You could do this on a separate plain sheet of paper. It is a good idea to set it out in pencil first, and then ink it in when you are sure you've got it right).

### Research

(Optional - this means, you don't have to do this if you don't want to).

If you are interested in the Prophet's family, you could try looking in other sources to add many more names to this family tree.

## 3. THE NIGHT OF POWER (LAYLAT AL-QADR)

### Fact Questions

1. What did Muhammad like to do in Ramadan?
2. Why was Muhammad so respected?
3. What is the Muslim name for the 'Night of Power'?
4. How old was Muhammad on this night?
5. Very briefly, what happened on this night?
6. Name the cave where Muhammad had his call.
7. What did the command 'Iqra!' mean?
8. Name the angel who came to him.
9. Name two other people who had also seen this angel.
10. Who was the first person to believe the Prophet's message?
11. Name her Christian cousin.
12. Give three facts about him.
13. Name the next three first believers.
14. What was tested during the Prophet's 'wait'?

### Understanding

Do the work set in 'Discussion Topic'.

### Special Text

Write out the words of Surah 96:1-5, with a nice border as before.

### Dictionary Work

Look up LAYLATUL-QADR: What do we know about the date of this night?

Look up I'TIKAF and explain what this means.

Look up JIBRIL and give two more names used in the Qur'an for this angel.

Look up WARAQA : What warning did he give the Prophet?

Look up ABU BAKR : List three facts about him.

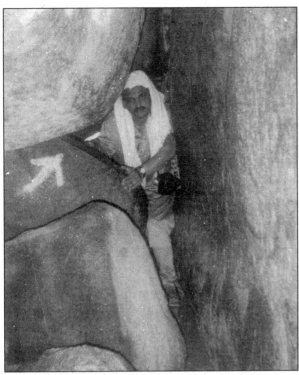

*The cave on Mt. Hira.*

## 4. THE REVELATIONS

### Fact Questions

1. Give the word for 'awareness of God'.
2. List three 'moments of truth'.
3. How does enlightenment often change a person?
4. What is the biggest 'moment' for a Muslim?
5. Which two things in life really change?
6. When people are convinced God really exists, what do they 'hand over'?
7. What is the word for submitting to God? (If not sure, look back at Unit One).
8. Who was an impatient Prophet? (His Muslim name is Yunus).
9. What does 'nazala' mean?
10. What is 'wahy'?
11. Why did the Prophet's friends write the messages down?
12. List four facts about the revelations.
13. How did the Prophet feel when he received his messages?
14. In what way was the Prophet God's 'instrument'?
15. What did people challenge him to do? (A miracle is something that happens that is outside the normal process of nature).
16. What did the Prophet challenge the doubters to do?
17. What did Allah say about the Prophet's character?

### Note

Miracles are regarded as acts of God that somehow break the laws of nature, or intrude upon them in some way, in order to bring about an amazing event. Examples in the Old Testament are Moses' staff changing into a serpent, the Ten Plagues, the Splitting of the Sea; Elijah raising a dead boy to life. Examples in the New Testament are all the many healings performed by Jesus, three people raised from the dead - Jairus' daughter who had just died, a boy being carried in his funeral procession to his grave, Jesus' friend Lazarus who had been dead for four days; the stilling of the storm; Jesus walking on water; feeding five thousand people with five loaves and two fishes.

The Prophet Muhammad was also involved in many special healings and feedings; he was credited with many miracles.

Religious people tend to have a strong belief in miracles, on the grounds that Allah can do as He wishes, and may intervene to disturb the laws of Nature as He wills. The case of the Virgin Mary having the baby Jesus is referred to several times in the Qur'an, with the statement: 'Allah has only to say 'Be!', and it is so.' (eg.Surah 3:47).

However, the Qur'an gives many clues that God does not readily break His own created laws on our behalf. We are urged, over and over again, to think about the 'natural miracles' or 'signs' of the created universe, for in them are 'significant insights for those who are wise'. (Surah 4:5).

Humans are never forced to believe in God; they are always given freedom of choice. When non-believers tried to persuade the Prophet to do a miracle in front of them so that they could believe in him, he refused.

'Say: 'My Lord is high above these things. I am only a man and His messenger'. (Surah 17:90-93).

'Yet they say: 'Why are not signs (or miracles) sent down to him from his Sustainer?' Say: 'The signs are indeed with God, and I am indeed a clear warner of the consequences of going the wrong way'. (Surah 29:50).

The Prophet stated: 'I have no control over what may be helpful or hurtful to me, but as Allah wills. Had I the full knowledge of the Unseen, I should increase the good and evil should not touch me. But I am only a warner, and an announcer of good tidings to those who believe. (Surah 7:188).

Muslims with great reverence for the Prophet also praise and respect him for the miracles associated with him. However, the Prophet himself did not emphasize such things, and always gave all glory and honour to Allah.

Important point : As is obvious from the cases of other miracle-performing people who pray constantly and are close to God, miracles certainly do not prove that the person doing them is in any way a divine being to be worshipped.

## Understanding

Do the work set in 'For Your Folders' and 'For Discussion'.

How would you answer a non-believer who suggested that the Prophet was probably either mad, or an epileptic?

## Dictionary Work

Look up TAQWA: What is a muttaqeen?

Look up the Prophet YUNUS: What happened to him?

## 5. PREACHING IN MAKKAH

### Fact Questions

1. What three things did the Prophet try to make people realise?
2. When will people who don't believe have to start believing?
3. When are people no longer forgiven?
4. What was more important to a Muslim than family or tribe?
5. Which people should always be treated with dignity?
6. What was the reaction of the Makkans (Meccans) to the Prophet's message?
7. What did they accuse the Prophet of?
8. Name one of the Prophet's uncles who became an enemy.
9. Who was Bilal, and who rescued him?
10. Name one of the Prophet's uncles who was a famous warrior.
11. Who was the Prophet's protector?

### Understanding

Do the work set in 'Things to do' and 'For Your Folders'.

### Dictionary Work

Look up BILAL: Who was his master? What did Bilal become?

Look up MU'ADHIN: Explain what this word means.

Look up ADHAN: Explain what this word means.

## Art Work

Draw a minaret and mu'adhin. (There are examples in the dictionary on p.2).

## 6. THE NIGHT JOURNEY (LAYLAT UL-MIRAJ)

### Fact Questions

1. Which of the Prophet's loved ones died when he was around 50?
2. Which town rejected the Prophet? (Apart from Makkah).
3. What does 'miraj' mean?
4. What do Muslims call the 'Night of Ascent'?
5. What are the two possible meanings of 'the farthest place of worship'?
6. What was al-Buraq?
7. From which city did the Prophet ascend through the Heavens?
8. How many Heavens did he pass through?
9. Name four other prophets he saw in the Heavens.
10. Which one did he say looked most like himself?
11. What important decision was taken?
12. What was said about Allah in surah 6:103?
13. What was going on around Allah's Throne? (Surah 40:7)?

14. What do Sufis say about this journey?

### Dictionary Work

Look up LAYLAT UL-MIRAJ: When is this usually celebrated?

Look up AL-AQSA and give three facts about it.

Look up JERUSALEM and give three facts about it.

Look up BAIT UL-MAQDIS: what word does 'maqdis' come from?

### Art Work

Draw the Dome of the Rock, given in the dictionary on p.9.

### Note

Laylat ul-Miraj, the 'Night of Ascent', is usually celebrated on 27th Rajab. The Prophet was a guest in the house of Abu Talib's daughter Umm Hani. He slipped away to pray at the Ka'bah, and dozed off to sleep in the Hijr. Suddenly, he was summoned from his sleep and taken to Jerusalem, from whence he ascended through the heavens to the Throne of God (surah 17:1). It is so unlike other records of the Prophet's life that Muslim scholars are

divided in opinion as to whether it was a miraculous event that really happened, or should be thought of as taking place while the Prophet was in a trance, or was a vision. One tradition suggests that as he left his bed he tipped over a cup of water, and when he returned from the heavens, the liquid was still emptying. Another tradition tells of how one incident on his journey involved his taking liquid from a water-bag carried by an animal on a caravan journey without the owner knowing, and when the owner later arrived in Makkah with the caravan, it was seen to be so. Tradition also states he was awoken by angel Jibril, and carried to Jerusalem on a winged creature called a Buraq (the Lightning), a strange horse with wings and a human head. As he and Jibril rose through the heavens they saw other prophets, including Musa, Ibrahim, Yahya and Isa, and prayed with them. Discussion with Musa involved how many times per day Muslims should pray, and it was as the result of this that the number was fixed for all time as five. Neither the Prophet nor the angel could approach close to the Throne of God, which was surrounded by brilliant light. This experience, be it miraculous journey or vision, occurred shortly after the Prophet's loss of she who was both his dear wife and his closest friend, Khadijah, and his uncle Abu Talib, in the Prophet's 'year of sorrow'. Like the first 'Night', it changed his life again and brought him fresh hope and vigour.

Umm Hani actually begged the Prophet not to tell anyone, as she feared he would simply be ridiculed-as was indeed the case. However, Abu Bakr earned his title as-Siddiq, (Witness to the Truth), when he insisted that no matter how out unlikely it sounded, if the Prophet said a thing was so, then it was so.

# 7. IN MADINAH

*Fact Questions*

1. What five things did the visitors from Yathrib pledge?
2. What was the Prophet's journey from Makkah to Yathrib (Madinah) called?
3. Where did the Prophet hide?
4. Who brought him food there?
5. Who stayed behind in his bed in Makkah, as a decoy?
6. How did a spider and a pigeon 'help' the Prophet?

7. How did the Prophet choose where he would stay?
8. What became the new name of Yathrib?
9. What does AH stand for?
10. Explain what is meant by 'muhajir' and 'ansar'.
11. In Madinah, what had to come before loyalty to one's tribe or family?
12. Why were some Jews angry about Islam?

13. Which town did Muslims first face when praying?
14. What was Yom Kippur, and what did Jews do on that day?
15. In what ways did Allah change: (a) the qiblah, and (b) the fast?
16. When was the Muslim fasting month?
17. What did this test?

## Understanding

Do all the work set in 'Thinking Points' and 'For Discussion'.

## Dictionary Work

Look up HIJRAH: What does the word mean? What year was 1AH?
(Look up and read CALENDAR).
Look up JEWS: Which of the Prophet's wives were Jewish?

## 8. MUHAMMAD THE RULER

### Fact Questions

1. Although the Prophet was now a ruler, did he live like a rich man or a poor man?
2. Give three examples of humble things he did.
3. What had to come first to a Muslim?
4. Why was slavery not forbidden outright?
5. Describe briefly the Prophet's normal food.
6. Why were the marriage laws changed?
7. How many wives did the Prophet marry after Khadijah died? (No-one is absolutely certain about the exact number, but these are the wives known about for sure)
8. Describe briefly the Prophet's sleeping quarters.
9. Who was his youngest wife?

10. What special title was given to the wives?
11. Who once 'rode the Prophet like a horse'?
12. What is the Sunnah?

## Understanding

Do all the work suggestions in 'For Your Folders', 'Things to Do', and For Discussion'.

## Dictionary Work

Look up AISHAH and give five facts about her.
Look up SUNNAH and copy out the note.
Look up PROPHET'S WIVES and list the eleven names about whom there is no doubt.
Which wife was the Prophet's cousin?
Who was the mother of the Prophet's son Ibrahim?

## Art Work

Create a diagram showing the names of the Prophet and his wives. You could do a flower with many petals, or a tree with many branches, or a necklace with many pendants, etc, etc.

## 9. THE ROAD TO MAKKAH

### Fact Questions

1. Every citizen of Allah should have this.
2. On what four things should there be no discrimination whatsoever?
3. Who opposed the Prophet at the Battle of Badr?
4. Why were the Makkans surprised at the outcome of this battle?
5. Which battle did the Muslims lose?
6. What wound did the Prophet receive?

7. What three things did the Prophet learn about battles?
8. What happened in 629?
9. What happened in 630?
10. What did the Prophet do when he entered Makkah?
11. What is the ban in Makkah, to this day?

## Understanding

Do the work set in 'For Your Folders' and 'Thinking Points'.

## Dictionary Work

Look up BLACK STONE and give three facts about it.

Look up KA'BAH: How did the Prophet 'cleanse' it?

## Art Work

Draw the Black Stone - on p.11 in your dictionary.

## 10. THE FAREWELL

### Fact Questions

1. How many Muslims went on pilgrimage in 632?
2. Where did the Prophet give his famous Sermon?
3. Muslims were asked to live in a certain way with each other. What way?
4. Which two things of every Muslim were to be regarded as sacred?
5. All believers were asked to be this.
6. What two things did the Prophet 'leave behind'?
7. What did the Prophet say about a new message?

8. Who called the crowd to prayer?
9. What happened when the Prophet went home?
10. Who led the prayers when he became too ill?
11. Where did the Prophet die?
12. Who could not believe he had died?
13. Who took control and became new leader?
14. Give the dates, according to Muslim tradition, of the Prophet's death.
15. Where was he buried?

## Understanding

Do the work suggestions in 'Thinking Point', 'For Your Folders' and 'Talking Point'.

## Dictionary Work

Look up LAST PROPHET and explain what is meant by 'chain' and 'seal'.

## Special Text

Write out your own copy of the Last Sermon, or see if you can buy a special card or poster with the Sermon on it.

*The pillar at the summit of Mt. Arafat.*

## The Last Sermon

On 9th Dhul-Hijjah 10 A.H. the Prophet Muhammad (pbuh) made his final address to 120,000 of his followers from Mount Arafat after the Hajj:

'O people, listen to my words carefully, for I do not know whether I will meet you again on such an occasion.

O people, just as you regard this month, this day, this city as sacred, so regard the life and property of every Muslim as a sacred trust. Remember that you will indeed appear before Allah and answer for your actions.

Return the things kept with you as a trust to their rightful owners. All dues of interest shall stand cancelled and you will have only your capital back; Allah has forbidden interest, and I cancel the dues of interest payable to my uncle Abbas ibn Abd al Muttalib.

O people, your wives have a certain right over you and you have certain rights over them. Treat them well and be kind to them, for they are your partners and committed helpers.

O people, beware of Satan, he is desperate to divert you from the worship of Allah, so beware of him in matters of your religion.

O people, listen carefully. All believers are brothers and sisters. You are not allowed to take things belonging to another Muslim unless it is given to you willingly.

O people, none is higher than the other unless it is higher in obedience to Allah. No Arab is superior to a non-Arab except in piety.

O people, reflect on my words. I leave behind me two things, the Qur'an and my example (the Sunnah), and if you follow these, you will not fail.

Listen to me carefully! Worship Allah and offer Salah, observe Sawm in the month of Ramadan and pay Zakah.

O people, be mindful of those who work under you. Feed and clothe them as you feed and clothe yourselves.

O people, no prophet or messenger will come after me and no new faith will emerge.

All those who listen to me shall pass on my words to others, and those to others again.'

### Allah revealed the following verses on that day:

'Today I have perfected your religion for you, completed my favour upon you and have chosen Islam as the way of your life.' (5:3).

The Prophet's mosque, Madinah.

# Beliefs

## 11. GOD

### Fact Questions

1. When does Allah always forgive us?
2. Can we find out about God just when we feel like it?
3. How close is Allah to us?
4. Which is Allah's favourite nation?
5. What is the one secret we can hide from Allah?
6. Name one great prophet equal to God.
7. What is the awareness that brings people to Paradise?
8. Which groups of people were promised reward in the Afterlife?

### Understanding

Read through the unit and do the work set in 'For Your Folders' and 'Things to do' numbers 1 and 2.

### Dictionary Work

Look up the Beautiful Names of God in the Dictionary, and appendix p.79. Write five sentences on what these names teach us about God.

Choose five of the names, write them out with their meanings, and learn them by heart.

### Artwork

Do 'Things to do' No.3 - the Scroll.

### Notes

Some definitions about belief in God:

- **Animism** - the belief that things have spirits, or souls. All people and animals have souls (life forces); certain rocks, trees, springs, etc. may be occupied by a spirit entity.
- **Atheism** - the conscious decision to belief that there is no such thing as God.
- **Agnosticism** - the belief that one cannot know whether God exists or not. One should keep an open mind.
- **Deism** - the belief that God does exist, through the use of reason.
- **Theism** - the belief that God does exist, and has been revealed through Holy Books and prophets.
- **Polytheism** - the belief that there are many gods, whether or not one is supreme.
- **Monotheism** - the belief that there is only One God.
- **Pantheism** - the belief that everything that exists is part of 'god', and separate souls or spirits are part of the one complete Soul.

### Belief in God, His unity - Tawhid

This is the most basic and fundamental of beliefs. It can be approached from two main question-points; firstly, does God exist at all, or is the whole notion nonsense, and secondly, if there is such a concept as 'divinity', how many divine beings are there? Is there only one - or are there two opposing equal forces, like light/darkness, or good/evil? Or are there a whole order of

divine beings, perhaps running into millions, for all we know?

Each of these points of view has had its supporters throughout the earth's history. One thing that is quite certain is that the belief in some Divine Entity has existed as long as we have proof of human existence - thanks to various burial customs that suggest strongly a belief in life after death. But is it all just wishful thinking?

The plain fact of the matter is that the existence of God cannot be scientifically proved. Perhaps we could say 'yet' - but maybe it will never be proved. Maybe it is not intended to be. However, there is an enormous amount of circumstantial evidence, and millions of pages of theological argument to consider.

## CLASSICAL ARGUMENTS FOR THE EXISTENCE OF GOD, AND ARGUMENTS AGAINST

- **First Cause** - for: that unless something it is caused, it does not exist. Everything in our universe is caused. Something must have caused it. Whatever that cause was, that we may call God, even if we have no idea of what God is.

Against: Those who do not believe in God as the origin of the Universe suppose it to have existed from infinity, in other words, to have had no beginning. It's easy enough to claim this - it can hardly be proved (any more than the existence of God as the First Cause can) - but it defies our logic.

- **First Movement** - for: that unless something is moved by forces acting upon it, it does not move. Everything in the universe is in motion. Whatever it was that set the whole lot off, that we may call God.

Against: There is no proof that what started off all the movement in our universe was a Divine Being. Maybe it was the impetus of the Big Bang, the primal cosmic explosion? Why call it God? As before, this cannot be proved. It may have been simply some force of science.

- **Contingency** - the reverse of the First Cause argument - for: If a thing might not have existed, it is called contingent. You are a contingent being, because you might never have existed. If your parent had sneezed at the wrong moment, it would not have been you but some other sperm that fertilised your mother's egg. Needless to say, by 'you' in this context, I am talking about you as a physical body - whether or not your soul existed independently of your body before you were born, and what plans God might have for you had such a thing happened, are a different matter altogther. We might call these 'contingency' plans.

Is it possible that our earth might not have existed? Of course it is - it is therefore contingent. Is it possible that our entire solar system might not have existed? Of course it is - it is therefore also contingent. It must exist for a reason, a cause. Is it possible that the entire cosmos with all its universes might never have existed? We suppose so - therefore the whole lot is contingent. Thus, there must have been something which caused it all to be, and that we call God.

- **Necessary Being -** this is also called the Ontological argument (from the Greek word 'ontos' - 'being'). For: God must be 'necessary' because a scale of values exists - some things are bad, some are better, some are much better, and at the top there is that which is best. Can there be two 'bests'? No, not by definition of what we mean by best. That which is at the top of our values, we may call God. And He must exist, because that which does not exist cannot be the best; if it doesn't exist it cannot be regarded as supremely anything. Therefore if there is a supreme of the scale of values, God, or Allah, must exist.

Against: Unfortunately there is a descending scale of values as well as ascending - bad, worse, the worst. If you argue that God is the Supreme Good, you must also accept that 'He' is the Supreme Evil. If you just pick and choose which of the virtues you will apply to God, that is your personal choice. Hence this leads to dualism, and all other sorts of speculations.

- **Design -** this is also called the Teleological argument, because it looks forward to an end, aim or goal (from the Greek word 'telos' - 'end'). For: The universe in every aspect of its laws and their physical manifestation show order and pattern - in other words, design. They do not appear to have come about by accident. Even if it is true that things have evolved, they have evolved to a pattern, and seem to be moving towards an ultimate goal, even if we do not know what that goal is.

Against: The goal might simply be the perfection of that form of life in its environment - which might of course, lead to its total destruction if the environment suddenly changed - for example, the dinosaurs of ancient times, and the many many modern species whose habitat is being destroyed by human activity.

These five arguments are known as the Classical Arguments, and ever since they were argued out in the Middle Ages by St. Thomas Aquinas (for the Christians) and Ibn al-Arabi (for the Muslims), they have raged on, and not really been improved on.

- **The existence of the concept of God.** For: We can deduce the real existence of God from the fact that 'He' as a concept has entered human consciousness at all. Why should such a concept have ever arisen, if there has never been such an Entity? Is it possible to conceive of something which does not exist at all, and has never been part of human experience?

Against: Opponents to this argument point out that this is nonsense - we are able to conceive of all sorts of monsters that do not and have not ever existed. Every fan of film special effects can easily imagine Monsters from the Black Lagoon. Those who wish to pursue the argument point out that all these creations of rather weird minds simply have their origins in other things like them - such as reptiles, dinosaurs, etc - which they have used piece-meal in their mental creations.

- **Personal religious experience.** For: We can deduce the real existence of God from those who have religious experiences of their own - who feel aware of the presence of God, who perhaps have visions, or see angels, or have moments of mystical awareness, or have flashes of insight into the future, etc. Where could all these experiences come from, if not from God?

Against: Unfortunately it has to be admitted that mental institutions have a high proportion of such in their care. 'Jack the Ripper' heard the 'voice of God' exhorting him to cut bad girls' throats. Thus the atheist rests his/her case. It is always unsafe to base beliefs on emotions, feelings, mystical states or states of altered consciousness - one of the major criticisms of such religious manifestations as the present emphasis on 'spiritual phenomena' such as the 'Toronto blessing', emotional soul-singing, speaking in tongues, and New Age Christianity, or the trance-states inducted by Sufi dhikr.

One of the ways that chants, incantations, and emotionalism etc. work is to 'numb' the mind, to deliberately alter its state of consciousness, to promote 'alpha' states, all of which can easily result in images and impulses that are not true ideas but merely visual images, intuitions and feelings. The person may *feel* a dramatic sense of well-being, an 'openness to God' or being 'at one with God', or 'at one with nature' or the universe - but this is deceptive. Altered mind states make us open to things other than God, including evil matters and entities that come clothed in beautiful disguises.

When we cut to the bottom line, no matter how brilliant our brains, or how sensitive our insights and intuitions - it still comes down to a matter of faith, in the sense of accepting things that apparently cannot be proved.

## Content of belief

When it comes to *what* believers believe about their God or gods, these are hardly matters that can be forced on a person. People believe what it seems right to them to believe. They follow their own sense of logic, and their own conscience. They use such mental equipment as they have. They can hardly do more. Others, of course, settle for a slavish acceptance of what others, probably those in authority over them in some shape or form, tell them.

Therefore, you are at liberty to examine the religious beliefs and systems of any or all of the world's faiths, and use your own brains. Muslims believe very strongly that 'truth stands clear from error' (Surah 2:256). They believe that God does exist, and that there is only One God, one Supreme Being, the Almighty (or Allah - the translation into Arabic of 'almighty'). They believe that all things, good and evil, must of necessity have their origin in Him, and that there must be a reason why the universe is as it is, and why people are as they are, and why the tests of their lives come along as they do.

They do not choose between a universe started off by a Big Bang or some other theory and a universe created by God, but a started-off universe whether by Big Bang or any other origin with God, or no universe at all.

The actual arguments regarding physical things like the origin of the universe, or the theory of evolution, are irrelevant to the existence of God. Muslims may take them or leave them, and generally consider it better to adopt a 'wait and see' attitude to the claims of science. They see the evidence of cause and design in everything. They are aware that everything is contingent, and as regards their own lives or fortunes, they could be changed in a flash. They believe humans should be humble, and be aware that however much they know, there are a million times more things that they don't know.

They will never accept that God has a partner, or sharer, or would ever intermingle His 'substance' in the world of physical matter by engendering half-human offspring. They do not believe that any other thing could possibly have power over God - whether it was a sacrifice, the pleas of the devout, a rival spirit entity, or a lucky charm! No-one can possibly 'know better' than God, or have more compassion than

God. They do not believe that any other mind has the right to pass ultimate judgement, for they do not have the knowledge of background and circumstances as God has. We do not have the right to assume that such-and-such a person is evil, or a saint - how do we know?

All these things are part of what a Muslim calls tawhid, the One-ness of God.

### How can we know about the 'nature' of God?

We can only have a very limited awareness of it. Muslims are extremely careful never to associate any image or thing with God. 'Nothing is like unto Him' (Surah 42:11). There is in the whole of creation nothing that is like Allah, or partakes oι Allah, or is in any way associated with Allah. Allah is inexpressible. It is even misleading to call God 'Him', which implies sexuality.

All the references that seem to suggest that God has a body which is physical, and has mouth, tongue, eyes and ears, etc., should be interpreted symbolically. Did God 'speak' to the Prophets, or 'sit' on a throne? Or do these passages mean rather that God's revelation was conveyed to the human mind, and that God has almighty power?

Muslims believe, however, that important clues have been revealed in the 'Beautiful Names' of God - none of which are names as such, but which refer to His attributes, and express His lordship of the universe and His providence in it. Since God Himself revealed these names as part of the Qur'an, Muslims can study and use them as true guides to the 'character' and 'personality' of God.

You will often hear Muslims talk about the 100 Beautiful Names, but in fact, if you take the trouble to count up all the Names mentioned in the Qur'an, there are more than 100. It is also not true that you only get 99 names on a chart, since the 100th name is known only to the camel, and that is why it seems to have a superior smile! That is a silly joke.

Not all of the names are comfortable. True, God is as-Salaam (the Source of Peace), al-Wahab (the Bestower), al-Basir (the All-Seeing), al-Wali (the Protecting Friend) and al-Afuw (the Pardoner); but He is also al-Muntaqim (the Avenger), al-Mani (the Preventer), al-Khafid (the Abaser), al-Muhsi (the Reckoner) and al-Mumit (the Annihilator).

At no time, in the entire 23 years of the Revelation to Muhammad, did Allah ever refer to Himself as Father. This must have been deliberate. A Muslim can certainly call God 'Rabb' or 'Master', but not 'Abb' or 'Father'. One can only guess for the reason for the omission of this familiar way of referring to God. The most likely reason is that it has obvious physical connotations, and can lead people astray. It became a commonplace title for God after the coming of Jesus, and since the success of Trinitarianism in the Church, has led to all sorts of completely unprofitable speculation. God is not our Father, except in the symbolic sense that He is our Creator.

Many Muslims make a study of the given Names of God the starting point for their thoughts about God, and many recite them regularly as reminders.

## 12. TAWHID AND SHIRK

### Fact Questions

1. What does the word Tawhid mean?
2. What do we mean when we say Allah is Creator?
3. What does Transcendence mean?
4. What does Immanent mean?
5. Why do you think that Surah 112 would not be accepted by a Christian?
6. What is meant by Shirk?
7. Why is thinking that you can persuade God to do something you want Him to do, really shirk?
8. Why is using lucky charms shirk?
9. What do Muslims say about the claims Christians have made about their prophet Jesus?
10. What is the Arabic name for Jesus?

### Understanding

Do the work set in 'For Your Folders.

### Special Texts

Write out Surah Ikhlas (Surah 112) with a decorative border, and learn it.

Write out the 'Transcendence' verse - 6:103, and one of the 'Immanence' verses - either 2:186 or 50:16.

### Dictionary Work

Look up TAWHID. What does it say about the 'sex' or 'gender' of God?

Look up KUFR. What are the literal meanings of this word?

Look up SHIRK. It suggests some things that people have made into 'idols'. Can you give examples of heroes, sects or hobbies which have almost become idols? What is wrong with people claiming that their football team, or favourite pop star, is 'god'?

Look up TAKFIR. Why is it often associated with unpleasant extremism?

### Note

Some characteristics of Allah

- **Omnipresence.** One of the chief characteristics of Allah; it means that He is present everywhere, from the most minute scale even smaller than the atomic level, to the vastest reaches of existence. 'To God belong the east and the west; wherever you turn, there is the Presence of God; for God is All-pervading, All-Knowing.' (2.115,142) 'Most certainly We shall relate to them with knowledge, for We were never absent (at any time or from any place).' (7:7)

- **Omnipotence.** One of the chief characteristics of Allah; it means to have power over all things, absolute control over all affairs. 'Whatever God grants to humanity out of His mercy, no-one can withhold; and what He withholds no-one can grant apart from Him. He is the (source of) Power, the All-Knowing.' (35:2).

- **Omniscience.** One of the chief characteristics of Allah, it means that He knows everything in every sphere of existence, no matter how great or small, universal or intimate. 'God has the key to the Unseen, the treasures none know but He. He knows whatever is on land or in the sea; no leaf falls without His knowing it; there is not a grain in the darkness of earth, or a green or dry thing, but it is carefully noted.' (6.69). See also 31:16; 67:14.

## 13. CREATION

### Understanding

Read through the unit, and do the work set in 'For Your Folders', Things to do' and 'Talking Points'.

### Dictionary Work

Look up FIRST CAUSE. Is there any part of our universe which is not contingent?

Why does the Big Bang theory not answer the question of Creation?

Look up AL-GHAYB, and explain what this means.

## Note

A mind-boggling Universe.

The sun is a giant in our solar system. It is so huge that 1,300,000 earths could fit inside it. But compare the sun to some of the supergiant starts in our galaxy, and it suddently looks tiny indeed.

For instance, imagine putting various supergiant starts right where our sun is. There are some so mammoth that they would engulf the entire orbit of the earth. We would be inside the star! The star called Betelgeuse would extend nearly to Jupiter. And if the star Mu Cephei sat where the sun is, it would swallow Saturn - although Saturn is so far away that it took the Voyager 2 space-craft four years to get there from Earth,travelling about 20 times as fast as a speeding bullet.

Our galaxy, the Milky Way, has been called a giant spiral galaxy. Appropriately so. The sheer immensity of this great glowing pinwheel of over 100,000,000,000 stars, spinning majestically in the blackness of space, is staggering to the human mind. If we could stand on one edge of our galaxy and send a beam of light toward the opposite edge, it would take over 100,000 years for that light to cross the galaxy even though that beam would hurtle toward its goal at awesome speed: 186,000 miles every second. In other words, the Milky Way has a diameter of 100,000 light-years.

Yet, our neighbouring spiral galaxy, Andromeda, is over twice the size of ours and may contain some 600,000,000,000 stars. What is more, astronomers have discovered a mammoth galaxy they named Markarian 348. It is some 13 times as large in diameter as our Milky Way galaxy, measuring about 1,300,000 light years across!

Even the behemoth Markarian 348 would look small next to the galaxy recently discovered at the centre of a cluster of galaxies called Abell 2029. Scientists believe that this is the largest galaxy they have ever seen. It is over 60 times as large as our own galaxy. It is some 6,000,000 light-years across and is home to a mind-numbing swarm of some 100,000,000,000,000 stars. According to a report in The New York Times, this is also one of the most luminous galaxies ever observed. And it is not the chaotic product of random forces. "This is an organized mass of light and energy," one of its discoverers said of it. "It's a very large, organized galaxy."

Our brains cannot even begin to grasp the immensity of these collections of stars or the vast distances involved. So, what about the creative, organizing force behind it all? "Raise your eyes high up and see. Who has created these things? It is the One who is bringing forth the army of them even by number, all of whom he calls even by name." (Isaiah 40:26) If the creation is awesome, how much more awesome is the Creator!

## Research

To discover the distance light covers in one light year, do the sum:

186,000 (miles)

x 60 (seconds)

x 60 (minutes)

x 24 (hours)

x 365.25 (days in a year)

# 14. ANGELS, JINN AND THE DEVIL

## Fact Questions

1. List five things we learn about angels in the three verses quoted at the start of this chapter.
2. What are the jinn thought to be?
3. What are jinn said to be made of?
4. What does surah 72 tell us about some jinn?
5. Name one thing that jinn and humans have in common.
6. What does the word 'angel' mean?
7. What does surah 41:30-32 teach about angels?
8. Give two examples of human beings who have seen the angel Jibril.
9. Make a list of the angels named here, and state their functions.
10. Give the other name of Satan or Shaytan.
11. Why did Shaytan become the enemy of human beings?

## Understanding

Do the work set in 'Talking Points', 'For Your Folders' No.2, and 'Thinking Points'.

## Dictionary Work

Look up SHAYTAN. What is the literal meaning of his name?

Look up JINN. How does it compare their creation to that of humans? What sort of places were they said to be attracted to?

Look up EVIL. What definition is given here?

Look up FREEWILL. How does our freewill affect our life after death?

## Art Work

Draw a book lying open to show two pages. On one side, list some of your good deeds or intentions for the last week; list some of your bad deeds or failures on the other side.

## Note: Angels

It is impossible for humans to perceive angels as they really are — they belong to the realm of al-Ghayb, the Unknown. They are the means by which the spiritual realm of Allah can have an effect on the physical world of matter. When they are sent with messages to humans, they may assume human shape, but this is not their real form. They are often represented as having wings, but this presentation is by no means consistent. Attempts to depict or draw angels are forbidden in Islam.

## Jinn

The plural noun jinn is taken from the verb 'janna' implying veiled or concealed from sight. It signifies beings that are hidden from human senses.

Jinn appear to be a lesser order of beings than humans, although they have freewill like humans. They inhabit the same universe, but on a different 'plane'

Occasionally they attempt to possess human bodies, and have to be exorcized. They are not always malevolent, however, and surah 72 mentions jinn that were converted to Islam. Many people who are aware of them treat them gently and find them helpful, although they can be mischievous.

## 15. HUMAN BEINGS

### Fact Questions

1. What do the names Adam and Hawwah (Eve) mean?
2. What was Adam made out of?
3. Does God look like a human being? (Some Christian paintings depict Him as an old man, usually a white man, often not wearing many clothes).
4. What is the name of the theory that human beings descend from animals?
5. What is a ruh?
6. What is meant by a soul's time-span?
7. What does reincarnation mean?
8. When will soul and body be reunited again?
9. 'Reincarnation' means that a soul can be reborn again in another body (human or animal) on earth. (If you got it wrong, please correct it). What does Islam teach instead?
10. What does Islam teach as the purpose of human lives?
11. Why do humans not remain equal?
12. What is meant by a khalifah? (Note: the function of stewardship, or responsibility, is called Khilafah).

### Understanding

Do the work set in 'Thinking Points', 'For Your Folders', and 'Things to do'.

### Dictionary Work

Look up RUH. What is suggested are the different fates for the ruh of good or evil people, after the moment of death?

Look up RESURRECTION. What comment is made on the difficulty for Allah

in raising our bodies? How will our new bodies compare to our old ones?

Look up KHILAFAH. What does this mean?

Look up CALIPH. (ie. Khalifah). Name the first four men to rule Islam after the Prophet.

## 16. RISALAH / PROPHECY

### Fact Questions

1. What is a Rasul?
2. What is risalah?
3. Who is the real founder of Islam?
4. Who was the first Prophet?
5. How many prophets are named in the Qur'an?
6. Name the five major prophets.
7. Why was Muhammad called the 'Seal' of the prophets?
8. Explain what is meant by the Sahifa, Tawrah, Zabur and Injil.
9. Which of these books has been completely lost?
10. Give examples of three things that

have happened to the original texts of the other books.

11. What does 'Umm al-Kitab' mean?

12. What were the Qur'an revelations intended to do?

13. Why are the surahs in the order they are today? (This was not their original order, as revealed to the Prophet).

## Understanding

Do the work set in 'For Your Folders' and 'Thinking Points'.

## Dictionary Work

Look up and list the prophets named on p. 80.

Look up PROPHETS IN THE QUR'AN: which three are not named in the Bible?

Look up NABI and RASUL. Explain the difference between the two terms.

Look up NAZALA and explain what it means.

Look up LAST PROPHET, and copy out this important note.

## Art Work

Draw a scroll and copy out the list of statements in 'Things to do'. Now cross out the wrong statements. (Answers at the end of the book).

## Note: Prophets

'Say: "We believe In God, and in what Has been revealed to us, and what was revealed to Abraham, Isma'il, Isaac, Jacob, and the Tribes, and in (the Books) given to Moses, Jesus, and the Prophets, from their Lord: We make no distinction between one and another among them, and to God do we bow our will (in Islam)." (3:84)

'O People of the Book! Commit no excess in your religion: nor say of God aught but the truth. Christ Jesus the son of Mary was (no more than) an apostle of God, and His Word, which He bestowed on Mary, and a Spirit proceeding from Him: so believe in God and His apostles. Say not "Trinity": desist: It will be better for you: for God is One God: Glory be to Him: (Far Exalted is He) above having a son. To Him belong all things in the heavens and on earth. And enough is God as a Disposer of affairs.' (4:171)

## Note: Seal of the Prophets

The prophet Muhammad was granted this 'title' in 33:40. Just as a seal (Khatam) marks the end of a document, so Muhammad was the last of the long chain of messengers from Allah. The term khatam is synonymous with khitam, the end or conclusion of a thing. The revelation granted to Muhammad (i.e. the Qur'an) has therefore to be regarded as the culmination, the end of all prophetic revelation.

## 17. ISA (JESUS)

### Activity

Read through the interview, twice - make use of another reader to do this with you. On the second reading, change over parts.

### Fact Questions

1. What is a virgin?

2. Does the Bible or the Qur'an mention Mary the most?

3. Who had no father or mother?

4. What did the Parable of the Prodigal Son teach?

5. Who wrote the Christian books?

6. What do some Muslims think about St.Paul?

## Understanding

Do the work set in 'Things to do', 'Thinking Point' and 'For Your Folders'.

## Dictionary Work

Look up ISA. Name his mother.
Look up SACRIFICE. Can a sacrifice ever 'bribe' God?
Look up INJIL. Explain what this is.
Look up MARYAM. Who was she descended from?
Look up MAHDI. Explain what the Mahdi is.

## Special Text

If you have a Qur'an, look up and write out Surah 35:18

## Note: Christmas celebrations

Some Muslims marry Christians, or live alongside Christian people. Christmas is the festival held on December 25th in most Christian societies to celebrate the birth of the Prophet Isa, (who, of course, they worship as the Son of God). Other Christians celebrate this festival on other dates, for example, January 6th. The actual date of Isa's birth is unknown. 25th December was chosen by the Church because it was already a midwinter festival, the rebirth of Sol Invictus, the Rising Sun, after the shortest day, December 21st. Hence some Christian groups, for example the Jehovah's Witnesses, refuse to celebrate on what is really a pagan occasion from the times of jahiliyyah. Many Muslims do not know what attitude to take if they are living in a Christian society. Should they regard it as shirk and have nothing to do with it?

It is worth remembering that many of the first Muslims were Christians originally (e.g. Salman, Ubaydullah, etc.). One of the Prophet's companions, Asma bint Abu Bakr, once asked him if it was appropriate for her to be kind and dutiful to her non-Muslim mother. He ordered her to be so. Islam urges maintaining good relations with people. There is no harm in giving Christian friends (or relatives) gifts-the Prophet did not instruct his followers not to do so. A Muslim could suggest that Christians wishing to give gifts to Muslim children or friends could keep the gift back until the next 'Id. If this would be offensive, simply explain to the Muslim child receiving the gift that it has no religious value. Obviously no Muslim can celebrate the notion of God becoming incarnate, or being born as a human being; however, there is no harm in respecting a day that commemorates the birth of a great prophet.

## 18. AL-QADR; PREDESTINATION AND FREEWILL

### Fact Questions

1. Explain the difference between a cause and an effect.
2. If the universe had no cause, would it have existed?
3. Give two examples that show the 'fine detail' of God's knowledge.
4. What is the nafs?
5. Which part of us makes choices?
6. What are the four things humans have choices over, on which we will be questioned on Judgement Day?
7. Which is the hardest - the path towards good or the path towards evil?
8. Who tries to influence people away from the good?

9. Why is it pointless to use 'lucky' charms?
10. What are the 'five rules' of Allah?

## Understanding

Work out the 'chain' as far as you can for:

(i) a table   (ii) a cup of tea   (iii) an elephant

Do the work set in 'For Your Folders', 'Thinking Points' and 'Things to do'.

*Special Text* - Copy out either 35:2 or 10:107 with a decorated border.

## Dictionary Work:

Look up FREEWILL. Why is there no good or evil without it?

Look up AL-QADR. Explain what al-qadr means.

What does 'predestined' mean?

How might a person who had committed murder use predestination as an excuse?

Why did Allah send prophets?

What does the concept of Judgement depend on?

Why are mistakes and misfortunes important too?

Look up and explain: TAWAKKUL, SABR, ISTIKHARA.

## Note: On Freewill and Fatalism

Belief in that everything, good and evil, comes from Allah is the Muslim concept of al-Qadr, the key doctrine of Allah's complete and final control over the fulfilment of events, or Destiny. This is famous for being one of the most difficult of all theological problems. It is not a problem limited to Islam - the same complicated arguments have raged through Christian history too.

How does one balance the idea of God knowing absolutely everything with the idea that a human being has been granted freewill? If God knows in advance everything that will happen to a person, then that person's life must be entirely predestined. Furthermore, if God does not intervene to stop particular courses of action or their outcomes, then one can say that He alone is responsible for them. The problem of freewill versus predestination is linked to the problem of theodicy, or the problem of evil. Who is responsible for evil, if God is ultimately responsible for everything? This leads to such cases as a thief pleading his innocence, because he was surely predestined to steal, and therefore it was hardly his fault, and so on.

Many people believe that Muslims are fatalists, who believe that since 'everything is written' ('maktub'), and that God knows everything in advance - therefore it must all be predetermined. No human brain has been able to untangle this problem satisfactorily - but it is a mistake to assume that Islam is a fatalistic religion. Fatalism is an abuse of Islam - for the entire system of God sending revelations to humanity through the mediation of chosen prophets indicates that humans are expected to listen and then make choices, and adjust their lives accordingly (Surah 6:91; 23:73).

Freewill is the fundamental ingredient

of human activity, and the most difficult of God's gifts to understand or appreciate. Freewill makes sense of human morality - without it there is no such thing as good or evil conduct, for we should simply be automatons.

The whole concept of future judgement depends on personal choice and responsibility. Even if you argue that from the outset God always knows what the ultimate fate of each individual soul will be, (which He must do if He is omniscient), and that He allows each soul a lifetime as a human in order to prove it to himself/herself, it does not answer the question of why God should choose to go through the exercise.

The most satisfactory conclusion is that God does indeed know everything and every possibility, but humans do not. Therefore, if a human chooses a particular thing, there will be a particular outcome leading to a particular conclusion. If the human chooses a different course of action, then the outcome and conclusion will be different. If you choose to swallow a whole bottle of painkilling tablets, you will die this afternoon; but if you choose to swallow only two, it may cure your migraine and you may live to be a hundred. God, like a 'master-computer' knows all the possible outcomes but He leaves the choice to you. One relevant passage in the Qur'an states : *'Truly, Allah does not change the condition of a people until they change what is in themselves'.* (surah 13:11). This certainly seems to indicate that humans have the power to change through their own freewill, and these decisions after their fates.

That is not a perfect answer, but no-one has ever given a perfect solution to this problem. The real answer lies in the realm of al-Ghayb. All devout believers can do is to ask for guidance along their path of life.

They may not be able to see the road way into the distance, but they pray that God will show them the next step, one step at a time.

## 19. AKHIRAH/LIFE AFTER DEATH

*Fact Questions*

1. What is the Arab word for Life after Death?
2. Which is the longest and most important - life on earth, or life after death?
3. What is the purpose of life on earth?
4. What four important things are being tested in our lives?
5. Look at 'the Record' section.
   (a) What are you responsible for?
   (b) How do we earn merit?
   (c) What is the Record for?

6. Explain what Muslims mean by 'time-limit' for testing.
7. How does a person gain forgiveness?
8. When do all people stand alone before God?
9. Why did God send messengers?
10. What are the different fates for:
    (a) Those who are sorry for what they have done wrong?
    (b) Those who are not sorry?

### Understanding

Do the work set in 'Talking Point' and 'For Your Folders'

Look at the 'For Discussion' topics. Do you agree or disagree with the statements given there? Explain why.

### Dictionary Work

Look up TESTS. Give three examples of tests that involve suffering, and three examples of tests that involve wealth.

Look up JUDGEMENT DAY. What is the Arabic word for this? Why are our 'books' (Record) shown to us?

Look up REPENTANCE. What is the Arabic word for this? What does 'repentance' mean?

Look up KAFFARAH. What does this mean? Give an example of something you could do as an act of kaffarah.

Look up FORGIVENESS. Copy out the last sentence.

### Notes: On the Afterlife and Judgement

● **Akhirah. The Hereafter, Life after Death.** This is one of the key fundamental beliefs of Islam, and provides one of the motivations for being Muslim. The fact of life after death is taken as axiomatic, but the form(s) it will take are not known to humanity. *'In Heaven I prepare for the righteous believers what no eye has ever seen, no ear has ever heard, and what the deepest mind could never imagine'* (32:17, and hadith qudsi). Descriptions of conditions in Paradise and Hell are given in detail in the Qur'an, but many scholars take the principle that these are to be interpreted metaphorically, since the Qur'an itself states that *'We will not be prevented from changing your forms and creating you again in forms you know not'* (56:60-61).

The Qur'an reveals that a person's future life will depend very much on three things - what they believe, how they have lived, and the mercy of Allah. All one's deeds during lifetime are recorded in each person's 'book' by two recording angels, and will provide the basis of judgement. All judgement is entirely individual, and no one will be able to excuse or buy off the fate of another - which will be entirely dependent on Allah's mercy.

It is worth pointing out that Muslims who suppose their future state in the life to come is entirely dependant on the balance of their good and bad deeds are not understanding the teaching that Allah may choose to forgive any number of sins, great and small, as He wills. It is not for us to

judge or condemn others-we do not know the mercy of Allah, or His decisions. Muslims who occupy their time trying to accumulate 'good points' by endless repetition of phrases and other ritual practices would do far better to examine their moral and ethical standards, and the good deeds they do to and for others.

• **Day of Resurrection.** Muslims believe that the whole of humanity will be resurrected at a time when God wills. Those who think it impossible for God to recreate human bodies forget the miracle of their first creation. Surah 75 states that God can re-create us, even to our individual fingerprints. However, our resurrection bodies will probably bear no resemblance to our earthly bodies ('*I will create you in forms you know not of*' - 56:61). At this time, each individual will be shown his or her 'book' revealing all good and evil aspects of their lives, and will face judgement. Fortunately for us, however, God does not judge like human beings; although always just and fair, He is also Supreme Compassion and Understanding, so no believer need lose hope, or feel certain that he or she will be condemned.

• **Judge.** It is not for us to judge others. Allah is our only real Judge, who has full knowledge of all our circumstances, conscious and unconscious. Sometimes we think people to be great saints, whereas there are many things in their lives and characters, unknown to us, that show them really to be sinners, proud, self-righteous; etc. Sometimes we think people to be great sinners, whereas there are many things in their lives and characters, unknown to us, that show them to be struggling hard, generous, compassionate, and so on. God represents Perfect Justice, a fairness always tempered by His mercy. Human judges should act as far as possible according to

His principles, and be beyond corruption. The Prophet was well aware of the differing standards of different judges. A Muslim judge would rather mistakenly excuse a guilty person than mistakenly condemn an innocent one.

• **Judgement Day.** The Day of Resurrection when all humans will discover their eternal fates. Humans do not necessarily get what they expect, or what they have deserved; for Allah has full knowledge of all our circumstances and intentions, conscious and unconscious (16:61; 34:45). His perfect justice is always tempered by His mercy, and those who showed repentance during their lifetimes are forgiven, if it is His will. According to many hadiths, it is always His will, alhamdu lillah! However, those who have wronged others do not escape the justice of having this put right--there is no overlooking of sins and hurts caused. Allah knows everything. Our books recorded by our angels are shown to us, so that we can be in no doubt of what we have done. This is not to inform God, or help Him judge us-He already knows everything; it is to make it clear to us. Some people who have believed themselves to have lived wonderful lives will discover occasions when they unwittingly (or even uncaringly) hurt others; the hurt ones will be recompensed for this.

## 20. JUDGEMENT, HEAVEN AND HELL

*Fact Questions*

1. What four things put some people into Hell, according to 74:39-47?
2. Give one way in which humans are different from the animals?
3. Are we more or less 'aware' after death, according to Islam?

4. What is meant by Barzakh?
5. Who is Azrail, and what does 'he' do?
6. What is the name of the Place of Reward and the Place of Punishment? Give the names in both English and Arabic.
7. List five of the things said about Paradise, and three of the things said about Hell.
8. What is the alternative view about Paradise given in 'the Afterlife' paragraph One.

## Understanding

Do the work set in 'Thinking Points' and 'For Your Folders'.

How do the Muslim teachings given here differ from:

(a) Those who believe that death is the end, and all life and knowledge ceases;

(b) Those who believe that sinful people can be reborn and come back and try again in other bodies (reincarnation - this is the belief of Hindus and Buddhists, amongst others)?

## Dictionary Work

Look up PARADISE
(a) What is its Arabic name?
(b) Where does this word come from?
(c) What is the other English name for Paradise?

Look up END OF THE WORLD, and copy out the note.

## Note: On Belief in Afterlife

- This belief has been widely held since humanity's earliest known history.
- It has not been universal, and ideas about it have differed.
- Prehistoric people buried objects from life, so presumably expected some form of life in which they could be used, somehow.
- Dreams suggest that there is a part of a human which can leave the body and wander elsewhere, in sleep, and do things not possible in the waking life, eg. Fly, traverse huge distances in a flash, visit and talk to those who have died, etc.

The main beliefs about life after death have been:

- Although something survives, it is not eternal. Spirits haunted graves and places known in life, and could be left food and drink or offerings. They would gradually fade away.
- The souls of the dead went to a grim underground place to spend eternity in misery and remorse (eg. the Greek Hades, the Hebrew Sheol).
- The souls of the dead would transmigrate into new bodies, either better or worse states depending on how they had lived.
- This process could go on forever, (reincarnation), or it could end in 'union with God', or annihilation of the self -

the drop of water falls into the ocean and becomes ocean.

- If souls continue after death, there is no reason why they should not also have existed before birth. 'Eternity' does not just mean 'from now on', but 'for the whole of time', in both directions - before and after.
- The soul does not exist at all, and therefore belief in any kind of life after death is meaningless. The only way we partially continue is through our offspring.
- Although we cannot prove the reality of the soul by pure reason, we can believe in it for moral reasons, based on the notions of mind and conscience.
- Both Christianity and Islam teach the real existence of the soul, its continued existence after the death of the body, the resurrection of some sort of body at the Time of Judgement, and a future fate involving reward or punishment. The punishment will be for as long as God wills, and need not be eternal; some believe in the complete destruction of all that which is evil, including that within an individual soul - ending up with a purified soul that may then find peace.
- Modern studies of Out-of-Body Experience (OOBE) and Near Death Experience (NDE) strongly suggest that there really is a soul and it can leave the body and act and think independently of it.

# 21. THE HOLY QUR'AN

## Fact Questions

1. What is a surah?
2. How many surahs are in the Qur'an?
3. Which is the first surah?

4. With what words do all surahs except surah 9 begin?
5. Why do surahs have peculiar names?
6. What is a hafiz?
7. In which language was the Qur'an revealed?
8. Who was the Prophet's chief secretary?
9. Who looked after the oldest Qur'an?
10. What four things should Muslims not do whilst the Qur'an is being recited?
11. What are the three preparations?
12. What is a kursi? (Can you draw one? - See Dictionary p.39)
13. Why are Qur'ans usually kept covered?
14. What is calligraphy?

## Special Text

Find p.56 and write out al-Fatihah in English. Give it a decorated border.

## Dictionary Work

Look up QUR'AN
(a) How long did it take to be fully revealed to the Prophet?
(b) What does 'Qur'an' mean?
(c) What is the Arabic for 'Mother of Books'?
(d) What is an ayah, and what does this word mean?
(e) What does al-Fatihah mean?

## Research

If you have a Qur'an - Look up Surah 9. Why do you think this surah does not start with the usual dedication - 'In the Name of Allah, the Compassionate, the Merciful'? If your Qur'an has a commentary or footnotes, you should find some suggestions there. (Yusuf Ali and Muhammad Asad's translations have such notes).

## 22. HADITHS

### Fact Questions

1. What is a hadith?
2. What does 'haddatha' mean?
3. Explain the difference between Prophetic hadith and Hadith Qudsi? (Look back at Unit 6 where we had the word Quds before).
4. Name the two chief hadith collections. (These were compiled around 300 years

after the Prophet's actual lifetime).
5. Name the four next most important.
6. Who wrote the first biographies (life stories) of the Prophet?
7. How many hadiths were listed in: (a) Bukhari (b) Muslim and (c) in circulation by the third century AH?
8. What is a hadith 'chain'?
9. How might a Muslim know a hadith was faulty?
10. Name one wife of the Prophet who was an eminent scholar.

### Understanding

Do the work set in 'Things to do' and 'Thinking Points'.

### Dictionary Work

Look up HADITH:

(a) What is the Arabic word for 'chain'?

(b) What is a sahifa?

(c) Which is the earliest known collection of hadiths?

(d) When did Imam Malik die?

Look up HADITH QUDSI. What does 'qudus' mean?

Look up BAIT UL-MAQDIS. What is this? What is this mosque also called?

Look up ISNAD. Give one way a person could tell if a hadith was not genuine.

### Note: The Hadiths

The Hadiths are the second source of knowledge of God's will which is held in great respect by Muslims. The Hadiths (which means 'sayings') include:

- sayings of the Prophet

- actions or practices of the Prophet

- silent approval of the action of another by the Prophet.

The Hadiths contain the Sunnah or rules of life. These are divided into three groups:

Sahih (sound)

Hasan (good)

Dai'f (weak)

or

Saqim (infirm)

These divisions indicate the genuineness that scholars attribute to the account. Unlike the Qur'an, the Hadiths are not the word of God and therefore can be criticized. Any hadith which does not agree with the principles of the Qur'an must be deemed false - no matter how well-meaning.

Sunni Muslims have six main collections of Hadiths. The six collections are named after the collectors:

| | |
|---|---|
| Bukhari | Al-Tirmidhi |
| Muslim | Al-Nasa'i |
| Abu Da'ud | Ibn Majah |

The authenticity of the collections was based on two lines of scholarship: the first, isnad, checked the chain of authorities cited, while the second, 'ilm ar-rijal, extended this by checking the details of these authorities in huge biographical dictionaries.

# Worship

## 23. IBADAH

### Activity

1. Copy the list of Islamic/Arabic words given below. Go through this section and give one word which suggests the meaning of each one in English:

Ibadah Kufr Shirk Tughyan Iman Amal Ihsan Jihad Din Shahid Niyyah

### Fact Questions

1. If 'abd' means 'slave', what does Abdallah mean?
2. What is meant by 'ibadah'?
3. If you deny the existence of God, which sin is that?
4. If you believe other things have power like God, which sin is that?
5. If you are so over-confident you make others feel small, which sin is that?
6. What did the Prophet say about ihsan?
7. What aspects of our lives are not covered by Din?
8. What is a martyr?
9. Explain what is meant by 'the real jihad'?
10. Why do Muslims believe 'intention' to be so vital?

### Understanding

Do the work set in 'Talking Points' No.2 'For Your Folders' No.1.

### Special Text

Copy out the hadith about iman and amal at the bottom of p.48.

### Dictionary Work

Look up the NAMES OF GOD in the dictionary, p.79. We learn most of our lessons about the Nature of God from these names. What do these particular names mean?

Abd al-Azim Abd al-Karim Abd al-Qadir Abd ar-Rauf Abd al-Wali Abd ar-Rahman.

(You may be more familiar with Abd-al as Abdul).

Can you give examples of what these Names teach us about Allah's nature and 'character'?

Look up ABD AL-MUTTALIB. Who was he? Can you guess why his name has not become a popular Muslim name?

Look up KUFR and SHIRK and check that you know what they really mean.

Look up TYRANNY. What did the Prophet say was 'the most excellent jihad'?

All families need leaders, but families with 'tyrants' are often not too happy. Is there a tyrant in your house? (Make sure it isn't YOU!).

Look up IMAN. Can you remember a lady in the Prophet's family whose name meant 'tranquil'? Why does belief in God make us tranquil?

Look up AMAL. What is faith worthless without?

Look up IHSAN. Is there any part of your thoughts or actions that God couldn't know?

Look up SHAHID. How does a person become a shahid?

Look up DIN-UL-FITRAH and copy out the note.

Look up NIYYAH. When does Allah allow this to count just as much as an actual action?

## 24. SHAHADAH AND ADHAN

*Fact Questions*

1.  What are the 'Arkan'?
2.  A 'creed' is a declaration of faith, from a Latin word 'credo' which means 'I believe'. What is the Arabic for 'I believe'?
3.  Why do you think shahadah has to be the first pillar?
4.  What two things do all Muslims believe?
5.  Make a list of the are seven things in the 'Faith in Detail'. Do 'For Your Folders' No.1.

    The famous 'Ship of Life' Calligraphy shows an Arab dhow (boat) made up of the words of the 'Iman-i-Mufassal.'

*The ship of life. The 'boat' reads:*
*'I believe in Allah, and His angels, His books, His prophets, the Last Day, predestination, good and evil, and resurrection after death'. The 'sail' reads: 'There is no God but Allah and Muhammad is His messenger'.*

*Imam Hamza Yusuf hears the Shahadah of a new American Muslim.*

6.  If a person is born into a Muslim family, when should he or she first hear the shahadah?
7.  Who summoned the faithful to prayer?
8.  Explain the difference between the Mu'adhdin and the Adhan.
9.  What phrase is added during the dawn prayer?

*Art Work*

Copy out the diagram (or make a better one of your own), showing the five pillars that hold up Ibadah. Underneath each pillar choose one word for each to state what they mean: eg. shahadah = witness.

*Understanding*

Do the work set in 'For Discussion', 'Things to do' and 'For Your Folders' No.2.

## 25. PREPARATION FOR PRAYER

*Fact Questions*

1.  What are the seven things Muslims do in order to prepare for prayer.
2.  Explain what is meant by: Wudu Tayammum Qiblah Mihrab

*Calling the adhan.*

3. Why might travelling Muslims carry a small compass?

## Understanding

Do the work set in 'For Your Folders' Nos 1 and 2; 'Thinking Points' and 'Things to do'. You could use the dictionary p.74 to help you with the pictures.

## Dictionary Work

Look up GHUSL. What is this and when is it necessary?

Look up and check the meanings of WUDU, TAYAMMUM, QIBLAH and MIHRAB.

## SOME SUGGESTED THOUGHTS TO GO WITH WUDU

Muslim prayers are performed after ritual washing. This washing is both external and internal:

1. wash the hands to the wrists three times and rinse the mouth three times with water from the right hand.
1a. ask God to forgive sins of deed or word committed knowingly or unknowingly
2. wash the nostrils three times
2a. ask for purity to enable the worshipper to smell the sweetness of heaven
3. wash the face three times
3a. ask for the darkness of sin to be removed so that the worshipper can see God's light
4. wash the right arm to the elbow three times
4a. ask to receive the records of the worshipper's deeds in the right hand on the Day of Judgement.
5. wash the left arm to the elbow three times
5a. ask not to receive the record in the left hand as sinners will
6. wash the head with the inner side of the fingers once
6a. ask for the worshipper's head to be covered with mercy
7. with forefingers in the ears, wash the back of the ears with the thumbs
7a. ask that the worshipper should only wish to hear good and not evil.
8. wash the back of the neck once
8a. ask that suffering may not hang around the neck
9. wash the right foot to the ankle.
9a. ask that the worshipper should be led in the path of the righteous
10. wash the left foot to the ankle
10a. ask that the worshipper should not be led into the paths of hell.

If there is no water, or if it is unusable, or if the worshipper is sick, then Tayammum, or dry wudu, can be performed. This is done by placing dust on the hands, blowing it off and then doing the motions of washing the face and arms with the hands.

## Art Work

Draw the mihrab shown in the dictionary on p.45, or design one of your own.

## 26. SALAH

### Fact Questions

1. How many times per day should Muslims perform salah (also called namaz in Urdu)?
2. Write out the names of the five prayers, and state the times between which they should be said.
3. What do Muslims face while praying salah?
4. Look at the picture on p.54. Why do you think these Muslims are praying in the street?
5. Look at the prayer timetable for Start Times. These were recorded for the first two weeks in July, in Hull, north-east England.
   (a) What time was the start of fajr on 7th July?
   (b) What time was sunrise that day?
   (c) Fajr = Dawn. How long, therefore, was there between the first light of dawn and the actual sunrise?
   (d) Why is sunrise earlier on 1st July than on the 14th July?

(This is a geography question. You need to know the date of midsummer day, and what happens to the daytime after it in the northern hemisphere).
   (e) Why is sunset later on 1st July than on 14th July? (More geog).
6. How should prayer mats be treated when not in use?

### Understanding

Do the work set in 'For Your Folders', 'Thinking Points' and 'Things to do'.

### Art Work

Draw a 24 hour clock face, and divide it up for the five prayers on one day in the chart.

### Dictionary Work

Look at the clocks shown in the dictionary on p.60. You will often see clocks like this in the mosque showing people the prayer times for that day. Most Muslims are used to eastern ways, so they often read them from right to left. The sixth clock face shows the Jumu'ah time. Look up Jumu'ah and explain what this is.

## 27. THE RAKAH

### Fact Questions

1. What is a rakah, and how many compulsory rakahs are there in each prayer?
2. Explain what is meant by: takbir al-Fatihah ruku qiyam sujud salam
3. Write out and learn the Arabic words for 'Allah is Supreme'.
4. Write out and learn the Arabic words for 'In the Name of Allah, the Compassionate, the Merciful'.

5. What are the two special requests asked for in al-Fatihah?
6. Allah is 'Lord of................'? and 'Master of..................'?
7. Can you work out which words are the Arabic for those two phrases? (Clues: Rabb = Lord; Malik = Master or King).
8. Did the Prophet think public prayers (those said together in congregation) should be short or long?
9. Why do Muslims bow or kneel at prayer?
10. What are the 'five bones' that touch the ground during sujud?
11. What are the two meanings of the head-turning during the salam?

### Useful Prayer-Card

For practising Muslims.

If you have never done this, it is quite a good idea to make a prayer-card. It might come in very handy for future reference, if you ever introduce someone new to Islam. Get some A4 card and make a pencil line down the middle. On the left, write in the Arabic things said during the rakah, and put the translation (given on pp56-57) on the right. You could combine this with question 4 given above.

### Understanding

Do the work set in 'For your Folders' and 'Things to do'.

### Art Work

Look at the pictures on p.58. Draw your own version of each prayer position and label them.

### Dictionary Work

Look up RAKAH. What is the 'greeting to the mosque'?

Look up BISMILLAH. When does this refer to a party?

Look up BISMILLAH AR-RAHMAN AR-RAHIM

(a) Give two examples of when a Muslim might use this phrase.

(b) Which surah does not start with these words?

Look up DARUD, and explain what this is.

### Art Work

Draw your own Bismillah (This could be on a special card).

A Mihrab is also called a qiblah niche. It shows the direction of Makkah.

A Muslim often owns a Prayer mat-to make a clean space on which to bow down;

A compass

finds the direction of Makkah. With the compass comes a small leaflet showing how to set it so that whenever you are, the compass will point to Makkah.

A string of beads, to use for prayers after Salah; you could recite the Names of God, or phrases praising and thanking God.

## 28. IMAMS AND FRIDAY PRAYERS

### Fact Questions

1. What is the imam in the picture doing?
2. What is the Arabic word for 'sermon' or 'short religious talk'?
3. Which is the day for special congregations in the mosque?
4. Where do most women pray at this time?
5. What is an Imam?
6. What four qualities are expected in an Imam?
7. How many rakahs are said in a Friday prayer?
8. Why do praying women sit apart from the men?
9. What provisions are sometimes made for women in a mosque?

### Special Text

Copy out surah 62:9 with a special decorated border.

### Understanding

Do the work set in 'For Discussion.'

If you are a practising Muslim, look at the section called 'Concentration'. Many Muslims break these 'unwritten rules' when they go to pray. Nobody is perfect. However, explain why it is bad Islamic manners to:

(a) Chat to a friend while waiting for prayer to start.
(b) Recite Qur'an loudly while waiting for prayer to start.
(c) Make a big show with loud takbirs, rocking during sitting prayers, yawning, loud sighs, etc, etc.

### Dictionary Work

Look up WOMEN. (many people find it very strange how so many mosques have become 'prayer-clubs' for Muslim men. Look again at Surah 62:9 and check out

# THE MUSLIM IMAM'S WORK

The mosque is clean. We take off our shoes when we enter.

I wear traditional dress in the mosque

We have to wash before we pray.

It is important to pray regularly.

I teach children Arabic

I love to hear people declare their faith.

At 'Id, all Muslims put on their best clothes to pray at the mosque.

Sometimes I am invited to parties to celebrate a baby's birth.

A Muslim wedding is a very special occasion.

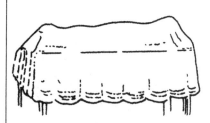

Funerals are sad times for all the family.

I often give talks in schools.

Sometimes I meet with other religious leaders in the community.

Imam Mukhtar Maghrawi giving a lecture.

other relevant passages if you like). Does the Qur'an ever give the command to pray to men only? What did the female companions of the Prophet usually do?

Some women think men don't want them there in the mosque because there's no room for them. Could this be true? Is this a good or bad thing?

(Note: There is a whole section of the role of Shi'ite Imams in units 70-72).

## 29. DU'A

### Fact Questions

1. What are du'a?
2. Look at the four common sorts of du'a people pray. Can you give an example for each?
   (eg. thanks for Mum getting better; help to face a bully; forgiveness for upsetting sister; request for guidance when I start a new job).
3. What is a subhah (tasbih)?

4. Why does it have 99 beads?
5. What do Muslims remind themselves of during prayers?
6. What is the best kind of du'a?

### Understanding

Do all the work set in 'Talking Points', 'For Discussion', 'Things to do', and 'For Your Folders'.

### Art Work

If you have a photograph or picture of someone making du'a prayers, you could stick it in your folder. If you have no photo, you could draw a picture of someone at du'a prayer.

## 30. ZAKAH

### Fact Questions

1. What does the word 'charitable' mean?
2. What is sadaqah?
3. What is zakah, and how is it different from sadaqah?
4. How much of one's surplus income is subject to zakah?
5. What are the aims of zakah?

6. What six kinds of people may receive zakah money?
7. Give two reasons why zakah is usually paid in secret.
8. What does Surah 2:264 say about people who like to get public praise for their giving?
9. Who is the true Owner of all our wealth?
10. Can you think of some things or ambitions that do often become the 'masters' of certain people? Money is usually top of the list, so we'll take that for granted - but what else can 'enslave' people?
11. How is the real value of something increased when you give it away?

## Understanding

Do the work set in 'For Your Folders', 'Talking Points', and 'Things to do'.

## Dictionary Work

Look up ZAKAH.
(a) What is meant by 'nisab'?
(b) What happens when people just 'save' money?
(c) If you were farming in the UK - sheep or cows - how much zakah should you pay on these animals?

## 31. SAWM

### Fact Questions

1. What is sawm (or siyam)?
2. What is the name of the Muslim fasting month?
3. When does a day's fast begin and end?
4. What are the three things that have to be brought under control?
5. Why is Ramadan even harder for smokers? (Well, it serves them right!)

6. What is even more important than the going without?
7. Look at the second hadith given here. Why do certain people 'gain nothing but hunger and sleeplessness' when they fast? (ie. give examples of what you think they are doing wrong).
8. Write out the six aims of fasting.
9. Why can't a Muslim 'cheat' Allah?
10. How could a Muslim make up for not being able to fast?
11. Why is Ramadan a special month, apart from the fasting?
12. How many days earlier does Ramadan come each year, and why?
13. Explain what is meant by: iftar suhur.
14. Why is Ramadan harder
   (a) for people who are working
   (b) in a hot summer
   (c) for those who live away from the equator?

## Understanding

Do the work set in 'For Your Folders'.

## Dictionary Work

Look up FASTING:
(a) Are eating, drinking, smoking and sexual intimacy completely banned during Ramadan?
(b) How could someone who had missed the fast in Ramadan make up for it?
Look up CALENDAR:
(a) Which is Muslim Year 1?
(b) It's easy to calculate the Muslim date with a calculator. Put the year, subtract 622, multiply by 33, and divide by 32. 1997 = the Muslim year 1417.
What will the year 2000 be?
Look up LAYLAT AL-QADR.
(a) What happened on this night?
(b) What does 'Qadr' mean?
(c) When is it usually observed?

(d) Explain why this is not a universally accepted date.

(e) What do many Muslims do during this special night?

## 32. HAJJ

### Fact Questions

1. What is the Hajj?
2. What does 'Hajj' mean?
3. What is the 'Hajj duty'?
4. What are the dates of the Hajj?
5. What is an Umrah?
6. Where is the Hajj Terminal airport in Saudi Arabia?
7. How do Muslims who intend to do Hajj make up for it if they can't go?
8. Give three facts about the Hajj Terminal.

### Understanding

Do the work set in 'For Your Folders'.

## Press Report

The Muslim News, April 24, 1998

# More than 100 die in Hajj stampede

As we go to print, the official figure for those who died in the stampede at the Jamarat Bridge, in Mina, three miles from Makkah, on April 9, is 120. Most of the dead (who died soon after dhuhr on the last day of Hajj) were elderly and came from Indonesia and Malaysia. Over 2 million people performed Hajj this year from over 100 countries.

One Egyptian pilgrim told the Saudi Gazette that the rush on the Bridge was immense just before dhuhr prayers. Pilgrims were seen waiting at the entrance on this exceptionally hot day, for a long time. When the police started letting them on to the top, the stampede began. Many elderly pilgrims and women started fainting and falling on the ground. "By the time I got to the passage at the top, I saw hundreds lying on the sides of the bridge," he said. The massive rush takes place every year on the bridge from 12 noon to 3.30 p.m. The pilgrims have to rush to finish the stoning at the three-pillars to catch their buses for the return to Makkah. The Saudi Government provides extensive security and medical support to ensure safety but a stampede is becoming common.

Last year, 343 pilgrims died and more than 1,500 were injured when a fire engulfed 70,000 tents in Mina. In response, the Saudis set up more than 10,000 fire-resistant tents and banned the use of gas cylinders.

In recent years, tragedy has dogged the Hajj season. In 1990, 1,426 pilgrims died in a stampede when a huge bottleneck developed at the entrance to a tunnel in Makkah. In 1994, 270 died in another stampede at Jamarat.

Meanwhile, 28 people died after a bus carrying Iranian Muslim pilgrims collided with a petrol tanker in Birecik in Sanliurfa province in southern Turkey, near the Syrian Border.

The authorities in Uzbekistan prevented Uzbek Muslims from leaving the country to perform Hajj. They claim many of the pilgrims are leaving illegally for Hajj. This year, the former Soviet Republic allowed only 3,500 to perform Hajj. Meanwhile, Saudi Arabia paid for about 1,500 Muslims from the former Soviet Union to attend the Hajj. The pilgrims included those from Russia (including Tatarstan and Chechnya), Azarbayjan, Kazakhstan and Uzbekistan. They have also paid for a group of British Muslim converts to go for the Hajj.

## 33. HAJJ BACKGROUND

### Fact Questions

1. Give the Arabic name for the Mount of Mercy.
2. In which plain is it to be found?
3. What happened here, according to tradition?
4. Why did Allah forgive Adam and Eve?
5. What did they do, in gratitude?
6. What is the main theme of 9 Dhu'l Hijjah?
7. Who is the second prophet remembered on Hajj?
8. Name this prophet's two wives.
9. Name his eldest son.
10. What did Ibrahim dream that Allah wanted him to do?
11. What happened at Mina?
12. Why did Ibrahim throw stones?
13. Why didn't Ibrahim kill Ismail?
14. What was the reward granted to him?
15. How did Hajar and Ismail nearly die?
16. What are Safa and Marwah?
17. Who showed Hajar a spring of water?
18. What is that spring now called?
19. What is the Maqam Ibrahim?
20. Describe briefly what we think the first Ka'bah looked like.

### Understanding

Do the work set in 'Talking Points' and 'For Your Folders'.

### Dictionary Work

Look up HAJJ, and draw the Hajj pictures. Look up ADAM:

(a) What is the name for Eve in Arabic?
(b) Why may they be considered 'equal'?
(c) Who refused to honour Adam?
(d) What were Adam and Eve forbidden to do
(e) How did Shaytan deceive them?
(f) What is meant by tawbah?

### Note: The Christian Doctrine of Original Sin and Salvation

In Christian doctrine the sin passed down by Adam and Eve was known as the Original Sin. All future human beings were born carrying the stain of this sin, from which they could never be pure enough to break free. God, because of His great love and compassion towards humans, became 'incarnate' (became a human being) in order to be their Saviour or Redeemer. The Son of God was both human and divine, therefore could identify with humanity, and also be greater than humanity and hence able to redeem them.

Islam rejects the notion of inherited original sin, and claims we are all judged fairly for our own lives. Therefore the whole idea of a Redeemer, or a Christ dying a sacrificial death in order to save us, is not necessary. Muslims do not believe God had a human son. They believe Jesus was a great prophet and

*The extended Ka'bah shrine, packed with pilgrims.*

Messenger, but only son of God in the sense that we are all 'sons' of God. Muslims claim this is what Jesus actually taught. For example, the Lord's Prayer begins 'OUR Father, which art in Heaven'.

If Islam is right, and the notion of a divine Trinity is wrong, the whole of the edifice of Christianity is undermined-hence the enmity of Christian theologians towards Islam.

Look up IBRAHIM:

(a) Where did he come from?

(b) What did his name al-Khalil mean?

(c) How did he prove that his father's idols had no power?

(d) What do we call a person who wanders from place to place and has no settled home?

(e) What country did Ibrahim's wife Hajar come from?

(f) Why did people offer sacrifices to idols?

(g) Why was Ibrahim's dream mistaken?

(h) What did Ibrahim sacrifice instead?

(i) What feast do Muslims celebrate each year in memory of this?

## 34. ARRIVAL

### Fact Questions

1. What is the chief aim of the state of ihram?

2. What do men in ihram wear?

3. What do women in ihram wear?

4. What three things do ihram cloths symbolise?

5. What does ihram also remind Muslims of?

6. What is the rule about sex and marriage in ihram?

7. What is different about the soap the traders sell to pilgrims?

8. Why do some people carry umbrellas to Saudi Arabia - one of the driest places in the world?

9. What is the ruling for ladies' faces?

10. What are people forbidden to cut?

11. What do pilgrims wear on their feet?

12. Why is the Hajj a relief for wild animals?

13. What is the prayer of arriving pilgrims called?

14. What is the tawaf?

15. What does 'Labbayka, Allahumma!' mean?

16. Do all pilgrims have to touch the Black Stone?

17. What does the sa'y symbolise?

### Understanding

Do the work set in 'Thinking Points'.

### Dictionary Work

Look up IHRAM:

(a) Draw the male pilgrim

(b) How does ihram indicate equality?

(c) What are the ihram rules aimed at encouraging?

Look up TAWAF:

(a) If you arrive at the Ka'bah at 2am, should you have a sleep first before doing tawaf?

(b) What arrangements are laid on for the aged and disabled?

## Special Text

Make a neat copy of the Talbiyah Prayer, and give it a decorated border.

## 35. SIGNIFICANT PLACES

### Fact Questions

1. What does 'Baitullah' mean?

2. How are the prophets Adam and Ibrahim connected with it?

3. What did the Prophet Muhammad find inside it?

*An old photo of the Ka'bah.*

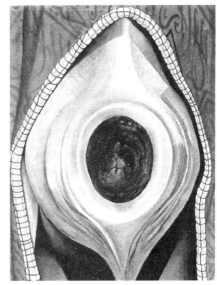

*The Black Stone set in silver.*

4. What is inside it now?

5. How many qiblahs are inside it, and why?

6. What is al-Kiswah?

7. What happens to it at the end of Hajj?

8. Briefly describe what the Black Stone looks like.

9. The Ka'bah, and the Black Stone, existed long before the time of the Prophet Muhammad. Give one piece of evidence to prove this.

10. What is the 'meteorite' theory?

11. If you look at the picture of the Ka'bah, you will see a long corridor running along the 'top' side. It joins the two hills, Safa and Marwah. Who first ran desperately between those two hills, and why?

12. What is the name of the well shown to her by the angel Jibril?

13. State two things that pilgrims might do at this well.

14. What happens on the Plain of Arafat?

15. Which is the most important part of Hajj?

16. What do pilgrims do at Muzdalifah?

17. What can you see at Mina? (see the picture on p.73).

Pilgrims climbing Mt. Arafat.

## Dictionary Work

Look up BLACK STONE:

(a) What is it called in Arabic?

(b) Where is it set?

(c) How was the Prophet Muhammad connected with it?

## Art Work

Draw the picture, if you have not drawn it earlier. (You could stick in a photograph or picture-postcard if you have one).

Look up MOUNT ARAFAT:

(a) What is the date when the Hajj wuquf takes place?

(b) What do pilgrims pray for at this time?

Look up MINA:

(a) When do pilgrims camp here?

(b) What do they do with some small stones?

Look up MUZDALIFAH:

(a) How many pebbles do pilgrims collect here?

(b) Which prayers are said at Muzdalifah?

Look up JAMARAT:

(a) How many jamarat are there?

(b) What does throwing the stones represent?

Look up ZAMZAM: Whose vision led to its rediscovery after its loss?

## Art Work

Draw the picture of a jamra.

## 36. THE STAND BEFORE GOD

### Fact Questions

1. What is the Arabic name for 'the Stand'?

2. How long do the pilgrims stand before Allah?

3. How does missing the Wuquf affect a person's Hajj?

4. Look at the pictures. Why do you think so many people are carrying umbrellas?

5. What happens on 10th Dhu'l Hijjah?

6. What happens to the carcases of all the slaughtered animals?

7. What do pilgrims do at the end of their ihram?

8. What title may pilgrims take?

9. In which town is the Prophet's tomb?

10. In whose room was he buried?

11. Who else is buried in that room with him?

12. What happened on Mt Nur?

13. What happened on Mt Thawr?

14. Which mosque has two mihrabs, and why?

15. Where is Aishah buried?

16. Who were the Wahhabis, and why did they destroy the 'grand mausoleums'? (A Mausoleum is a grand monument erected over a grave).

## Understanding

Do the work set in 'Things to do' and 'For Your Folders'.

## Dictionary Work

Look up WUQUF:

(a) If you miss the wuquf, what does your Hajj become?

(b) Which prayers start and end the wuquf?

## Art Work

Draw the picture

Look up DHU'L HIJJAH:

Is it the first or last month of the Islamic year?

Look up MUHARRAM:

Which month of the year is this?

Look up ASHURAH:

Which member of the Prophet's family died on 10th Muharram?

Look up WAHHABISM: Copy out the note.

Look up BURIAL: Why did the Wahhabis disapprove of the Mausoleums?

Look up GRAVES: What did the Prophet recommend?

# Festivals and Special Days

## 37. FESTIVALS

### Fact Questions

1. What does the word 'Id mean?
2. Why is the practice of 'regularly repeating' important?
3. List some of the good things brought about by the festivals.
4. Is the Islamic calender based on the sun or the moon?
   (therefore, explain why Muslim feasts come 10 or 11 days earlier each year).
5. Make a list of the six 'special days' in Islam.
   (Look at the section headings for this).
6. When is the Prophet's birthday celebrated?
7. What happened on Lailat ul-Qadr? (This can also be spelled Laylat al-Qadr).

8. What happened on Lailat ul-Miraj?
9. What is the Lailat ul-Bara'at?
10. What is the Arabic name for New Year's Day?
11. What does it commemorate, and who started this practice?
12. What is the special name for Muharram 10th?
13. What three events are celebrated on this day?
14. Why is it an extra-special day for Shi'ite Muslims?

### Understanding

Do the work set in 'Talking Point'.

### Dictionary Work

Look up 'ID:
   (a) What is the greeting used on 'Id days?
   (b) Design and draw your own 'Id card (or, you could stick in one that you received, if you have one).

Look up FEASTS:
   What sort of things do Muslims celebrate with feasts?
   Note: These are not 'Ids, because they do not recur regularly; they are one-off events.

Look up MAULID AN-NABI:
   (a) How do some Muslims celebrate this day?
   (b) Why do you think some Muslims feel it is wrong to make too much of it?

Look up LAYLAT UL-QADR:
   (a) Why is this the most important night in Islam?
   (b) What is meant by i'tikaf?

Look up LAYLAT UL-MIRAJ:
   Why is it called the 'Night of Ascent'?

Look up LAYLAT UL-BARA'AT:
   (a) What do many people do on the following day?
   (b) Why is it also known as the 'Night of the Decree'?

Note: 'Id or Eid
   This word gets spelled both ways because it starts with an Arabic sound for which there is no equivalent in English.

## 38. 'ID UL-FITR

### Fact Questions

1. When does this feast take place?
2. How do Muslims know when it is the right day to celebrate it?

3. What do many Muslims send to friends and relatives?
4. What is the zakat-ul-fitr?
5. How long is the holiday in some Muslim countries
6. How does the 'Id congregational prayer differ from the usual Friday ones?
7. In what sort of places is this prayer held?
8. Why might some people visit the cemetery (graveyard)?

### Understanding

If you are a practising Muslim family, give a brief description of how you celebrated your last 'Id. (Living or working in the West, your celebrations may have been 'dampened' by work and school routines here. Or were they? Or, how did you make the day special anyway?)

Do the work set in 'For Your Folders'.

## Dictionary Work

Look up 'ID UL-FITR:

Give two other names used for this festival.

## 39. 'ID UL-ADHA

### Fact Questions

1. When does this feast take place?

2. Which Prophet's obedience does it commemorate?

3. How long does the feast last in some Muslim countries?

4. What does the feast represent?

5. What sort of animals might be sacrificed at this feast?

6. Which is the most usual in the West?

7. Where are the animals slaughtered in the West?

   (Private slaughtering at home is forbidden by law).

8. How is a sacrificial animal killed?

9. Why is it killed in this particular way?

10. What is the word for meat which comes from creatures killed in this way? (Note: True Muslim meat is always killed in this way, and not just at festivals).

### Understanding

Do the work set in 'For Your Folders' and 'For Discussion'.

### Special Text

Copy out Surah 22:37 (given on p.80), and give it a nice decorated border.

### Note

Do you know how animals are usually slaughtered for the meat market in the West? Many non-muslims believe halal killing to be cruel, and complain about this method; but they usually do not know themselves about the non-halal methods, in order to compare them fairly. Keep your eyes open for information, press-cuttings, etc. It would be useful to 'cut and paste' a page for your folder. The animals regularly eaten in the West are sheep, cows, pigs and chickens. In France, they eat frogs legs and snails and horse-meat, and in some places people eat whale-meat, and in China they eat dogs.

(There is more work on this subject in Unit 44).

### Dictionary Work

Look up 'ID UL-ADHA:
(a) Give two other names for this feast.
(b) How can Muslims join in if they do not sacrifice an animal themselves?

### Research: Find out

How much does a whole sheep cost at your butchers? (It is around three carrier-bags of meat).

# 'Islamic Relief's Alternative 'Id celebrations' By Muhammad Sajjad

April 11 saw Islamic Relief bring their national concert tour to the Wembley Conference Centre in north-west London as part of the celebrations for 'Id al-Adha. The evening was primarily set up as a children's programme, where fun and games would occupy most of the function.

Nevertheless, there was a very serious point to the event. Islamic Relief were trying to bring across to the public that while most of the Muslims were celebrating this auspicious occasion of 'Id in a jovial manner, there were many Muslims out there who were not so fortunate. This point was emphasised clearly by Dr.Hani al-Banna, Founding Director of Islamic Relief. "No one would like to see our children naked, sick and in poverty", he said. He spoke of the distress of many Muslims in Third World countries. He later pleaded with elders in the audience to donate money generously to Islamic Relief so

that they may help those in need. "The one who helps himself is the one who gives", he said.

Having been set up in 1984, Islamic Relief has provided a vast amount of humanitarian support around the world, varying from victims of war to those suffering from famine and drought. Their current agenda is called the Orphan Welfare Programme and is designed to help those children who have become separated from, or lost their families as a result of natural catastrophes like flooding and cyclones. They currently have an aid agency in Bangladesh where they are helping many such victims, as they very movingly illustrated on a short video. Similarly they want to help many such children in Pakistan, India, Bosnia and Palestine, to name but a few places.

Throughout the evening, many Muslim music groups performed a variety of different acts, from nasheeds and Islamic rap to a traditional Palestinian dance. The evening was headlined by a group called The Sham, who are from Birmingham and have featured greatly on the new Islamic Relief Charity Album, 'Our Children Our Future'. In addition, there was an auction, which raised close to a thousand pounds for Islamic Relief, as well as

a raffle in which the first prize was an Umrah ticket donated by Emirates Airlines.

The guest speaker at the event was Iqbal Sacranie, Secretary General of the Muslim Council of Britain (MCB), an umbrella organisation set up last year to act as a focal point for more than 250 Muslim groups and individuals in the UK. He spoke on the good work that Islamic Relief was doing in supporting Muslims in need around the world. "We as Muslims should be seen as doing good work," he said, and spoke of his happiness that Islamic Relief were part of the MCB.

The UK Manager of Islamic Relief, Fadi Itani, spoke on the Islamic principles relating to helping those less unfortunate than us.

"Islamic Relief is related to the message of the Prophet. We all try to do our best, but our community are complaining that we are losing our future," he spoke referring to the many young Muslims who are presently undergoing terrible hardship and whose futures look very bleak. "We must find them an alternative, and Islam has an alternative," he added.

The evening was enjoyed by everyone, yet the strong message that Islamic Relief tried to bring through remained very poignant right until the end. The organizers hope to repeat this function every year, and hope that these functions will act as a spring-board for Islamic Relief's good work around the world.

# Lifestyle and Social Practice

## 40. SHARI'AH

### Fact Questions

1. What is meant by 'taqwa'?
2. What does taqwa alter?
3. What is the one thing that brings true justice?
4. What does 'shari'ah' mean?
5. For what is the shari'ah the criterion?
6. The Four Principles sum up the whole concept of shari'ah. Write them out neatly, with a decorated border.
7. What is the Ummah?
8. What are the ideals that form the basis of Islamic morality?
9. What is a madhdhab?
10. Explain what is meant by 'keeping the gate closed' and 'keeping the gate open'.

### Understanding

Do the work set in 'Thinking Point', 'For Your Folders' and 'Things to Do'.

### Dictionary Work:

Look up TAQWA:
What is a muttaqeen?
Look up SHARI'AH
(a) What two things are shari'ah rulings based on?
(b) Who is the leader of the chief Shi'ite madhdhab?
Look up SUNNAH: What does this mean?
Look up SUNNI: What is a Sunni Muslim?
Look up SHI'AH: Who were the Shi'ites originally following?

### Note: The Sunnah

Sunnah, pl. Sunan. Lit. 'a form', (from 'sanna' - to shape, form, establish); the customary practice of a person or group of people. It has come to refer almost exclusively to the practice of the Messenger of Allah. The Prophet's example, or way of life. Everything he said, did, approved of or condemned.

The original principle was that those who followed the Prophet's sunnah would be rewarded for it, but there was no punishment or censure for those who did not. The Prophet was very clear that no-one should be coerced into making compulsory anything that was not compulsory. Attempts to preserve his way of life in exact detail in societies that have changed considerably are misguided and extremist. In any case, some Muslims seem rather quaint in which examples of sunnah they accept and which they reject. Many insist

on not eating with knife and fork where it is normal to do so, yet think nothing of using a modern toilet instead of crouching over two bricks! The real importance of following sunnah lies not in such trivial detaiis, but in following the Prophet's way of compassion, gentleness, honesty, courage and truth (33:21). At the time that Imam Malik, may Allah be pleased with him, compiled the Muwatta', there was no sense of setting the sunnah of the prophet apart from the sunnah of Madinah, so that the actions of its knowledgeable people were given even more weight than the behaviour of the Prophet related in isolated hadith. This has always characterized the Maliki viewpoint.

## Madhdhab

A 'school' of religious law, or a system of fiqh. Four madhhabs (correct plural 'madhahib') have been accepted as authoritative by Sunni Muslims. The Hanafi (from Abu Hanifa 669-767), the Maliki (from Malik ibn Anas 717-795), the Shafi'i (from al-Shafi'i 767-820), and Hanbali (from Ahmad ibn Hanbal d.855). Shi'ite Muslim groups developed their own system of law and moral precepts from their sixth Imam, Jafar al-Sadiq (d.765). Abu Hanifa placed his emphasis on broad interpretations based on individual reasoning and analogy; Imam Malik taught that the ways of the elders of Madinah should be uncorrupted by new converts or 'modern' influences; al-Shafi'i brought greater clarity to the bases of making legal decisions, using general principles as well as specific Qur'anic commands-the Prophet's practice as recorded in hadiths was more important than the practices of various communities; ibn Hanbal developed al-Shafi'is thought, and emphasised methods of choosing hadiths carefully - but preferred even weak hadiths to strong analogies. Jafar as-Sadiq regarded consensus as valid only if the opinion of the Imam was included, because of the belief that Imams were infallible, and did not need to resort to analogy. In this century, most Muslims follow one or other

of these schools, but although these eminent teachers are so highly venerated, it is not to be assumed that no further thought can be added to theirs.

Each of the scholars who founded the schools of thought after named them was simply a great scholar. They did not aspire to any higher position. There was nothing special about the number four-there were many other eminent scholars, some of whom were contemporaries of those four (e.g. Imam al-Layth ibn Sa'd of Egypt). None of the four made any special claim to be followed. A school of thought is a matter of deductions of rulings and verdicts from Qur'an and hadith statements. The four Imams all drew from the Qur'an, but had different knowledge of and approaches to the hadith. They had eminent disciples who gave a continuity to their 'schools,' but in each school we may find scholars who differed on specific questions. There was no rigidity about following any one Imam in all questions and matters. If they had known later generations of Muslims would be divided into narrow 'schools' they would have been horrified - they were the first to admit they were liable to error. A Muslim may choose which of their opinions they agree with, or even not belong to a 'school' at all.

# 41. QIYAS

## Fact Questions

1. What is the chief problem when following the shari'ah?

2. Why do Muslims feel that these issues matter?

3. Why can't Muslims just pick and choose the rules?

4. What is meant by 'qiyas'?

5. When is qiyas used?

6. What is a binding decision called?

7. What is the exercise of reason called?

8. What is a mujtahid?

9. What is an ayatollah?

10. What is fiqh?

11. What four principles have always to be taken into consideration?

12. Why is it important to have limits?

13. What is Shari'ah intended to provide?

14. It is important to know the names of the five categories of behaviour in Islam. Write out their Arabic names, and explain what each means. Give an example for each category. (Try to think of your own examples too).

15. How might a Muslim decide whether or not any modern action is halal?

## Understanding

Do the work set in 'Thinking Points' and 'For Your Folders' No.3.

## Dictionary Work

Look up QIYAS: Write out the note.

Look up IJTIHAD: What does this exercise of reason make use of?

Look up FIQH: What does this word mean?

Look up AYATOLLAH: Name the Ayatollah who led the Islamic revolution in Iran.

Look up FARD: What is the word for 'voluntary'?

Look up FARD KIFAYAH: Give some examples of these.

Look up HARAM: Why is any thing or substance or activity forbidden?

Look up BIDAH: What do we mean by bidah?

## 42. MANNERS AND GREETINGS

### Fact Questions

1. Explain what is meant by 'taharah'.
2. Which parts of the body need special attention?
3. Which pet causes most problems to Muslims in the UK, and why?
4. Why do Muslims keep a jug or bottle of water in the toilet?
5. At which times is a full bath or shower necessary?
6. What was the Prophet's recommendation about body hair?
7. Why are Muslims usually not shy to take their shoes off in public?
8. Look at the Table Manners section: Can you find and list ten 'rules'?
9. What is the usual Muslim greeting and reply, and what do these words mean?
10. Why do many Muslim men not shake hands with women, and vice versa?
11. Write out the Arabic for:
    (a) 'If God wills' and (b) 'Praise be to Allah'

### Understanding

Do the work set in 'For Discussion' and 'For Your Folders'.

### Dictionary Work

Look up: AL-HAMDU-LILLAH. When might Muslims say this?

Look up DOGS:

(a) Why do Muslims normally not keep them in the house?

(b) In what circumstances might they keep a dog?

Look up HAMD: Whose name includes this word?

Look up INSHA ALLAH: When might a Muslim say this?

## 43. MUSLIM DRESS

### Fact Questions

1. What are Muslim men and women both asked to 'guard'?
2. Why do Muslim women try not to meet the eyes of male strangers while walking in the street?
3. What sort of clothes still leave a woman 'naked'?
4. What do Muslims generally believe about sexual freedoms?
5. What is meant by 'hijab'?
6. Why do so many women prefer traditional Islamic dress to western clothes?
7. Explain what is meant by 'purdah'.
8. What is a chador?
9. Give four 'rules' for Muslim men's clothing.

### Understanding

Do the work set in 'For Discussion' and 'For our Folders'.

### Dictionary Work

Look up AWRAH: There are a lot of different ideas as to what this word means. Give two of them.

Look up BURQA:

(a) In which regions of the world are these mainly worn?

(b) Do a quick sketch of one.

Look up CHADOR

(a) Where might you see this worn?

(b) Do all Iranian Muslim women wear them?

Look up CLOTHING:

(a) Sometimes you see Muslim women with their faces all covered up except their eyes. Why do most Muslim women not veil their faces?

(b) What is the proper way for a Muslim

man to react when faced by a 'sexy' lady?

Look up HIJAB:

(a) Draw the typical veil.

(b) What is the intention of it?

Look up PURDAH: What is this an extreme version of?

Look up MAHRAM: Who are a woman's mahrem?

Look up KHULWAH: What does this mean?

## Art Work

If you have collected up or drawn pictures of Islamic dress from various parts of the world, this is a good place to display them.

## Notes: On Dress

There are few specific rules concerning dress in the Qur'an and therefore the clothes that Muslims wear tend to be influenced in part by the cultural practice of the country in which they live. However, the following points are observed:

- Men and women must cover their bodies from the neck to the ankles.
- The clothes should be sufficiently loose so that the shape of the body is not made improperly apparent.
- For certain tasks men may uncover to the waist and from the knees down.
- Although men are not required to cover their heads, women do so when outside of their homes and in the presence of men who are not close relatives. Some women also choose to cover their faces (although during the Hajj all women must uncover their faces for the actual pilgrimage).
- Men should not wear silk (which is understood to mean fine clothes) or gold jewellery. Women may wear these things but not in order to entice men. For the same reason men and women should lower their eyes when they meet.
- Nudity is forbidden even within a single sex group; the only exception is made for medical reasons.

## Purdah

An Urdu word referring to the practice of complete social separation of men from women unless they are members of their immediate family, an extreme extension of the sensible requirements that women should never be left alone with men who might take advantage of them. Many Muslim women achieve purdah when out in public by dressing in such a way that they cannot be seen. Islam requires modest

dress, but does not lay down the style - this is frequently a matter of local custom. Purdah can be oppressive and an abuse of Islam when it is forced upon women who do not wish to dress in this manner, sometimes by law backed up with a police force!

## Segregation/Seclusion of Women

It is not true that women are required to be kept at home all the time-and this is not attempted in most of the Muslim world. Muslim women are requested not to hang about in public places unnecessarily, or to encourage unwanted attention. Women may certainly go out, and move within women's circles especially, visiting their friends and relatives and receiving visitors. The notion of complete segregation, leaving women to have their own gatherings away from those of men, is mainly social tradition. What is forbidden in Islam is for a man to be alone in an enclosed area with a woman whom he could legally marry - including his first cousins. At least one other person should be present, usually a woman, preferably his mother or sister, in order to prevent any temptation to sexual misconduct. It is an unfortunate fact that some girls and women even need protection from men in their own families, and in these circumstances it would be most advisable to seek not to be alone with them, either. As

for men and women being present in the same school, class, lecture hall, meeting, or place of work, this is perfectly permissible in Islam, provided the women are wearing correct Islamic dress. Islam is the middle way between the lax and the too-strict. It was normal, at the time of the Prophet, for women to attend prayers at the mosque.

## 44. FOOD LAWS

### Fact Questions

1. What is the meaning of 'haram' and 'halal'?
2. Which animal meat is totally forbidden to both Jews and Muslims?
3. Can you list six products which are regularly made from this animal in the West? (eg: sliced ham).
4. Give two examples of flesh-eating animals no Muslim should eat.
5. Muslims should not eat animals that died in certain ways. List six of those ways.
6. Why should a Muslim not eat 'black pudding'?
7. Give two examples of lawful meat-animals.
8. What weapon is normally used to kill in the halal method?
   (A different weapon might be used in a hunting situation).

9. What is the Islamic position on factory farming and animal experimentation?

10. What do Muslims do as they slaughter an animal?

11. How does Halal slaughter show kindness and compassion?

12. Make a list of foods that you eat regularly which are halal.

13. Can you find out the name for Jewish halal meat?

14. Read 'Social Consequences' and check your answer to No.3.

15. Why do many Muslims examine the lists of ingredients on packeted food?

## Understanding

Do the work set in 'Thinking Point', 'For Your Folders' and 'For Discussion'.

## Dictionary Work

Look up HALAL:

What are the characteristics of that which God allows for us?

Look up HARAM: Why are certain substances or actions forbidden?

Can you give an example of a haram substance which is not food or drink?

Can you give an example of a haram action?

Look up FOOD LAWS: What do Muslims say is wrong with the animal-fat content of a food? Find out what gelatine is, and which foods regularly use it.

Look up SLAUGHTER: Copy out the last sentence.

## Food Laws

In the Qur'an the rules about food and drink are clearly laid out:

*'O you who believe! Eat of the good things that We have provided for you, and be grateful to God, if it is Him you worship. He has only forbidden you dead meat, and blood, and the flesh of swine, and that on which any other name has been invoked besides that of God. But if you are forced by necessity (to eat non-halal food), without wilful disobedience, nor transgressing due limits, then you are guiltless. For God is Oft-forgiving Most Merciful.'* (11: 172-3).

Food which is permitted is halal, while that which is forbidden is haram. Halal ('lawful') also means that the food must be properly acquired.

Also haram is the meat of any animal which:

*'.....has been killed by strangling, or by a violent blow, or by a headlong fall, or by being gored to death, or that which has been (partly) eaten by a wild animal; unless you are able to slaughter it (in due form);'* (from 5:4)

## Meat has to be slaughtered in a special manner:

1. The intention must be to sacrifice the meat in the name of God.

2. The blessing 'Bismillah Allahu Akbar' must be said.

3. The four arteries of the throat should be severed with one clean cut.

Because of this, meat which has been ritually slaughtered by Jews and is kosher is also halal.

The restrictions on halal slaughtering also apply to any other products which may have animal derivatives in them. Carnivorous animals, rodents and reptiles are also regarded as haram.

Muslims are instructed to keep food covered to avoid disease and also not to use any articles for eating made with pure gold or pure silver.

Eating must be preceded by 'Bismillah' or 'Bismillah al-Rahman al-Rahim' - 'I begin in the name of God, the Merciful, the Beneficent.'

## Pork

Pork, or flesh of the pig, is a meat declared haram by Allah (2:173; 5:3). This follows the law given in the Tawrat to Musa (see Leviticus 11:7-8; Deuteronomy 14:8 in the Old Testament). The same law was followed by the Prophet Jesus and the first Christians (see St. Matthew's Gospel 5:19) but relaxed by later Christians (see Acts 10:3-7).

Apart from the fact that Allah forbade eating this flesh, it seems to be a meat which has the greatest content of germs and parasites, most of which are contagious and some of which are fatal. The pork tapeworm (balantidium coli) is the largest protozoan affecting humans. It lodges in the intestine. Trichina roundworms (Trichinella Spiralis) are now very common in Europe and the USA.

Muslims living in non-Muslim communities should be aware that any product including 'shortening' or 'animal fat' probably means pork lard. Gelatine can be made from the skin or bones of the pig; insulin is sometimes made from pigs' pancreas; pepsin in cheese-making is usually derived from pig.

The Christian dismissal of the rule against pork was based on a dream experienced by St. Peter. Muslims maintain that no dream, no matter how pious the dreamer, should be used as basis for legislation opposed to God's revealed law.

## 45.  GREEN ISLAM

### Fact Questions

1. What is the Arabic for a 'custodian' or 'deputy'?
2. Give one example for each of the ways in which humans damage, pollute or destroy their environment.
3. What happens when disruption is caused to the natural systems of the world?
4. What is Allah's attitude towards His creatures?
5. What is the Muslim attitude to blood-sports?
6. What is the Muslim attitude to hunting?
7. What sort of weapons are Muslims allowed to use, and why are other sorts forbidden?
8. Give some examples of reasons why people do experiments on animals.

### Special Text

Copy out one of the hadiths and give it a decorated border.

### Understanding

Do the work set in 'For Discussion' and 'For Your Folders'.

### Dictionary Work

Look up ANIMALS:  Why is using leather not forbidden?

Look up HUNTING:  Why should hunting never be a 'sport'?

Look up IHRAM: When do Muslims enter this state?

Look up GREEN ISLAM: What are humans expected to be?

Look up KHILAFAH:  In your family, who do you have to look after?

What rules might you suggest for:

(a) a zoo

(b) a pet-shop.

Many people keep caged birds. Why might a Muslim argue that keeping pigeons and free-range chickens is halal, but keeping budgies or canaries is haram?

The Muslim News, April 24, 1998

## 'Protest against Halal Slaughter'

Animal Rights groups protested against sheep being slaughtered for 'Id al-Adha in Havering, Upminster, even though the animals slaughtered there were stunned before being slaughtered. Over 1,200 sheep were slaughtered for Muslims from East London.

Kamal Siddiqui, Chairman of Essex Islamic Trust, told The Muslim News that Muslims should "be allowed to practice their religion". Mr.Sarfaz Sarwar, from Basildon, Essex, said: "Why is it that no one objects to the millions of turkeys who are slaughtered during Christmas? Why just pick on Muslims?"

John Palmer, the Company Director of the abattoir where the sheep were slaughtered told The Muslim News: "We stunned the sheep before they were slaughtered, we had the Official Veterinary Service Official, we have had inspectors in from the Meat Hygiene Service and we have had a representative from the Ministry of Agriculture, Fisheries and Food."

Animal Rights groups have threatened to take the Prison Service to court after it was found that some prisons are providing halal meat to all inmates in some prisons. The Prisons Service emphasized to the Muslim News that the prisons cater for dietary needs of all faiths including Muslims who require halal food. "However, it has come our attention that some prison service establishments are providing halal meat to all prisoners regardless of their religious beliefs," said the spokesman for the Prison Service. He added: "This is not general practice and is not encouraged." The authorities are looking into the complaint.

The Evening Standard, 7.7.98

## 'If this is true, the meat is not Halal!'

Slaughterman? The term suggests some element of skill, but all that is required in a Muslim abattoir is the brutal ability to beat or wrestle an animal to the ground and then slit its throat. Twenty-four years ago, when I first saw Muslims slaughter a cow, it was still the ritual business of crating the terrified animal and turning it to hang head down before the knife was drawn across the throat and the belly simultaneously slit to let the intestines tumble out, and it took what seemed an age to die in the great spread of blood and guts. That was bad enough, but an improved standard of living has now made meat much more prominent in the Near Eastern diet, and conditions for animals in abattoirs have worsened by far with the demand for quantity.

They wait on floors slippery with faeces, watching what happens in the slaughter area, and are then dragged by ropes and their own tails, or beaten with iron bars, to get them near the drains into which their blood must flow; there, boys and men kick their legs from under them, jump on their backs - anything to make them fall so that their heads can be held back - and in this state of terror their throats are cut, more or less.

If more, then death is fairly swift - a minute or so of struggling to get to their feet, and then consciousness is gone; if less, then the loss of blood is slow and for as much as two or three minutes the bull or cow will make frantic efforts to stand, and then, too weak, succumb to the dreadful business of drowning in its own blood - perhaps five minutes in all.

It is evident that these brutal procedures brutalize those who inflict them. It is evident that the younger boys find the abattoir a place of fun - yes, fun - and that vindictive acts of cruelty excite them to do more.

This leads me to the perilous subject of ritual slaughter in this country - the halal of Muslims and the shechita of Jews - perilous because to criticize the practices of these minorities is to be accused of racial prejudice. Both methods involve the bleeding to death of the fully conscious animal. All slaughtered animals bleed to death, but in licensed abattoirs they are stunned and deeply unconscious before their throats are cut. It is hardly a method that we would choose for dispatching human beings - and in that context we would not describe it as humane - but it is significantly less cruel and less prolonged than halal slaughter; it is, moreover, better supervised.

The Ministry of Agriculture exercises little, if any, supervision over ritual killing for the Muslim and Jewish communities. Anecdotal evidence suggests that a shochet, a Jewish slaughterman, undergoes rigorous training and is unlikely to be careless or deliberately cruel; there is, however, irrefutable evidence that Muslim slaughtermen in Britain lack training and skill, and are unsupervised. The Muslim fraternity also practice private slaughter; it is illegal here, and is contrary to a European Directive (No.95/119/EC), but it is nevertheless common wherever Muslims live. Many readers will recall reports of the Parisian killing field in which French Muslims slaughter hundreds of animals on the Feast of Sacrifices, "a scene more fitting to the Dark Ages...to turn the hardiest stomach'" as the Daily Mail's man put it last year.

## True Conditions for Halal:

- The slaughter must be done in as kind and humane way as possible.
- The animal should be well cared for, fed and watered up to the time of slaughter.
- The animal should not be in a state of panic from seeing the conditions.
- The instrument for slaughter should be very sharp (knife usually, bullet in hunting).
- Proper prayer should be said over each animal, with proper respect.
- The blood should be drained out quickly.

## 46. DIFFICULTIES IN NON-MUSLIM COMMUNITIES

### Fact Questions

1. Why is clothing at school a problem for some Muslims?
2. Why do Muslims object to school showers?
3. Why do Muslims find school sex and moral education lessons a problem?
4. Give 3 reasons why some Muslims might object to Religious Study lessons.
5. How do school toilets and washrooms present problems to young Muslims?
6. What is the problem of Friday lunch-time to a Muslim?
7. Why would young Muslims (and Muslim teachers!) find the school day extra hard in Ramadan?
8. What is the Muslim preference regarding doctors?
9. What is the biggest 'pet problem' faced by Muslims in the UK?

### Understanding

Do the work set in 'For your Folders', 'For Discussion', and one of the 'Things to do'.

## Some Definitions

**Discrimination** - When someone is marked out as being different, and therefore not so valued, for some particular reason.

**Racism** - the belief in the superiority of a particular race, and antagonism (dislike, contempt, poor treatment) towards members of different races.

**Sexism** - discrimination against people on the basis of their sexual gender. (Only a certain sex can get a particular job, lodging, promotion, etc.).

**Ageism** - discrimination against people on the basis of their age. (Only a person younger than a certain age can get a particular job - usually because training is expensive, and the employer wants value for money).

**Multi-Ethnic** - a community made up of people from several different races. ('Ethnos' = Greek for 'race'). In the UK we have many races living together - English, Scottish, Irish, Welsh, Pakistani, Indian, Turkish, Armenian, Jewish, Bangladeshi, Chinese, etc., etc.

**Multi-Faith** - a community made up of people from several different faiths or religions. In the UK we have Christian, Muslim, Jewish, Hindu, Buddhist, etc. etc.

**Racial Harmony** - people of different races living peacefully together in mutual co-operation.

**Prejudice** - when someone is discriminated against, and treated unpleasantly, simply because of the personal likes and dislikes, usually quite unreasonable, of an individual.

## Some Difficulties Faced by Muslims

1. Praying five times a day.
2. Not many mosques to meet in for worship. (In many people's houses the front room has been turned into a 'house mosque').
3. Laws. Sometimes the laws of Islam do not agree with the laws of the United Kingdom. These are two examples: (a) In England it is illegal for a man to have more than one wife; (b) Gambling is forbidden in Islam, so is the charging of interest on loans of money.
4. Fasting. It is harder to fast when other people are eating and drinking around you.
5. Food. It is not always possible to get 'halal' meat. Neighbours may complain about the smell of curry. (But what does a Muslim think about the smell of bacon cooking?)
6. Expense of the long journey to Makkah for the Hajj. (Relations often club together to save enough money to send one member of the family.)
7. Language. Many Muslim women who have emigrated to the UK do not go out to work so they have little chance to practice their English. Children born in England grow up speaking their own language at home and English outside the home. They also have the extra work of studying the Qur'an in Arabic.
8. Ignorant people laugh at such things as the Muslim prayer positions and the clothes they wear. Some people even look down on them because quite often the colour of their skin is different. They forget (or do not know) that many brown people are not Muslims, and many white people are.
9. Festivals and holy days. It is difficult to get time off work to go to the mosque on Fridays and to celebrate festivals which do not count as national holidays.

10. A different life for women. Muslim parents tell their daughters,'You must wear these clothes...You can't go to youth clubs and mix with boys. ...You can't choose your own husband.' English society says, 'All that is out of date. Of course you must be free to do what you want. It's your life'.

## Press Report

The Muslim News, 24 April, 1998

### 'Protest against mixed swimming' by Sarah Sheriff

The mother of a 13-year-old girl is courting the displeasure of her daughter's school by unilaterally withdrawing her from swimming lessons. "This is not just of concern to me as a Muslim" the mother of 13-year-old Nosheen, told the Muslim News. "I think many parents would be concerned that girls at a vulnerable age who are very conscious of their bodies are being made to swim in mixed sessions." Although Muslim girls at the school are allowed to wear leggings and t-shirts in the mixed PE and swimming lessons, the mother was dissatisfied because her daughter felt uncomfortable wearing clothing which clung to the body when wet in the mixed swimming sessions. "My daughter does not wear hijab (head scarf) to school, but many other girls do. How must they feel when they have to take part in mixed swimming lessons?" she asked. "I am sure many of these girls' parents are unaware that this is happening, and the girls feel they have no choice in the matter and are helpless, and perhaps even lying to them."

Her daughter explained the difficulties faced by girls in the school. She told The Muslim News: "Swimming started for us last year when I was in Year 7. We weren't given any choice to have segregated swimming. I feel very conscious and embarrassed but my friends don't care. They've said to me: `Why did you tell your mum about this? Why didn't you lie?' I don't think their parents know that swimming is mixed. My PE teacher is not at all sympathetic." She added: "I enjoy swimming and go to women only sessions with my cousins, which I enjoy."

When she first became aware of her daughter's concerns in early March, Mrs. Younus wrote a letter of complaint to the Head of Year and requested that her daughter be excused from swimming. The PE teacher rang to say that the school was already meeting the basic obligations towards Asian and Muslim pupils by allowing them to wear t-shirts and leggings. "She suggested that if I felt so strongly about the issue, I should have put her in a single-sex girls school." Muslim parents at a primary school which acts as a feeder were horrified that a school with a high proportion of Muslim children should be insisting on mixed swimming. A 150 strong petition was drawn up and signed by Muslim, Hindu and Christian parents opposing the mixed swimming.

### Sex Education and Sexual Morality

When Muslim children are taught about performances of ablution, ghusl (bath) and prayer, they should learn, in an Islamic context, about the menstrual cycle, emission of semen and sexual intercourse. Generally a mother would explain to her daughter, and a father to his son. The degree of detail of what is taught varies from family to family. At the same time the children would be taught the etiquette of dress and behaviour, both in the home and outside it. They are taught to seek permission before entering their parents' room at the time they are resting. They are taught to avoid nudity, even when among their own sex. They are taught to dress and behave modestly in accordance with Islamic requirements when in the presence of people of the opposite sex outside the close family. They are taught to avoid activities and situations which could lead to immoral relationships.

In this way the children are prepared by gradual stages to exercise self-restraint and to find fulfilment in their own family life until they are old enough to assume the responsibilities of marriage for themselves.

Muslims do not necessarily disapprove of the factual content of school biology and sex education lessons. However, they do feel it is very important that it should be taught by a teacher who shares Muslim values and morality regarding such things as sex before marriage, unmarried people living together (cohabiting), promiscuity, homosexuality, etc.

# Rites of Passage and Family Matters

## 47. THE FAMILY

### Fact Questions

1. What is meant by the term 'extended family'?
2. What happens to many people when they become old?
3. Give an example of showing tolerance to a parent.
4. Give an example of showing understanding towards a parent.
5. Should Muslims ever use Old People's Homes?
6. How might a parent show 'false pride' in a child?
7. What might happen to children if their parents are over-protective?
8. How do most children react when they discover their parents are disappointed in them?
9. What happens when parents push their children too hard?
10. What happens when parents don't push their children hard enough?
11. Why is making sure a youngster learns a trade or skill as important as academic education?
12. At what age should Muslims begin prayer and fasting?
13. What happens when parents have 'favourites'?
14. What is a milk-brother, or milk-sister?
15. Briefly explain the difference between fostering and adoption.
16. Sometimes those who take on fostered or adopted children do not tell them about their real parents. What is the Muslim ruling on this?

### Special Text:

Copy out Surah 17:23-24, with a decorated border.

### Understanding

Do the work set in 'For Your Folders' and 'Thinking Point'.

### Dictionary Work:

Look up OLD AGE :
(a) What is meant by 'hikmah' and 'sabr'?

(b) Why did the old lady cry, and how did the Prophet cheer her up?

Look up CHILDREN: What did the prophet forbid?

## Notes

The Importance of the Family in Islam

In Islam the family is regarded as the basic unit of society. It should provide security - financial, physical and psychological - to all its members. If the family is functioning well, the individuals within it find satisfaction and inner peace. The old are loved and cared for, the young are cherished and taught Islamic values and manners.

Therefore Islamic moral and legal injunctions are directed towards the strengthening of family ties, and against anything that could weaken or break up the family. This is the key to understanding the Shari'ah in respect of marriage. On the Day of Judgement each individual will stand to be judged alone for his or her deeds.

However in this world, he or she is part of a family - initially as a child, then as a husband or wife and parent and probably eventually as a grandparent. He or she may also be a brother or sister, a nephew or niece, uncle or aunt or an in-law - part of a whole web of relationships by kinship or marriage which draws people together and increases their mutual love and support.

Therefore marriage, which is at the root of every family, is not regarded at any stage as a matter for only two individuals.

### Faith within the Family

The family is also considered very important in sustaining the faith and transmitting it from one generation to another. It is learned by children from the words and behaviour of their elders - their responses and reactions to day-to-day events and crises, and from the practice in the home of some of the 'Pillars of Islam - the five daily prayers, fasting, zakah and general charitable acts.

Faith in Allah is in fact the only thing that has more weight than family ties. Children are expected to obey their parents in all affairs, even if they are non Muslims, unless they instruct them to do something contrary to Islam, when it becomes their duty to disobey, but tactfully.

Faith is also one of the factors in the choice of a marriage partner. Marriage of a Muslim woman to a non-Muslim man is unlawful. A Muslim man may marry a woman who follows a revealed religion (Jewish or Christian), but if the difference in religion is likely to cause strains in the family, faith should have priority.

### The Extended Family

The Muslim family comprises not only of parents and their children. It includes

grandparents, unless and aunts, cousins and relatives of similar degree. Keeping up these ties is strongly encouraged, and breaking them is condemned:

"Know your relations, so that you may fulfill your duties to your kinsmen; and your duty towards your kinsmen is love for your family which will increase your wealth and lengthen your life."

(Hadith from Tirmidhi)

In most Muslim societies the extended family lives close together - either in the same house or compound, or in the same neighbourhood.

## Dependency and Inheritance

The extended family is held together not only by ties of goodwill. It also involves financial responsibilities.

It is the duty of members of the extended family, in order of closeness, to assist financially any other member who needs help. Therefore a family member, male or female, who is elderly, widowed, divorced, disabled or sick, or for any other reason without financial means can depend on his or her relatives for support according to their means.

Likewise when a Muslim dies, his or her relatives will inherit a part of his or her estate in a fixed proportion in accordance with regulations laid down in the Qur'an.

The general rule is for a male to inherit twice the share of a female in the same degree of relationship (e.g. a son inherits twice the share of a daughter). At first sight this may appear unfair, but if it is viewed in the light of the greater financial responsibilities of men in supporting their own families and taking care of other dependants, it will be apparent that this is not so. However, many modernist Muslims regard this as one of the areas of teaching where the actual conditions of the society should be taken into consideration.

A Muslim may, make a will in respect of not more than one-third of his property, in favour of a person or persons who are not among his automatic heirs, or as a charity or waqf.

## 48. BIRTH AND INFANCY

### Fact Questions

1. In a perfect world, why would no Muslim babies ever be illegitimate?
2. What is meant by 'Ummah'?
3. What is the first word a Muslim would like a baby to hear?
4. Explain the meanings of the words 'adhan' and 'iqamah'.
5. What is the tahnik?
6. List three things that might happen at an aqiqah.
7. What sort of name should not be given to a Muslim baby?
8. Give the meaning of: Abdul Rahman Abu Hussain
   (You can also look up Kunya Name in your dictionaries).
9. What would little Hussain's mother be called?
10. What is meant by 'khitan'?
11. Why is late khitan not recommended?
12. What is the 'Bismillah'?

## Understanding

Do the work set in 'Fcr Your Folders', 'For Discussion' and 'Things to do'.

## Dictionary Work

Look up ABD: Why is the name Abdul on its own incorrect?

Look up AQIQAH: Are any of these practices compulsory?

Look up BIRTH CEREMONIES: What is the word for 'charity'?

Look up BISMILLAH: What does this mean?

Look up KHITAN:

(a) Which prophet first received this command from Allah?

(b) When is it usually done?

(c) Which country has a tradition of circumcising boys late?

(Please note that it was never requested that girls be circumcised in any way. It has been an ancient tradition in certain countries - notably the Sudan, Egypt and Somalia, and seems to have started at the time of the Pharaohs. Some Muslims have maintained that it is an accepted part of Islam, because apparently some of the Muslim women were circumcised at the time of the Prophet. However, the notion of cutting off the female sex organ is abhorrent and is really a cruel mutilation, and the Prophet disapproved it. Circumcision of boys only removes a tiny flap of skin that covers the tip of the penis; it improves health, cleanliness and sexual pleasure. The only female circumcision that should be even contemplated is if a grown woman herself wished it.

(Note: - Birth control (Contraception), Family Planning and Abortion are dealt with in Unit 66).

## 49. MARRIAGE

### Fact Questions

1. Why do some Muslims feel it is preferable to marry a relative?
2. What is meant by an 'arranged marriage'?
3. Why do Muslims think young love can be dangerous?
4. Are forced marriages ever allowed in Islam?
5. What is a 'mahr'?
6. When might a wife choose to return a mahr to her husband?
7. Explain briefly what happens at a Muslim wedding.
8. What is a 'Wali'?
9. True or false:

   Marriages are 'made in heaven'?

   Marriages are always 'till death do us part'?

   Marriages are always happy?

Marriages need hard work, tolerance and loyalty?

Physical marriage goes on after death?

10. When might a Muslim bride who wore a fairly plain dress for her wedding really dress up?

11. Did the Prophet marry any of his cousins?

12. What money rights should a Muslim wife have?

13. Do Muslim men only have to marry Muslim women?

14. Wives of which religious faiths are forbidden to them?

15. What is the most important thing in a Muslim marriage?

16. In what ways is a husband or a wife a 'best friend'?

## Understanding

Do the work set in 'For Your Folders' and 'Talking Points'.

*Traditional Asian bride.*

## Dictionary Work

Look up ARRANGED MARRIAGES: What do parents do?

Look up CELIBACY: What does this mean? Is it approved in Islam?

Look up DOWRY (MAHR): Who pays it to whom? What things are not approved in Islam?

Look up MAHREM: Explain what this is. Can you list your own mahrem?

Look up NIKAH: Outline some Asian cultural practices often done by Muslims in the West.

Look up WALIMAH: What is the real purpose of a walimah?

Look up PROPHET'S WIVES:

(a) Name one of his wives who was his cousin.

(c) What does 'Umm al-Muslimun' mean?

## Note: Arranged Marriages

Marriages are generally arranged in Muslim communities (as is the case for two-thirds of the people of the world), although this is not laid down in the Qur'an, and no one should be forced into marrying against his or her will. A boy's parents will look out for a suitable partner for their son, and will approach the girl's parents before she is asked for her consent.

Arguments can be put forward both for and against arranged marriages, but most people seem to prefer whatever is the accepted social norm. Generally, difficulties only arise where there are conflicting ideas within society. Some Muslims growing up in the West, for instance, may be envious of their Western teenage friends who have the freedom to go out with the opposite sex and to marry whoever they want. But here is the other point of view:

It is not always harmful for the young

*A Bosnian Muslim Wedding.*

to benefit from the experience of their loving parents, who usually look for compatible partners rather than the short-lived romantic ones.

Some western girls, incidentally, confess to being secretly envious of arranged marriages as at least it lessens the risk of growing old in loneliness, as well as freeing them from having to kiss so many frogs before they find a prince!

(Hesham El Essawy, letter of 30 October 1984)

In arranged marriages, the couple have to grow to love the one they marry, rather than marry the one they love, but this still produces loving relationships which are often more stable than their Western counterparts. The tenderness and love experienced between husband and wife are seen as part of Allah's intentions for men and women, as this passage from the Qur'an shows;

'*And of His signs is that He created for you, of yourselves, spouses, that you might repose in them, and He has set between you love and mercy.*' (30:20)

Part of the arrangements includes coming to an agreement about a sum of money, called the mahr. This is paid by the bridegroom to the bride, as a token of his appreciation of her. It then belongs to the wife to do with as she pleases. The wife then owns something to her own right even if

she had nothing before. expenses and setting up the newly-weds in their home. It is sometimes paid partly in goods. If the payment delayed, the amount should be stated clearly on the wedding certificate. It has not been paid before the husband dies it is taken from the estate before distributing it among those who are entitled to inherit from the deceased. This gives the woman some measure of financial security.

Marriage is a contract; if it fails, the couple are free to divorce, and remarriage is up to the individual and not necessarily arranged by parents.

Arranged marriages to relatives, such as cousins, are common in some Muslim societies, but are not particularly encouraged in Islam. They can work well, but it can lead to terrible unhappiness if the marriage fails for any reason, and the couple are unable to be divorced because of the trauma it would cause the wider family. It is true that the Prophet did marry two cousins, but they were his fifth and seventh choices and had both been previously married to someone else.

## 50. MEN AND WOMEN

### *Fact Questions*

1. List the five commitments of a mother given here.
2. What are the three rights her child should have?
3. Which things should Muslim mothers take responsibility for?
4. What is the role of the father expected to be?
5. Why do Muslim women not consider being a housewife to be inferior?
6. What are the four rights of a husband?
7. What did the Prophet say was the 'best of treasures'?
8. Who did he say were the 'best Muslims'?

9. What does a Muslim woman regard as her 'rights' as she passes through the various stages of her life?

10. (a) Are Muslim women allowed to go out to work?

    (b) Which of the Prophet's wives were businesswomen?

    (c) Which one was his boss for a time?

11. How should a Muslim woman discourage harassment?

12. Should Muslim men help out in the home? If not, why not? If you think they should, why?

    Turn to the section Equality and Empowerment of Women p.105.

13. Give reasons why some women have become treated like inferiors.

14. In the Qur'an, what does it really mean every time it says 'man'?

15. Identify one female ruler named in the Qur'an.

16. What is the aim of female Muslim scholars?

### Special Text

Copy out the equality hadith, and give a decorated border.

### Understanding

Do the work set on p.103, 'For Your Folders' and 'Thinking Points'.

Do the work set on p.105 in 'Talking Point', and 'For Your Folders' No.2.

### Dictionary Work

Look up KHADIJAH : How did she make money?

Look up EMPOWERMENT OF WOMEN : Are the religious and moral duties of men and women any different in Islam?

Where are these ideas not readily accepted?

*Sr. Ruqaiyyah giving a lecture.*

Look up EQUAL RIGHTS :

(a) Why do women need extra physical care?

(b) What is the obligation of a divorced man?

### Note: The Rights of Husband and Wife

### The Husband

1. A wife should obey the orders of her husband, so long as they are in keeping with the will of God.

2. She should never, in any circumstances, betray her integrity, either in chastity or financial affairs.

3. She should refrain from any act which would cause him pain or distress.

4. Her outward appearance should be pleasing to him. She should keep herself clean, and dress modestly.

5. To obey her husband's wishes and acknowledge his rights count as jihad for her.

6. She should not leave his house without

his permission, or let anyone into his house without this permission.

7. A wife should not deny her husband his physical satisfaction - for he has agreed to have a sexual relationship with nobody else but her.

8. A wife should take care of the home to the best of her ability, and maintain its safety, hygiene, and halal diet.

### The Wife

1. A husband should maintain his wife, protect her, and always seek her welfare and happiness.

2. He should never betray her, either in chastity or in his financial dealings, and not place her at risk.

3. He should refrain from any act which would cause her pain or distress.

4. His outward appearance should be pleasing to her. He should keep himself clean, and decently dressed.

5. Knowing his wife should obey him, he should be careful not to make any unreasonable, hurtful or callous requests, or expect her to do anything contrary to the will of God.

6. Knowing that his wife should not let people in or go to places he does not approve of, he should for his part not leave her lonely, or drive away her friends or family, or deprive her of reasonable company, or bring into the house people she really does not like.

7. A husband should not deny his wife her need for love and physical satisfaction - for she has agreed to seek no-one else but him.

8. A husband should provide generously, help her when this is needed, and set a good and noble example to the children.

## 51. POLYGAMY

### Special Text

Copy out surah 4:3 and give it a decorated border.

## Fact Questions

1. Explain what is meant by: polygamy polygyny monogamy

2. Why should polygamy be pretty rare in Muslim societies?

3. When is polygamy not allowed in Islam?

4. Explain what polyandry is, and why it is forbidden to Muslim women

5. Why might a Muslim man consider taking on an additional wife?

6. What are the four main disadvantages to polygamy?

## Understanding

Look up Surah 4:3 and 4:129 (on p.104). How would you answer someone who stated that Allah had recommended polygamy?

## Dictionary Work

Look up POLYANDRY:
(a) What is meant by 'surplus women'?
(b) Which country apparently has the most of these?

Look up POLYGAMY. It was the normal practice in many countries before the coming of Islam. Islam disapproved of an uncaring polygamy, and set limits, but it was not actually forbidden.

In which circumstances is it still allowed?

## Note: Polygamy

According to Islamic teaching, men are allowed to marry up to four wives; but women may only have one husband. Muhammad himself is said to have had at least 12 wives during the last part of his life, although he was married to Khadijah alone for the first 25 years of his married life. In Muhammad's time, polygamy was a good way of providing for widows and their children, at a time when many husbands were killed in battle.

Today, polygamy is not very common among Muslims, for a number of reasons. The first wife can write a clause into the marriage contract, insisting that she should remain the only wife, or to be divorced if the husband insists on polygamy. Polygamy is expensive, not only to keep a number of wives, but also to pay their dowries. Also the Qur'an advises men to have only one wife unless they can be sure to treat all their wives equally (which is virtually impossible):

'...then marry such women as may seem good to you, two or three or four. If you fear that you will not act justly, then (marry) one woman (only) or someone your right hand controls. That is more likely to keep you from committing an injustice.' (4:3).

Note: Muslim men were expected to *marry* any slave women they desired and not force a sexual relationship on a helpless girl who did not wish it.

'You will never manage to deal equitably with your wives no matter how eager you may be ( to do so).' ( 4:129)

## No Hurt

One of the first principles of Muslim behaviour is that one Muslim should not deliberately hurt another, of whatever sex.

If they hurt a fellow Muslim or wrong them, they will have to face Judgement for it one Day. Islam tries to balance the needs of all concerned. Many Muslim couples suffer from all sorts of misfortunes including serious illness and inability to produce children and so forth, but they try to accept such trials when they come, and may find that their love and marriage relationship is actually strengthened by their compassion for each other.

## 52. DIVORCE

### Fact Questions

1. What is the difference between talaq and khul?
2. How is the talaq procedure sometimes abused?
3. What are other possible ways divorce procedure could be abused by unscrupulous men? (Look at Conditions Necessary).
4. What are the conditions for which a wife may seek a divorce?
5. How is it possible for divorce to be in all the categories, of wajib, makruh, mubah, mandub and haram?
6. Explain what is meant by 'iddah'. What is it for?
7. What is the usual procedure for the custody of children?

### Understanding

Do the work set in 'For Discussion' and 'For Your Folders'.

### Dictionary Work

Look up DIVORCE:
Why could it be said that 'departure from Islam' is always the real grounds for divorce?

Look up KHUL: What does a woman give up?

Look up DOWRY:
(a) What is the Arabic name for it?
(b) How might the dowry system be abused? (Six ways are listed here)

Look up LI'AN: How does is work?

Look up ZINAH: What is it, and what penalty was actually ordered in the Qur'an?

Look up TALAQ: What should family and friends be doing during the three months?

Look up IDDAH: Why does a pregnant woman's iddah end at a different time from anyone else's?

## 53. DEATH AND BURIAL

### Fact Questions

1. Why should Muslims try not to be too grieved by the fact of death?
2. How should a Muslim regard death?
3. When might Muslims feel particularly close to departed loved ones?
4. Look at the passage 75: 3-4. What is so special about the skin of the finger-tips? (Have you read Sr.Ruqaiyyah's little book 'Fingerprints', based on this very fact?)
5. What does this verse reveal about life after death?
6. Explain what is meant by Barzakh.
7. Look back at p.42. What meaning is given to 'barzakh' there?
8. Go back to pp.108-109.
   (a) What sort of wash is given to a dead Muslim?
   (b) How many cloths are recommended for shrouding?

### Understanding

Do the work set in 'For Your Folders', 'Things to do' and 'Talking Points'.

### Dictionary Work

Look up DEATH
(a) Copy out the first sentence.
(b) Why are our deaths no surprise to Allah?

Look up BURIAL: What happens to the bodies, and what to the souls?

Look up GRAVES: What did the Prophet recommend?

Look up GHUSL: Who else needs ghusl, apart from the corpse?

Look up SHAHID: Explain what this means.

Look up RAWDAH: What is it, and why do many Muslims disapprove of it?

## Research

You could find out where the Muslims in your community are buried, and visit their graveyard. It is courteous to remember and pray for their souls.

## Note: Some 'Death' issues

*When God wills:* Muslims believe that God knows the time of our deaths from our conception in the womb, or even before. Muslims should not worry about 'how long they have got', but make sure they live every day available to them in the best possible way, making the fullest use of its opportunities to love God and do good works. Since they believe in a scheme of things not limited to the physical world, Muslims should not be frightened by the prospect of death, but accept that life on earth is one of God's gifts, and that He may recall our souls when He pleases. We should always be grateful for what we have-even if our circumstances do not seem favourable, and make the very best use of all the time we are granted. Death is simply the passing from one sphere of life to another, which, insha'Allah, will be better for us. Death is always by God's leave (3:145); every person will have a 'taste' of it (3:185; 21:25; 29:57); there may be a second death later (37:59) the first death is not the end of all things (45:24-26); sincere people will not flee from it (62:6-8); our forms after death will all be changed. (56:60-61).

## Urs

The death anniversary of a Muslim saint. Widely celebrated by Sufi Muslims, but disapproved of in strictly orthodox Islam. Those who write leaflets inviting Muslims to make a saint's tomb a place of pilgrimage, to let him know their desires so that he may be able to beseech on their behalf, and who solicit donations, are really committing shirk. It is wrong in Islam to beseech dead people on behalf of living people, to speak to Allah for them. However, visiting graveyards, and remembering good people is recommended. It is normal to visit the graves of any loved one to pray for them.

## Post-mortems

Examination of corpses to determine the cause of death is permitted, especially when a crime is suspected or to enable medical students and their teachers to learn about the effects of certain diseases. It is forbidden to show disrespect to the dead body. Islam forbids the disfigurement of those who die in battle, and does not allow the cutting up of bodies for no good reason. Muslims who die in hospital should make it quite clear if they do not wish their bodies to be used for learning purposes, or for removal of various organs for study, or for donation for the use by the living.

There is no reason in Islam, however, why Muslims should not donate organs such as kidneys, corneas, etc, since at the Resurrection Allah will gather together all of the person, no matter what the fate of the corpse. No Muslim need fear that death from explosion, or donation of organs will prevent Allah from re-constituting us. (75:3-4).

## Fatihah recitations after death

Some Muslims hold gatherings on the third, seventh, tenth, fifteenth or fortieth days after the death of a person, in which passages of the Qur'an are recited and meals served. However, these practices are not compulsory and were not done by the

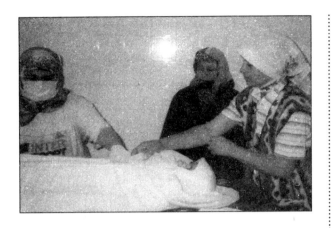

Prophet. They are simply expressions of respect towards the memory of the dead person, and condolence towards the bereaved left behind, and are really matters of culture and not of Islam. It is quite incorrect to imagine that the soul of the departed one will benefit from these gatherings and practices, or that the soul would suffer in some way or be punished if these things were not done. They are a matter of culture and custom, and a Muslim has done nothing wrong if these occasions do not take place. We can always cherish the memory of our deceased, and pray for them - but the intensity, or number of our prayers, or special gatherings, or complete readings of the Qur'an, are not the basis on which Allah will judge their souls, and will not affect the extent of His mercy. If a person believes he or she is more compassionate or just than Allah and therefore can beg, bribe or influence Him to change His will towards any particular soul, this is really a form of shirk. It is certainly misguided. There is nothing special that happens to the soul of the deceased on these days. A Muslim can remember and pray for a dead loved one at any time and in any place, without a social gathering.

# The Mosque

## Fact Questions

1. P.110. What is the Arabic for 'mosque' and what does this word mean?
2. Which prayer position uses the same word? (See p.59).
3. Does a mosque have to be a magnificent building?
4. Why does the actual place not really matter?
5. Why do some Muslim houses set aside a special place for prayer? In what way(s) is it special?
6. Briefly describe what the first mosque in Madinah was like.

## Understanding

Do the work set in 'For Your Folders' and 'For Discussion'.

pp.112-113. Do the work set for 'Things to do' and 'For your Folders'.

pp. 114-115. Do the work set in 'For Your Folders', 'Thinking Point' and 'For Discussion.'

## Dictionary Work:

Look up BARAKAH: What is it and where might it be felt?

Look up BAIT UL-MAQDIS: Why is this mosque called Maqdis, or Quds?

Look up IMAM: Who is allowed to act as one?

Look up I'TIKAF: How might the mosque be used for this?

Look up MADRASSAH: What are these for?

Look up MASJID: Where is the most important place of worship?

Look up and explain the following terms:

Mihrab  Minaret  Minbar  Qiblah  Salat Ul-Jumu'ah  Khutbah

## Art Work

Do a diagram of a typical mosque, labeling the various features.

## Research Work

(an optional extra).

Choose one famous mosque, and give a brief description of it. You could add any photographic or illustrative material you can find. It is possible to write to the Saudi Embassy for material on Makkah and Madinah, if you wish. Other beautiful and famous mosques are in Jerusalem, Damascus, Cairo, Istanbul, Rabat, Islamabad, Lahore, Delhi, etc.

A good opportunity here for a cutting out and sticking in session! Or a trip to any Muslim shop to see what 'goodies' they have.

Each Nation has given the mosque its own national characteristic.

Tunisia

Pakistan

Turkey

Egypt

Dar-al-Islam, Abiquiu, New Mexico.

Working Mosque—the oldest surviving mosque in the U.K.

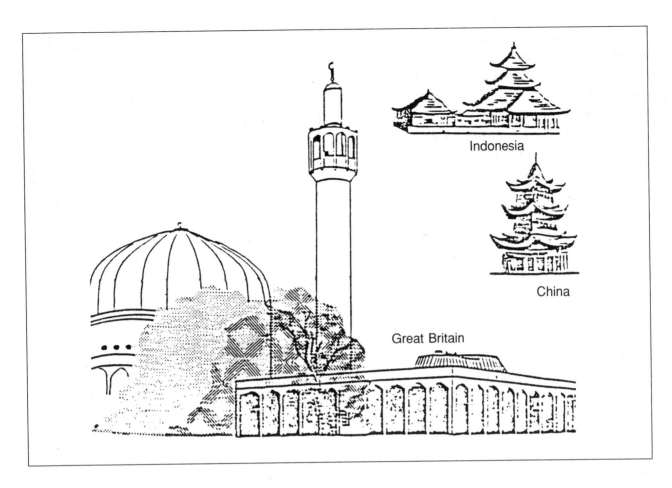

Indonesia

China

Great Britain

## Note

*The Madrassah :* There is no "church" structure with a hierarchy of clergy, except among the Shi'ah countries such as Iran. For the Shi'ah the term "Imam" means a political as well as spiritual leader to whom allegiance is due.

The duties of the imam vary. Some only lead the prayers. Others also have welfare and educational responsibilities in the community. They are generally respected as men of learning to whom people may turn for assistance and advice on religious and other matters.

The madrassah (Islamic school) was from the early days of Islam a part of the mosque, or attached to the mosque. This is because learning and the search for knowledge are a very important part of Islam, the Prophet is reported to have said:

"The search for knowledge is a duty for every Muslim male and female."

"Seek knowledge from the cradle to the grave."

"Seek knowledge even as far as China."

"One learned person is harder on the devil than a thousand ignorant worshippers."

"Knowledge is the stray camel of the believer - let him seize it wherever he finds it."

It was reported that after the Battle of Badr the Prophet promised to release any prisoner-of-war who taught ten Muslims how to read.

A Muslim child normally begins with learning the Qur'an. It is regarded as the key to all other knowledge, and the criterion by which to assess and understand all other kinds knowledge.

The child usually begins at an early age to attend a madrassah where he or she learns to read and memorize the Qur'an - especially al-Fatihah and the other shorter Surahs recited in the salat.

Many students read the Qur'an from cover to cover under the guidance of the teacher. When a student has completed this and can read from any part of the Qur'an with reasonable fluency, it is customary in some places to hold a walimah, a feast attended by relatives, friends and neighbours. The student may be asked to read from the Qur'an for people to hear, and prayers are offered for him or her. Other students may go on not only to read but to memorize the whole Qur'an. This takes a number of years of patient endeavour. If they succeed they are given the title hafiz. Students who can read the Qur'an in Arabic are also taught its meaning in their own language. (The majority of Muslims are non-Arabs, therefore this stage is very important for their understanding of Islam).

There are many kinds of madrassah today, some in mosques and some in regular classrooms. In some countries they are conducted in the house of the teacher, or

out of doors under a tree. Some teach only the Qur'an and minimal Islamic knowledge. Others have well-developed syllabi including Qur'an, Hadith, Moral Education, Fiqh (Jurisprudence), Sirah (biography of the Prophet), Arabic language, and other relevant subjects. Some madrassahs are full-time and children may stay there for some years before going to primary school. Some are part-time to enable children to attend primary school in the morning and madrassah in the afternoon. Some madrassahs hold weekend classes, while the pupils attend regular schools on weekdays.

In some countries Islamic organizations have established nursery, primary and secondary schools where all branches of knowledge are taught, including the sciences. From the 8th and 9th centuries AD Muslims translated scientific works of the Greeks and other ancient civilizations into Arabic. For over six centuries thereafter they developed the sciences themselves, producing many valuable books. Some of these were later translated into Latin and other European languages.

The most famous institutions of learning during the early centuries of Islam were the Nizamiyyah University in Baghdad and Al-Azhar University in Cairo, both founded in the 9th century CE. Al-Azhar thus pre-dates the founding of the University of Paris (12th century) and the University of Oxford (13th century) and is the oldest university in the world to have survived without interruption to the present day. Al-Azhar is still functioning as a university, with a broad range of subjects including not only religious studies but the sciences and humanities.

# Muslim Morality

## 57. MUSLIM VIRTUES

### Dictionary Work

Do the Dictionary Work first for this unit.

Look up VALUES : Copy out the list.

Look up IMAN: Copy out this entry in full.

Look up AMAL: What does it say about the relationship between faith and action?

Look up FORGIVENESS: What sins does God never forgive?

Look up REPENTANCE: Give the Arabic word. What does this mean?

Look up GENEROSITY: What reward does a Muslim desire for his or her generosity?

Look up HOSPITALITY: What does this mean?

Look up ISTIKHARA: When might one make a prayer of istikhara

Look up TOLERANCE: Copy out the last sentence.

Look up TRUST: What does trust in Allah really mean?

### Understanding

Now read through Unit 57 in your text-book. Do the work set in 'For Discussion' and 'For Your Folders'.

## 58. WORK ETHICS

### Fact Questions

1. What is the main aim of Islamic economics?
2. List the five main qualities a Muslim at work should have.
3. What is strongly discouraged?
4. What were the actual working 'jobs' of these prophets:

   Dawud (David)  Nuh (Noah)  Isa (Jesus)  Musa (Moses)  Muhammad.
5. What did the Prophet say about merchant-traders?
6. What is a fard kifayah?
7. What are the chief duties of employers and employees towards each other.

### Special Text

Copy out one of the hadiths against begging.

### Understanding

Do the work set in 'For Discussion' and 'Things to do'.

## Dictionary Work

Look up FARD KIFAYAH;

Make a list of the kinds of work or employment that come in this category (that of being necessary for any Muslim community).

## 59. WEALTH ETHICS

### Fact Questions

1. Complete the hadith: 'He is not a believer who eats his fill ......................'
3. How can Muslims show moderation in: eating; dressing; in the home; in buildings; at weddings; at funerals; in hospitality?
4. What was the test that the Prophet warned his Ummah of?
5. What is riba, and why is it forbidden to a Muslim?

### Understanding

Do the work set in 'For Discussion' and 'For Your Folder'.

### Dictionary Work

Look up USURY:
(a) What is the literal meaning of 'riba'.
(b) How should a wealthy Muslim help the poor?
Look up WEALTH: What is the true wealth of a Muslim?

Look up WAQF: How might rich Muslims use their money for waqf?

### Note: Money matters

*Usury:* A rich person lending money at interest usually gets people deeper into debt. Muslims with wealth are requested to help the needy by lending what they need without interest. (See Allah's earlier revelations to Jews and Christians in the Old Testament Law in Exodus 22:25; Leviticus 25:36-7; and New Testament Law in Luke 6:34-5). Allah said: *'If the debtor is in difficulty, grant him time until it is easy for him to repay; but the best way for you is if you cancel the your repayment of yours debt altogether' (2:280). (For exploitation in trade dealings, see 2:274-5; 3:130; 4:161).*

The Prophet also forbade needy Muslims from trying to borrow at interest except in case of dire necessity (e.g. life is not possible without food, clothing and medical treatment); even then, the borrowing should be limited to the exact amount (i.e. don't borrow 100 when 90 is what is necessary), and the borrower should constantly seek to escape the predicament, perhaps by taking on extra work, or by fellow Muslims helping out.

*Islamic banking.* A system which supports the prohibition of riba. It is an important Islamic principle that there should be equality of risk. From a banking point of view this means that the risks and rewards should be shared between borrower, bank and depositor. Muslim banks should not finance goods or schemes which are themselves forbidden in Islam.

One of the chief dangers of banks is that those who wish to borrow money for whatever reason usually end up paying enormous sums of interest as well as repaying the loan. Banks are a business, not a charity. They make their income from the money they loan out. Hence many people become enticed into borrowing money which is going to entrap them in debts, sometimes for many years or even a lifetime. Furthermore, if the money was borrowed for a business venture that went wrong, the borrower is still saddled with the debt to the bank until all is paid off. This is avoided in the Islamic system. If the business fails, the bank shares the loss too.

## Research

If you have access to a Bible, look up the passages listed in the unit on p.121 which give the previous rulings of Allah on the subject of Riba.

## Comments

As a Muslim, how would you comment on the following:
(a) Muslims who read/sell pornographic magazines
(b) Muslims who sell alcohol
(c) Muslims who cheat and fiddle in business

(d) Muslims who get others into their debt and then demand repayment.
(e) Muslims who sell meat supposed to be halal when they know it is not.

## 60. PRACTICAL COMPASSION

### Understanding

Read through Unit 60 on pp.122-123, and do the work set in 'For Discussion' and 'For Your Folders.'

### Note

Special People and Organizations, Health and Nutrition.

There are four sections in the Syllabus which require detailed knowledge of one special person or organization dealing with specific issues:
- racial harmony (this is in the compulsory section)
- relief of poverty and suffering in the UK by Muslims
- the need for world development on the causes, extent and effects of poverty in the world
- the support of conservation of the planet and its resources.

### Some Suggestions

Many of these organisations are very new in the UK, and it is too soon for 'heroic individuals' to have made much mark, or have been recorded adequately. However, here are some suggestions with contact addresses and telephone numbers. Do not forget that many Muslim workers are involved in non-Muslim organisations, such as OXFAM, UNICEF, WHO, WWF, etc, etc. Islamic Relief Worldwide (IRW) - Fadi Itani, 151B Park Rd, London, NW8 7HT - Tel. 0171 722 0039

Islamic Foundation for Ecology and the Environmental Sciences, Fazlun Khalid, P.O. Box 5051 Birmingham B20 3RW Tel. 0121 523 4264

Racial Harmony - Commission for Community and Racial Equality Tel.: 0171 828 7022. Ruman Ahmed, Tel. 0171 598 4631

Muslim Women's Helpline - Tel. 0181 908 6715, 0181 904 8193

Muslim Aid - Ibrahim Ali; PO Box 3, London, N 7 8LR, Tel. 0171 609 4425

Islamic Propagation Centre International (IPCI), 481, Coventry Rd, Small Heath, Birmingham, B10 OJS. Tel 0121 773 0137  Fax: 0121 766 8577

Muslim Relief Fund - Islamic Cultural Centre, 146, Park Rd, London, NW8 7RG Tel 0171 724 3363

Helpline (an offshoot of the paper Muslim Voice) Tel.0181 427 1751

The Red Crescent - Contact through Red Cross, 9, Grosvenor Cresc, London, SWIX 7EJ. Tel 0171 235 5454.

Palestinian Return Centre (PRC) - Crown House, North Circular Rd, London, NW10 7PN. Tel 0181 453 0919. Fax.0181 453 0994

Human Relief Foundation - Jamal el-Turk, Suite 4, Aberdeen Centre, 22 Highbury Grove, London, N5 2EA. Tel.0171 226 2125.

An-Nisa (Women's Health Matters) - Humairah Khan/Aishah Khan. Tel. 0181 838 0311.

Children's/Women's/Health and Ethical matters - Michelle Massaudi, Tel. 0181 343 8266.

Islamic Concern (Medical/Ethical) - Dr Majid Khatme, Tel.0181 345 6220.

Sadaqa Jariyya (Continuous Charity) -

*Destruction in Bosnia.*

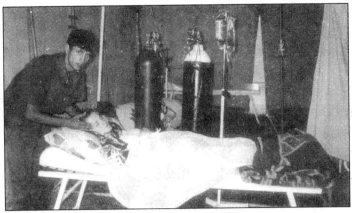

C/o Islamic Relief. Tel. 0171 722 0039 Fax. 0171 722 3228.

Muslim Hands - Shahid Bashir 205, Radford Rd, Hyson Green, Nottingham, NG7 5GT Tel. 0115 9117222.

Orphan Welfare Programme - c/o Islamic Relief, PO Box 13155, London NW8 7WW. Tel. 0171 722 0039

Medical Aid for Disabled people (MADP) in Sarajevo, Bosnia, c/o Islamic Relief

Hare Lip/Cleft Palate Operations, Lahore - c/o Islamic Relief, in conjunction with Child Care International (CCI) Birmingham.

Mother and Child Health Care, Ranypur, Bangladesh - c/o Islamic Relief.

Outpatient Centre, Ranypur, Bangladesh - c/o Islamic Relief.

Feeding Centres, E1 Obeid, Sudan - Islamic Relief, in conjunction with UNICEF.

School for Impaired Hearing - Islamic Relief.

Adult Literacy - Islamic Relief.

Own a Goat Project - Islamic Relief.

Community Action Programme (CAP) (formerly Rural Aid, Bangladesh) - Islamic Relief.

Water and Sanitation project - Islamic Relief.

### Some details from one example

**Islamic Relief Worldwide (IRW)** has been involved in many health related projects which aim to provide services to the local population as well as offering them advice and education in all related matters. Present activities include:

### Malnutrition

It is estimated that about 500 million people are chronically malnourished in the developing world. Islamic Relief has attempted to alleviate malnutrition at the local level through various projects. Two feeding centres have been established in the EI-Obeid area of Sudan which among other services provides supplementary feeding for malnourished children, pregnant and lactating mothers. A fish farm has been established near Zenica, Bosnia Hercegovina with the aim of producing fish which will be donated to vulnerable groups through institutions such as hospitals.

### Outpatient Clinics

These clinics provide general services such as vaccinations (Tetanus, measles, Tuberculosis, Polio, Diphtheria and Whooping Cough), diagnosing illnesses, a pharmacy etc. They also offer specialised services in paediatrics and gynaecology. The clinics provide an indispensable service in areas where the facilities available to people are minimal. Such clinics are operating in Sudan, Bangladesh and Albania.

The World Heath Organisation (WHO) estimates that during any two week period, at least a thousand million people, one in five are malnourished or in poor health. This statistic is amazing if one thinks of the modern technology available in today's world. Even though health is improving there is still a long way to go as shown by the statistics below.

- 17 million people die each year from curable infectious and parasitic diseases such as diarrhoea, malaria and tuberculosis in the developing world.

- In South Asia approximately a third of newborn babies are underweight.

- In Sub Saharan Africa there is only one doctor for every 18,000 people, compared with 390 in the industrial countries.

## Sudan

The food processing classes form another part of the vocational training programme in El-Obeid, Sudan. These are commercially oriented and teach students subjects such as cheese making and animal husbandry. These students often go into business with the skills they have learnt. Exhibitions are also held where the food produce is sold.

## Pakistan

Islamic Relief distributed 1,200 dry food packets, among the flood affected and destitute families living in the low-lying villages along the River Jehlum in the suburb of Pind Dadan Khan. Each packet weighed 10 kg and almost 6000 poor people benefited from this relief project.

## Albania

Islamic Relief distributed 52 tons of medical aid worth $100,000 to hospitals in the regions affected by the recent breakdown in state services. The aid was donated by MEDICARE, an Arab Trade Society in May. This brings the total value of relief goods distributed in the recent troubles to over $450,000.

In early 1997, a shipment of medical aid worth $300,000 was sent to Albania from Islamic Relief's Head Quarters in Birmingham. Some of it will be utilised in our clinic in Pogradec. Also 1,620 ready meals were provided in Tirana and Pogradec.

## Kenya

Heavy rains and floods in Kenya have washed away homes, roads and agricultural land killing thousands of animals and displacing thousands of people Islamic Relief's partner organization in Mandera, Kenya reported over 2000 people homeless and 99% of agricultural farms were destroyed. Islamic Relief currently sponsors orphans in Mandera, Kenya. The building of the orphanage was destroyed and surrounding land devastated. Islamic Relief immediately responded by allocating $3000 for the repair of the building and land.

## Bangladesh

A cyclone storm hit Bangladesh on Monday 19th may 1997. The cyclone was described to be the seventieth most devastating in the last three decades. More than a million people were evacuated to a safer area. Life saving medicine and floor covering material was distributed by Islamic Relief in Bangladesh.

## 61. JUSTICE, CRIME AND PUNISHMENT

### Fact Questions

(Note: Capital punishment comes later, in Unit 66).

1. Look at the four causes of crime given here. Can you give one example for each?
2. Write out the five main aspects of any punishment.
3. Why does a Muslim not just ignore wrongdoing?
4. How should a Muslim react if he or she has been wronged?
5. How is it possible for a judge to give a mistaken judgement?
6. How will Allah put that right?

### Special Texts

Copy out surah 35:45 and surah 42:40, with a decorative border.

### Dictionary Work

Look up CORPORAL PUNISHMENT:
(a) What does this mean?
(b) State three crimes that can be punished with corporal punishment in an Islamic society.

Look up FORGIVENESS:
What does this teach about the forgiveness of Allah?

Look up PUNISHMENT: How should a criminal be dealt with?

What is better than vengeance?

Look up HUDUD: What does this word mean?

Look up THEFT: How do the actions of thieves prove they are really unbelievers?

What is the penalty for unnecessary and unrepentant theft?

Look up QISAS: What is qisas?

Look up REPENTANCE: What is the Arabic word for this? When does Allah forgive us?

### Note

**The Hadd Punishments**

'Hadd' (pl. Hudud) means 'prevention', 'hindrance', 'restraint' or 'prohibition'.

The Hadd laws are the restrictive rules of God regarding lawful and unlawful conduct.

The Hadd punishments are the extreme limits of punishment beyond which a judge should not go. In other words, the punishments of the death penalty, amputation of a limb or limbs, or flogging of 80 or 100 strokes are the limits beyond which a person should not be sentenced. It does not mean that the judge automatically has to give those sentences. They may be reduced according to circumstances, the nature of the evidence, and the motivation of the criminal.

In other words, a thief could be sentenced to jail for theft, or community service; the worst penalty would be the hand-cutting. A thief should not, in Islam, face hand-cutting AND prison, or revenge etc. It would be illegal to put a thief to death for theft, as was the case in the UK until this century!

The same idea of LIMITS is true of all Hadd punishments; they are the extreme limit of the sentence. The Hadd does not have to be given if some lesser penalty seems appropriate.

## 62. JIHAD / WAR AND PEACE

### Fact Questions

1. What is the meaning of the word 'jihad'?
2. Give an example of when a Muslim might show: unselfish courage

obedience discipline duty constant striving

Your examples can come from any aspect of life - eg. at work, at home, in the family, nursing, in a non-Muslim environment, etc.

3. How does surah 22:40 show that Muslims should never attack the places of worship of the People of the Book?
4. What is Harb al-Muqadis (or Maqdis)?
5. When should jihad fighting stop?
6. How should one treat a wounded enemy?
7. How should one treat a captured enemy woman?

## Understanding

Do the work set in 'Thinking Point' and 'For Your Folders'.

## Dictionary Work

Look up JIHAD.

(a) In the Great Jihad, what are we fighting against?

(b) What aspects of jihad are involved for a khalifah for Allah?

(Look up KHILAFAH, too).

Look up MONGOLS, and ZIONISM: In what ways are they excellent examples of all that is not jihad?

Look up PACIFISM: When is it wrong not to fight?

Look up MUJAHIDEEN: What are they?

## Note

*Pacifism.* The notion that one should not fight, or do military service.

Muslims, although peace-loving, are not total pacifists because it is felt that there are certain circumstances in which it would be wrong not to fight. Muslims dislike cowardice, or attempts to brush off

responsibility or 'hide things under the carpet'. It is a Muslim's duty to defend the weak, the oppressed, the exploited, the downtrodden, and those persecuted for their religion. It is NEVER their business to persecute or become tyrants themselves. A 'double-danger' is that frequently those who do the most damage to Islam are themselves highly religious and devout Muslims who have rather intolerant and inflexible natures, who believe their distorted and extreme views really are the true Islam. The most effective way to counter this kind of unpleasantness is to show the true teachings and way of life set out by the Prophet, so that the grounds for criticism are removed.

## 63. PREJUDICE, NATIONALISM AND DISCRIMINATION

### Fact Questions

1. What does Islam say is the only true loyalty?

2. What was the Prophet's opinion of nationalism?

3. Millions of Muslim women do not wear the kind of hijab shown in the picture on p.128; millions of Muslim men do not grow beards. They are not compulsory in Islam, but sunnah. Explain carefully what is meant by sunnah. (You could look back at Unit 43; and look up Dictionary pp. 28 and 65).

### Understanding

Do the work set in 'For Discussion' and 'Things to do'.

### Dictionary Work

Look up PERSECUTION: What does

this mean? What example was set by the Prophet when he was personally persecuted?

Look up RACISM and TOLERANCE: What is taught in 88:21-22?

## Press Report

The Independent, July 2nd, 1998.

# HOME OFFICE ACCUSED OF RACISM

*By Ian Burrell Home Affairs Correspondent*

Jack Straw announced last night that he was not prepared to lift the ban preventing the American black militant leader Louis Farrakhan from entering Britain. The Home Secretary said his decision was influenced by violent scenes involving British followers of Mr.Farrakhan outside the inquiry into the murder of Stephen Lawrence this week.

A group of around 30 activists from Mr Farrakhan's Nation of Islam organization tried to force their way into the inquiry chamber in South London as police used CS spray to retain order.

In a faxed letter to the Nation's offices in Chicago, Mr Straw said he was"minded to maintain" Mr Farrakhan's exclusion from Britain.

The decision follows a review of Mr Farrakhan's case which began in the autumn. The original ban was enforced in 1986 by the then Home Secretary, Douglas Hurd, who feared that Mr Farrakhan's inflammatory language could spark racial unrest in the wake of the Broadwater Farm riot in Tottenham, north London.

Mr Farrakhan has called Jews "bloodsuckers", described Zionism as a "dirty religion" and revered Adolf Hitler as a "great man".

But last month, as The Independent revealed yesterday, the radical leader signed a statement in which he acknowledged that Britain was a multi-cultural society and promised to do nothing to incite racial hatred. The development prompted concern that the ban on Mr Farrakhan would be lifted.

The Nation of Islam leader has the opportunity to make further representations before Mr Straw makes a final decision.

Benjamin Muhammad, a spokesman for Mr Farrakhan said Nation of Islam lawyers would consider Mr Straw's statement before deciding whether to make further representations. he added: "This is a violation of human rights and the exclusion ... appears to have both racial and political overtones." He said it was unjust to relate Mr Farrakhan's entry status with the events at the Stephen Lawrence inquiry.

"The (British) government wants to ban the honourable minister Farrakhan who has violated no law and yet there has been no denial of privilege to the five men who killed Stephen Lawrence and that is a contradiction," Mr Muhammad said.

## Note

Orthodox Muslims (both Sunni and Shi'i) do not Recognise 'Nation of Islam' as being truly Islamic. Islam teaches tolerance and universalism.

### Jews

Those Jews who kept the pure faith, and might be regarded as the 'righteous remnant' referred to in their own scriptures, are accepted and recommended by Allah in the Qur'an (Surahs 2:62; 4:162; 5:132; 6:197; 28:53; 29:47). At the time of the Prophet, there were many Jewish converts. He hoped to convince the Jews of Madinah and bring them back to the truths of God's message, but they often acted treacherously and jealously for political reasons. Two of the Prophet's wives were Jewesses, Safiyah and Rayhanah, both widows of enemies defeated in battle. Some Muslims misguidedly feel the need to be hostile towards Jews in general, and interpret Quranic passages which referred specifically to particular Jews involved in treachery in and around Madinah as applying to all Jews, including those of today. This ignores all the teaching of love and tolerance towards the People of the Book, and the fact that individuals are always judged by Allah as individuals, and not as members of a particular race. No one person bears the sins of another.

It is important to remember that Jews, Christians and Muslims all worship the same One True God, the Creator, the Source of Revelation - even if human brains interpret things differently and adopt different practices in their worship.

# Prohibitions

## 64. SELF INDULGENCE

### Fact Questions

1.  Why do Muslims feel humble?
2.  What helps Muslims to succeed?
3.  When might anger be justified?
4.  Why are bitterness and remorse so dangerous?
5.  Why did Allah mention an ass in 31:19?
6.  What is meant by 'greed', and why is it wrong?

### Special Text

Copy out the first hadith, and give a decorated border.

### Understanding

Do the work set in 'For Discussion' and 'For your Folders'.

### Dictionary Work

Look up ANGER: What did the Prophet recommend?

Look up CHEATING: Give a definition and an example.

Look up DISHONESTY: Why is this a waste of time for a Muslim?

Look up ENVY: Why should a Muslim not be envious of others?

Look up SLANDER: What did the Prophet recommend?

## 65. DISHONESTY

### Fact Questions

1.  Can you give an example from your own experience of when you, or someone else, lied?
2.  Can you give an example from your own experience of slander?
3.  Make a list of six examples of dishonesty in everyday life.
4.  Why do all these answers to Nos 1 - 3 make a Muslim feel uncomfortable and unhappy?
5.  Give a definition of 'kufr'?
6.  In what ways are spiritualism, magic, astrology and lucky charms all forms of kufr?
7.  Why is belief in charms and superstitions actually contrary to Islam?

### Understanding

Do the work set in 'For Discussion' and 'For Your Folders'.

### Dictionary Work

Look up DIVINATION: How is this a form of shirk?

Look up MAGIC (sihr): How do jinn trick gullible people?

Look up SUPERSTITION: In what way can miniature Qur'ans or little texts sometimes be misused?

Look up GAMBLING: Why is this haram?

Look up THEFT: Why can a thief never claim to be a true Muslim?

## 'Lottery Dilemmas'

Muslims know that gambling is haram. That many devoutly "spend a pound" every week on the lottery, hoping the "divine finger" will point to them, is another matter. It should not surprise us that Muslims participate in the lottery. We are the poorest community in Britain today, and the poorest sections of society are likely to gamble most, in the hope of lifting themselves out of their plight. One only has to walk through any major city to understand why Muslims are prone to lottery mania.

The lottery poses dilemmas even for those who do not take part. Take the example of the local Muslim shopkeeper who set up his business to escape a life on the dole, after the collapse of the manufacturing industry in Britain. After some years of prosperity, the local supermarket has taken most of his trade. Faced with a choice of selling lottery tickets or losing his trade, it is not difficult to see why some are tempted by haram (thankfully the majority do not).

The lottery has become a national institution and is now beginning to permeate all aspects of social and economic life in Britain. The voluntary sector is increasingly becoming dependant on grants from the National Lottery Charities Board. With a progressive decline in local authority and welfare state funding programmes over the years, lottery money is destined to become the prime source of funding for voluntary groups and the poor. The deprived Muslim voluntary sector serving a poor community is faced with a stark choice; obtain funding from the national lottery for projects, or pack up, thus perpetuating the disadvantage; and where should new Muslim projects go for funding?

The Muslim community itself is not organized enough or willing to finance such services. Overseas Muslim donors have their own agendas. Should Muslim projects seek lottery funds? Should they use council services funded via lottery money?

There is another dilemma. The administration of the national lottery and its Charities Board are creating many jobs with good career structures. Should Muslim graduates who are already being excluded from so many employment opportunities, as a result of discrimination, avoid these jobs? Would Muslims engaging in these activities also be engaging in haram?

If the answer is that we would not have anything to do with lottery funds, then this poses another question. Is it haram for us to seek any kind of funding from the "public pot" (to which we also contribute) since this also contains income from haram activities?

What is haram and what is halal for Muslims living in Britain? Indeed, is it possible to avoid haram in a society where to engage in haram activities appears profitable. Should we all pack our bags and migrate? But which Muslim country is better? Nobody, it seems is debating these issues and guiding us on them.

Ironically, if all Muslims were to save one pound per week in a central pot, instead of spending it on the lottery, not only we would be following the Qur'anic injunction in 2:219, which asks us to refrain from gambling and spend anything above our needs on good causes, but we would also be able to finance most of our projects, thus creating employment for our children. In this way, we might eventually have more millionaires than if we played the lottery. The "divine finger" may then point to us collectively as an example for others. Until then what choice do we have? (Jahangir Mohammed).

## Gambling

Some things contain both harm benefit. If their harm outweighs their benefit, they are haram, or forbidden in Islam. Gambling may seem harmless fund at first, but it is like a drug leading the gambler into wasting more and more money. (2:219; 5:93). Therefore, such addictive things as casino gambling, card games for money, fruit machines, bingo, and National Lotteries are all haram.

## 66. DESTRUCTION OF LIFE

### Fact Questions

1. Why is it pointless for Muslims to worry if they might perhaps die today?
2. Give examples of why some people do wish to die before their 'time'.
3. Why do you think so many people fear death?
4. Why should Muslims not fear death?
5. When a person commits suicide, who else will go through terrible suffering, apart from the suicided person?
6. Islam teaches that all the sufferings people go through actually reduce the penalties and punishments we should receive for our sins in the Afterlife. How could this be used as an argument against euthanasia?
7. What are the grounds for giving the death penalty in Islam?
8. Why are murderers not always executed?
9. No penalty is given to ordinary Muslims who simply change their minds and leave Islam. However, how might it affect their eternal lives?

### Understanding

Do the work set in 'For Your Folders' and 'For Discussion'.

### Dictionary Work

Look up ABORTION: How do you think the modern use of ultra-sound equipment and screens has affected the notion that a baby's individual life begins after the 120th day of a mother's pregnancy?

Look up BIRTH CONTROL: What principles are acceptable in Islam?

Look up CAPITAL PUNISHMENT, DIYYAH, QISAS and FORGIVENESS. Explain how Islam limits personal revenge.

Look up DEATH: When does Allah know the time of our death?

Look up EUTHANASIA: When might a person's suffering be actually useful and important?

Look up SUICIDE: When is a person who commits suicide not held to blame?

How might Muslims help the souls of those who have committed suicide?

### Note: Suicide

Muslims believe that since every soul has been created by Allah, and is owned by Him, no person is allowed to damage or attempt to kill any body in which it is the 'guest'. To kill yourself is just as forbidden as killing another person unlawfully.

*'How can you reject faith in Allah, seeing you were without life and He gave you life; and He will cause you to die, and will bring you again to life." (2:28)*

Thabit b. al-Dhhah recorded that the Blessed Messenger observed: 'He who killed himself with steel, or poison, or threw himself off a mountain would be tormented on the Day of Resurrection with that very thing.' (Muslim 202)

Life may be full of hardships and terrible sufferings, but Muslims are taught to accept these as part of their test, and to face them with patience and humility. The real life of a Muslim is that to come in the Hereafter-human life on Earth is just preparation. Therefore, not even the very worst calamities that could happen in life should make a person commit suicide out of despair if their faith in God is genuine.

Anas recorded: 'None of you should wish for death for any calamity that befalls you, but should say: 'O Allah! Cause me to live so long as my life is better for me, and cause me to die when death is better for me.' (Abu Dawud 3102)

The real point is that the person who commits suicide is demonstrating that they have lost their faith in the reality of Allah and the Hereafter, and think, wrongly, that they are 'ending it all'. Furthermore, they are inflicting a life-time of terrible suffering on those who were not able to prevent their suicide. Many, many distressed people have held back from the brink of suicide by realising how much those who love them would be devastated by their fatal act.

To commit suicide out of shame has been considered honourable in some societies; in Islam, the desired course of action is humble apology followed by attempts to right the wrong, and not suicide.

Of course, a large percentage of people commit suicide as a result of clinical depression and mental illness, and this should not be regarded as the same thing as somebody just defying God's will.

The Law of Shari'ah concurs that if any people in those categories commit crimes they should not be punished; if they make agreements or enter into contracts in that state they should not be valid, and similarly while in that mental state they may not divorce a spouse or free a slave. Therefore anybody who unfortunately commits suicide while the balance of their mind is disturbed is not held responsible by Allah, but is forgiven.

'A'ishah reported the very important hadith: "There are three (persons) whose actions are not recorded; a sleeper until fully awake, a (person with) disturbed mind until restored to reason, and a child below the age of puberty.' (Abu Dawud 4384)

## 67. IMPURITY: SEX OUTSIDE MARRIAGE

### Fact Questions

1. What do Muslims not believe about sex?
2. What is a chaperone?
3. What is adultery?
4. What is the punishment ordered in the Qur'an for adultery?

### Dictionary Work

Look up CELIBACY and MONASTICISM: Explain what celibacy is, and the Muslim attitude towards it.

Look up CLOTHING: How does Muslim dress discourage adultery, and sex before marriage?

Look up GHUSL: How does a Muslim restore ritual purity after sexual intercourse, before the next prayer?

Look up KHULWAH and MAHREM: What do these words mean? What is the rule for Muslims?

Look up MUT'AH: What is it, and why are most Muslim women against this?

Look up SEX: What sort of sex brings sadaqah?

Look up ZINAH: What is this? Explain the difference between fornication, adultery and homosexuality.

### Understanding

Do the work set in 'For Discussion' and 'For Your Folders'.

*Moroccan style.*

## Notes :

*Adultery.* This is the sin of cheating on one's husband or wife. Sex after marriage with someone who is not your husband or wife. Fornication means sex before marriage.

Adultery is regarded as a shameful thing, and the theft of a marriage partner's honour as the worst sort of theft there could be. As marriage is a contract, it can be ended honourably if it goes wrong. But adultery is punishable in Islamic law by 100 lashes (17:32; 24:2-3, 4-10). The infliction of this hadd punishment was taken very seriously. It should only be administered after the act of adultery was physically observed by four reliable witnesses, who could identify each adulterer with absolute certainty. If perjury was committed, perhaps out of malice, then the one who gave false testimony should be lashed and his or her testimony never again accepted in the future. In some societies adultery is considered so shameful it is punished by

death - the practice that was considered normal at the time of the Prophet, and in the Old and New Testaments. The Prophet preferred mercy, but is known to have reluctantly condoned some executions when the guilty parties insisted on taking their punishment on this earth rather than waiting for God's judgement in the Hereafter. However, this was not the penalty laid down in the Qur'an. The Qur'an recommended that sexually promiscuous people should only marry each other.

## Some Definitions

- **Homosexual:** A person who prefers sex with another person of the same sex. The term applies to male or female, but there is another name for a female homosexual (see below).
- **Lesbian:** A woman who prefers sex with another woman.
- **Heterosexual:** The normal male/female sexual relationship.
- **Bisexual:** A person who will have a sexual relationship with either men and women, or both.
- **Trans-sexual:** A person born with the body of a man, but who feels that somehow he is a woman trapped in a man's body, and vice versa. These are the people who sometimes seek to change sex through hormone treatment and operations.
- **Transvestite:** A man who dresses in women's clothing, and vice versa. These are not necessarily homosexual, or wishing to change out of a 'wrong' body. Certain kinds of transvestites also have a historic tradition of association with pantomime and comedy, and as 'good luck' symbols at weddings in certain cultures ( eg: Pakistan)

All these are forbidden in Islam.

## Note: Temporary Marriage or Mut'ah

The origin of the idea of temporary marriage, or mut'ah, was to put an end to illicit sex. Under this arrangement, a man and woman could live together as husband and wife for a specified period and under specified conditions, at the end of which time they automatically separated. In support of this custom, surah 4:24 is cited.

Mut'ah was an established custom in Arabia before the advent of Islam, and it seems that the Prophet did not revoke permission at first. Later, however, either after the conquest of Makkah or the victory at Khaybar, he did issue an order of prohibition. This order was continued after his demise.

For example, Caliph Umar declared he would cancel, annul, prohibit and punish Mut'ah-al-Hajj and Mut'ah an-Nisa. (Muslim). He once declared from the pulpit: 'Should I know that someone had contracted Mut'ah, I shall straight away charge him with adultery, and mete out the punishment.'

Those who support mut'ah sometimes quote Abdullah ibn Abbas who gives the hadith: 'Mut'ah in a time of distress is as much permissible as are dead meat, pork and animal blood.' However, Ali reprimanded him for expressing this opinion and told him the Prophet had definitely forbidden mut'ah on 'the day of Khaybar.' He was backed up by Urwah ibn Zubayr.

Most Muslim women regard Mut'ah as little more than legalised prostitution.

## 68. SELF-ABUSE; ALCOHOL, DRUGS AND TOBACCO

Research - Go to a doctor's surgery, and see what pamphlets and information you can pick up on smoking, alcohol and drug taking.

Look up the following drugs and list their dangerous effects:

Cocaine ecstasy qat heroin nicotine amphetamines cannabis

### Fact Questions

1. How did Caliph Umar define 'khamr'?
2. Why do people who pray have to give up alcohol?
3. Why do some people favour making drug-taking legal?

(There is a special file on Drugs - See p.174)

### Understanding

Do the work set in 'For Your Folders'.

### Dictionary Work

Look up ALCOHOL: What were the three stages of prohibition?

Look up DRUGS: Why are they totally forbidden to Muslims (except for genuine medical use).

Note: Alcohol (khamr) is haram and may be used in medicine only if this is absolutely necessary.

## Intoxicants

*'O you who believe! Intoxicants and gambling, (dedication of) stones, and (divination by) arrows, are an abomination, Satan's handiwork. Refuse such (abomination), so that you may prosper. Satan's plan is to excite enmity and hatred between you, with intoxicants and gambling, and hinder you from the remembrance of God, and from prayer. Will you not then abstain?'* (5:93-4).

## 69. MODERATION, EXTREMISM AND FUNDAMENTALISM

### Note:

*Fundamentalism.* A problem has arisen in the West, because the word Fundamentalist means something different when referring to Christians than when referring to Muslims. In both cases, it means a person who refers back to the original Holy Text, and accepts every word of it to be true, and every command as valid. The problem is that in the Old Testament of the Bible, there are many items, narratives, stories and so on that are largely regarded as mythology, and not literally true. Different Christians vary as to which passages would come into this category. Most Christians would certainly not accept every single word of the Old Testament as being literally true.

Therefore, when we come across a Christian who does, that Christian is called a 'fundamentalist' and is regarded as being not only rather a 'simple soul', but worse - he or she is seen as someone who is perversely clinging to something which has been disproved by science, and therefore to persist in believing in it is regarded as stupid nonsense. An example would be the belief that the earth was flat, or that the sun revolved round the earth.

In Islam, it is somewhat different, for Muslims believe the Qur'an to be the directly revealed Word of God, not a book written by pious people about God which is full of their own ideas and mistakes and biases. Therefore, all true Muslims can be called Fundamentalists, since they regard all of the Qur'an as God's direct word, and all of it totally in keeping with all the scientific principles of the Creator.

What most people mean by 'fundamentalists' when applied to Muslims, is 'intolerant extremists.'

### Fact Questions

1. What was the Prophet's 'Middle Way'?
2. What things are prohibited in Islam?
3. Why did the Prophet recommend public prayers to be brief?
4. How did the Prophet react to a zealous Imam who prayed for too long?
5. Give examples of how long prayers, or too much time spent at the mosque, might cause suffering to others, and avoidance of duty?
6. What is an alim?

### Understanding

Do the work set in 'For Discussion' and 'For Your Folders'.

### Dictionary Work

Look up AMAL: How does Amal counter hyprocrisy?

Look up BIDAH and FARD: Explain what these things are.

Look up CONVERSION BY THE SWORD: How does this go against 2:256?

Look up DAWAH: What is the point of doing this?

Look up FUNDAMENTALISM: Why is this not always a bad thing?

Look up IJTIHAD: How does this help to control Fundamentalism?

Look up HYPOCRITE: What is the Arabic word for hypocrisy?

Look up TAKFIR: Explain what it is, and why it is against the spirit of Islam.

Look up TYRANNY, ZEALOTRY and EXTREMISM: How might even a very devout religious person be a tyrant?

## 70. THE SUCCESSORS - ABU BAKR AND UMAR

### Fact Questions

1. For what reasons were the first four caliphs chosen?
2. What sort of men were they?
3. What is meant by 'khalifah' and 'Rashid'?
4. Give four examples of their simple life-style.
5. What was the first duty of a caliph/khalifah?
6. What should a caliph's attitude be when faced with:

(a) a corrupt judge   (b) a homeless person   (c) an exploitative employer   (d) a refugee   (e) an orphan   (f) an underpaid worker (g) an over-charging landlord   (h) a business cheat   (i) a lazy worker (j) an illiterate child (or adult)   (k) an old person   (l) a sick person.

7. What was Umar's attitude towards the Christian and Jewish shrines in Jerusalem?

8. How did Umar's Jerusalem contract illustrate his tolerance?

*The Dome of the Rock, Jerusalem.*

## Special Texts

(a) Write out the first given saying of Abu Bakr. Why do you think that saying is good advice?

(b) Write out one of Umar's sayings.

## Understanding

Do the work set in 'For Your Folders'.

# 71. THE SUCCESSORS, UTHMAN AND ALI

## Understanding

Read through the unit carefully, and do the Quick Quiz.

Answer the questions set in 'For Your Folders' and 'Things to do'.

## Dictionary Work

Look us and read the entries on ABU BAKR, UMAR, UTHMAN, ALI and CALIPH.

Write a brief paragraph on whether you think a caliph following the Islamic rules of noble life would improve the world-situation of Islam today.

# 72. THE SUNNI-SHI'ITE SPLIT

## Fact Questions

1. Why did certain Muslims feel Ali should have been the first successor to the Prophet?
2. Name Ali's wife.
3. Name Ali's two sons by this wife.
4. Which country has Shi'ism as its State Religion?
5. What part was played in the history of Shi'ism by: Zainab (also spelled Zaynab) and Yazid.
6. What do Shi'ites do during the month of Muharram?

7. What is the difference between a Sevener and a Twelver Shi'ite?

## Understanding

Do the work set in 'Quick Quiz" and 'For Your Folder'.

## Dictionary Work

Look up SHI'ITE: From whom were Shi'ite Imams descended?

Look up SEVENER: What is an Ismaili?

Look up TWELVER: Give another name for this sect.

Look up HIDDEN IMAM: What happened to the last Imam in either sect?

Look up MAHDI: What is he expected to do?

Look up AYATOLLAH: What does this word mean? Name one famous Ayatollah.

Look up ASHURA:

(a) What is the date of Ashura?

(b) What did the prophet do on this day?

(c) What is the Sunni attitude towards the martyrdom of Hussein?

Look up KARBALA: In which country is this place?

# 73-74-75. SUFISM

## Fact Questions

1. What is meant by fiqh?
2. What is the other name for Sufism?
3. What are the six tasawwuf aspects of prayer?
4. Explain what is meant by
   (a) fana   (b) baqa   (c) shaikh.
5. How long does a mystical experience last?
6. What are the five main goals of Sufism?
7. Why are Sufis often tolerant of other religions?

8. Why was al-Hallaj executed for blasphemy?
9. What is a tariqah?
10. Name three Sufi orders.
11. p.74. What does Sufism attempt to 'save' Islam from?
12. Name one famous Sufi from pp 148-153, and either give two facts about him/her, or give one famous quote from their work.
13. What is a dervish?
14. What are dhikrs?
15. Give five examples dhikr practice.
16. p.152. Which is the largest Sufi order?
17. Name the first Khalifah of this order, and the fortieth.
18. Name a Scottish shaikh.

## Understanding

Do the work set in 'For Your Folders' and 'For Discussion' on pp. 151 and 153.

## Dictionary Work

Look up SUFISM: Give two possible explanations of the word's origin.
What does Sufism emphasize?
Look up DHIKR: What does this word mean?

Look up VISIONS: What are 'visions' What is the main effect of a vision?

# 76. WORLDWIDE ISLAM

## Fact Questions

1. How do we define a Muslim State?
2. Why do most Muslims insist there are NO real Muslim States in today's world - not even Iran or Afghanistan or Pakistan etc.
3. How could deep convictions regarding Islam and nationalism lead to disaster?
4. List the eight things Muslims cannot really accept in our modern societies.
5. Why do many leaders of modern 'Islamic States' fear their own extremists?
6. How many countries have over 80% Muslim population?
7. What are the main aims of:
   (a) Socialism (b) Pan-Arabism (c) Pan-Islam?
8. Why are millions of Muslims not interested in Pan-Arabism?

## Understanding

Do the work set in 'For Your Folders'.

## Dictionary Work

Look up CONVERSION BY THE SWORD: Why is this a nonsense in Islam?
Look up DHIMMI: What does this mean?
Look up MUSLIM BROTHERHOOD: Why is this movement feared by so many governments?
Look up PAN-ARABISM: What is the problem with this concept?
Look up PAN-ISLAM: What do many Muslims long for?

*Section Three*

# THE 'HIGH-FLIER' FILES

# File on 'Proofs' for the Existence of God

## THE PERFECT DESIGN:

Many people in the West were not convinced by materialist arguments, which undermined the credibility of the Bible and hence seemed to undermine the idea of belief in a perfect God. They retained their strong faith in a personal God, the Source of Divine Love who sees the smallest sparrow fall and knows us so intimately that even the hairs on our heads are numbered. In defence of God as the Creator, the Rev.William Paley (1743-1805), for example, argued in his book, 'Natural Theology', that every single thing on earth was so perfectly fitted to its natural environment that it was impossible for this to have occurred by chance. One could not simply throw up a handful of bricks into the air and expect them to fall down into the perfect and finished shape of a house, not even if one threw the bricks a million million times. For a house is designed; it is much more than a random assembly of bricks.

Paley also used the analogy of a watch. What is a watch? he asked. Well, it is something that tells us the time. But really, if you take the watch apart, it is just a collection of bits and pieces, springs and coils, cogs and wheels. A child could play around with them for ages and amuse himself by creating patterns with it, or an artist could create a work of art with its pieces. But only when it is put together in one specific way does it take on another function altogether: it begins to tell the time!

This could not have come about by accident; it had to be designed. Moreover, the fact that there is such a thing as 'time,' which obeys laws and can be measured, was a pre-existent condition for the creation of a machine for performing that task. The concept of 'watch' implies a knowledge and Understanding of certain intangible but existent concepts, intelligible only to a higher mind. The need to tell the time was not the reason why those cogs and coils were created, but it was the reason the watch was created.

If you wandered through some pleasant valley and found a heap of stones, you would think nothing about them but that they had arrived at their present place through natural causes. But if one day you came across other stones that were arranged in such a way that they formed the words, 'Welcome to Kansas City,' you would not imagine that this had happened by chance or accident, but would assume that some designing mind had arranged them in this manner --- a mind that understood the concept of communication of one mind to another through language, and such intangible things as the meaning of the concept of 'welcome'.

If the words happened to be in no known language - let us say 'Martian' - you would probably not even realise that they were words at all.

In nature, every creature fits so perfectly into its environment that surely it cannot be accidental. Consider the eye of a bird, for

example. A bird needs to pick up seeds and small insects, yet also to soar in the sky and see great distances; therefore it needs both far and near vision. And it does have both. If either were only partially developed or still evolving, the bird would fail to survive. Again, the archer fish needs an eye that can cope with refraction from the surface of the water, as well as the ability to shoot out a jet of liquid at the correct angle to knock down its prey, and it has both. If any of its faculties were only partially developed, the archer fish would not be here.

## LOADED DICE FOR 'LIFE':

Scientists trying to create 'life' in test-tubes know perfectly well that they can be successful in their experiments only if a great number of very special conditions occur at just the right time, in just the right proportions, under just the right conditions. These do not occur at random, and scientists use extreme care, effort and skill to set up these very conditions, according to their discovered knowledge and technology.

It is quite useless to claim that if all the ingredients were just thrown together and left (assuming, of course, that a selection of ingredients to remove any unwanted ones

had occurred first, which would certainly be cheating), in infinite time the desired result would come about by chance. There is no proof whatsoever for this rather remarkable assertion; it actually requires considerably more faith to believe in that than it would take to believe in God. If the required effect did appear to happen 'just spontaneously,' one would suspect the very strong possibility of what one might call 'antichance,' or 'loaded dice'!

## STATISTICS:

In 1953, Stanley Miller caused excitement when his experiments passed an electric spark through a collection of hydrogen, methane, ammonia and water vapour, which he presumed simulated conditions at the beginning of life on earth. His efforts did manage to produce four amino acids; thus it was claimed that the building-blocks of life had been created in the test-tube!

However, forty years further on, no scientist has yet been able to produce the full twenty amino acids needed. Scientists also point out that there is an 'oxygen factor' to consider. If there had been oxygen in the primitive 'air', the first amino acid could never have occurred; yet without oxygen, if it had occurred, it would have been destroyed by cosmic rays. The same energy that splits up compounds in the atmosphere would very quickly decompose any complex amino acids that formed 'by chance'. Miller himself had to admit that once he had created his four amino acids, he had to very quickly remove them from the area of the spark, which would have decomposed them.

Statisticians have now calculated that since the proteins needed for life have very complex molecules, the 'chance' of one forming at random is in the region of ten to the power of 113-a number larger than the estimated total of all the atoms in the universe! On top of that, no less than two thousand proteins serving as enzymes are needed to speed up the chemical reactions in each cell, and without this help the cell would die.

The structural units of DNA involve five histones (basic proteins) governing the activity of genetic material. The chances of forming even the simplest of these is said to be around twenty to the power of one hundred, another fantastic number. Moreover, proteins depend on DNA for their formation, but DNA cannot form without pre-existing protein. Which came first, the chicken or the egg? They must have developed in parallel, or evolved simultaneously, without either coming originally from the other.

As the biologist Edwin Conklin put it: 'The probability of life originating from accident is comparable to the probability of the unabridged dictionary resulting from an explosion in a printing shop.'

De Nouy was a mathematical genius who worked on the possibility of creating one molecule of protein containing only 2,000 atoms (instead of its normal much higher number) by chance. He further suggested accounting for only 2 different kinds of atoms in this molecule instead of 4, as in reality. He estimated that with 500 trillion 'shakes' per second, the time needed to form one such molecule by chance could be 10 to the power of 242 billion years. Since the earth has existed for only around 2 billion years, and the possibility of life on it for only around 1 million, de Nouy concluded that chance creation was therefore impossible.

## PURPOSE:

Thus, there seems to be undeniable evidence of purpose in it all. Many material things, which have no powers of thought or intelligence themselves, seem to cooperate somehow to produce ordered and stable systems, out of which all sorts of possibilities, such as life and consciousness, can arise. They seem to be achieving a purpose which they cannot possibly be consciously bringing about themselves.

There must surely, therefore, be a Designer or God whose intelligence actually guides things to achieve certain aims. It's all very well for scientists to suggest that in the 'primeval soup' of atomic particles in the universe, everything suddenly-or even over a vast period of time-sorted itself out to form the basis of our existence. But the conditions would all have had to exist prior to the fragments, and everything would have had to have come together at exactly the right moment. The 'primeval soup' theory totally ignores any explanation of where the original atoms came from anyway. And it is worth remembering that the vast majority of the laws of the universe are actually hostile to life as we know it; so the fact that life exists at all requires some plausible explanation in terms of antichance.

## A LOGICAL NECESSITY:

An early line of thought, favoured by St.,Anselm in the eleventh century AD - and the great Muslim philosopher Muhyiddin ibn Al-Arabi in the twelfth, was the attempt to prove the existence of God by logical reasoning alone. God was defined as the very essence of Perfection, Power, Goodness and Love. Therefore God, by definition alone, was by necessity the greatest possible thing that existed, the ultimate in the scale of values. Nothing greater than God could possibly be conceived of, for the simple reason that if anything could be thought of as more perfect or more good, then what had been simplistically though to be God could not possibly be Him. If anything were greater, then God was not God. By definition, God had to be 'that other than which nothing greater nor more good can be conceived'.

In every walk of life there is a scale of values. Not everything is the same; some things are better or of more value than others, and some are worse. There is an ascending scale of good, better, and best. If God is the Absolute, the Best, then by logic He must exist; if He did not, then obviously many existing things could be though of as being better or greater. It is absurd to think that that which is the greatest of all is imaginary. Therefore God is the Necessary Being and His non-existence is a logical impossibility.

Likewise, if God is supremely perfect, He must exist because if He did not, He could hardly be described as being perfect. If He is not supremely perfect, then He cannot be God. Perfection must have existence as one of its qualities, since that which does not exist cannot be perfect. Therefore, God must exist. The whole argument is contained within the logic of its own statements.

## WHERE DID THE IDEA COME FROM?

At any rate it is evident from mankind's continued contemplation of God that He certainly has been persistently present in human consciousness, leaving some very tangible proofs of His existence as may be witnessed in the long history of prophethood through the ages. From where could the idea of God have originated if there had never been any such thing? How could the notion possibly have entered human consciousness at all without God's being the cause of it?

## WHAT DOES 'REAL' MEAN?

The problem of attempting to prove the existence of God hinges upon what we mean by the word 'real'. For most people, anything 'real' is that which is subject to the laws of nature and limited by such elements as shape, mass, weight, position, and so on. If a thing is subject to any law of nature, then that law must be greater than it, and by the definition given above, it cannot be God.

This argument cannot, however, be used to prove that God does not have real existence, for we must admit that something far greater than any natural existing material object does exist - namely, the laws of nature. Surely the self-same argument that one would use to establish the existence and superiority of the concept of natural law to any physical thing is an argument basically similar to the argument for the existence of God, except that the argument for God's existence goes back a step further, for we cannot accept that the Power which created the laws of nature could be in any way limited by them.

In this case, the argument that God cannot have physical existence as we understand it is strengthened, since that would bind Him by His own laws. God is Real in the sense that He does exist and has limitless powers, although He does not exist as a limited physical object.

## THE ARGUMENT FROM MOTION:

Whatever is in motion is moved. If it is moved, it must have been set in motion by something which is already moving. That moving thing must have been moved by something else which was already moving, and so on to infinity. The whole of the universe is in motion, but this motion must have started somewhere. Whatever Immovable Mover it was that started it all in motion, this we call God.

## FIRST CAUSE?

We observe in our universe that if anything at all happens, it happens for a reason; that is, it has been caused to happen by something else. These other 'somethings' existed before the event or thing they caused to happen. And they themselves were set in action by previous causes.

Contemporary scientists are grappling with the recent discovery that at the sub-atomic level there does seem to be a certain element of uncaused activity, which looks, at first sight, as if it might threaten the tidy notion that everything must obey set laws, because everything is caused. However, against this unsettling notion it could be maintained that the apparent indeterminacy of sub-atomic reactions is no more than our ignorance. Once we have worked out the rules, it will be seen that all these apparently uncaused reactions do follow laws, after all.

## THE CONTINGENCY ARGUMENT:

If we put the theory of causation another way, we are saying that everything is as it is for a reason. In other words, everything is 'contingent'. A contingent thing is something that exists when it might not have. Take a table. We see the table and we assume that it exists. But is it possible that this table might never have existed? Of course it is. Consequently, it is a contingent thing. Why, then, does this table exist? Because someone chopped down a tree,

took the wood and constructed it; if they had not done so, the table would simply never have been.

And what about the tree? Is that contingent? Might it be possible that that particular tree would never have existed? Again, of course it is. The tree exists simply because someone planted it, or some bird dropped its seed in its place, or some seed simply drifted there on the wind. There is a direct cause for this tree. And could that cause never have happened? Of course! And so it goes on. Every single thing in our universe is contingent.

What about the universe itself? Is it possible that the whole universe might never have existed? Yes, of course it is! It doesn't matter which scientific theory you start your case from-primeval soups, atoms colliding, Big Bang theories; they can all be put forward as possible causes for the universe's coming into existence, if you don't want to accept the simple possibility that God created it.

The trouble with many scientists is that they stop the argument there; they do not go on to the further step and ask whether the ingredients of the Big Bang, whatever that was, or whether any other causal theories, are themselves contingent. The answer has to be, 'Of course they are'. So, once again, we are landed on the shores of 'infinity'.

## INFINITY?

If you don't want to believe in God, you have to accept that everything goes on back and back to 'infinity'. There are really only these two choices; either we accept that the series of causes does go on and on forever, and that there is simply no such thing as the beginning of the universe and existence (or, presumably, an end to it, since infinity must surely stretch in both directions); or we submit and say that there must have been a very First Cause, and that there was some time when the universe had not yet been caused and therefore did not exist.

If you take this second view, you naturally wish to know what the First Cause might have been. This is what a believer would call the Moment of Creation-the moment when God said 'Be!' and it was so.

## CREATION:

And God saw everything that he had made...

Creation is the beginning of the world, whether it be the whole universe or only the terrestrial globe; and the term naturally implies a creator.

What is, must have been made: this idea that the world had a beginning is presumably as old as humanity.

Sometimes the Creator makes the world out of already existing material, and sometimes engenders it, so to speak, out of Himself, but the more official Jewish Christian and Muslim view, is that God created the world out of nothing.

In the Bible there is a detailed account of the process of creation, followed by a continuous genealogy from Adam down to historical times. This makes it possible to calculate the Biblical date of creation, and in the seventeenth century Archbishop Ussher, the Irish Primate, worked out the accepted date, 4004 B.C. This of course referred only to the creation of the earth, though it was intended to have a universal application.

Present-day scientific opinion on the creation of the world, when by this we mean the earth, is not at all settled. One school holds that the earth, together with the other planets, condensed out of a filament of gas drawn from the sun. How

it was drawn out is a matter of opinion. Another school holds that the planets are the remnants of the hard core of a companion to the sun which exploded and, except for these remains, was entirely dissipated. Another again believes that the planets condensed at the same time as the sun from the same gaseous cloud, and are thus, so to speak, not children but brothers of the sun.

All agree that the earth first condensed somewhere about 3,000 million years ago. From there on, the scientific view is that the creation of the earth as we know it today is a serial and unending process. The oldest rocks solidified perhaps 2000 million years ago, and life emerged perhaps 1000 million years ago. Fish are about 300 million years old, reptiles 2000 million, and deciduous trees and grasses about 100 million. Mammals first became predominant about 50 million years ago. As for man, it is estimated that creatures more man than ape have been in existence for a million years, and that Homo Sapiens, true man, is at least 100,000 years old. This is a far cry from Archbishop Ussher's 4004 B.C.

The question of the creation of the whole universe is a very different one. Certain cosmological theories demand a starting point for the history of the universe as we know it. This beginning is also implied in one version of the theory of the 'expanding universe'. On the other hand some cosmologists, such as Hoyle and Gold, believe that the universe, while expanding, is infinite in space and time. That is to say, there is no reason for postulating by their theory a particular moment when the whole universe was created. They suggest on the contrary that there is and always has been a 'continuous creation'. But the whole topic is extremely open, and indeed it is one in which science is at the moment not much interested, regarding it as outside its province.

It is indeed possible that nothing useful will ever be said about the creation of the universe, because of the philosophical problems which are involved in any approach to the subject. These crop up as much when a personal creator is postulated as when he is not.

Consider this argument. Suppose God exists, and created the universe. He must have done it for a reason. Since He is omniscient, he must always have known this reason, and since before the universe was created there was no such thing as time and change, this reason must always have been a good one. Therefore if he was ever to create the world, he must have done it the first moment he was able to: therefore God and the world must have come into existence at the same time.

Another question already mentioned is: if the universe was created, was it created out of something or out of nothing? If out of something, then we must ask what this something was created out of. If out of nothing, then the process is unimaginable, and it becomes futile to try to make any statement about it at all.

Again, there has been no satisfactory

answer to the argument that if the world must necessarily have a creator to engender it and start it off, then this creator must himself need a creator. An infinite regress of this kind can only be avoided by juggling with the notion of time.

The truth is that clear thought about the idea of creation is almost impossible. Kant pointed this out more than 150 years ago. It is inconceivable, as he said, that the universe should not have had a beginning, that it should just stretch back into the past for ever. But it is also inconceivable that it should have a beginning, because we can not imagine anything genuinely without a preceding cause, and this is what the universe in its first moment of existence (or God in his first act) would be. This, said Kant, is a contradiction which springs from the fact that we are trying to think about al-Ghayb the unknowable, something which we cannot think about, because it lies outside the world by its very nature, whereas we can only think about what we have experienced in some way or another. This just argument applies equally to rationalists and to theologians. In this, as in many other things, we should be wiser if we followed Wittgenstein's maxim: 'Whereof we cannot speak, thereof we must keep silent.'

# *File on the Problem of Evil*

When people believe that there is a God and that He is the Supreme Force for Good, they are faced with the serious problem of the many painful and terrible things happening in our world that seem to be quite irreconcilable with any notion of a benign and compassionate Creator.

Simply expressed, the problem is this: If God really is Supreme, then He must, by definition, be able to do anything and everything. If He is Omniscient, then He must know everything that exists or occurs, down to the minutest details. If He is Omnipotent or All-Powerful, then there cannot be anything that He cannot do. Yet beyond any shadow of doubt, a great deal of suffering and evil exists, often in ways that are beyond our minds to accept. Obviously at least one of the proposed suggestions about God must be wrong.

If He is All-knowing, then He is certainly aware of human tragedies and awful sufferings; if He is All-Powerful, He could stop and eradicate all our problems if He so wished; if He is All-Loving, He should certainly wish to do so. The fact that evil and suffering exists therefore apparently suggest that either God is not All-Powerful and does not have the ability to do anything about evil, or that He is not All-Knowing and remains somehow unaware of suffering, or that He is aware of it and could do something about it, but does not do so and is therefore not All-Loving.

## IT'S GOD'S FAULT

One must pause to wonder why it is that suffering and evil exist at all. If God is truly the Creator, why did He create the possibility of such pain and despair and horror? Is there something limited in either God's power or His good intentions, or is there simply no moral aspect at all abroad in the universe, with things just happening as they do because that is the way it is?

Let's take a specific example of human suffering and think about its implications. Suppose there is a child being swept away in a flooded river, drowning because he cannot reach the bank and safety. If a bystander stood there watching with a lifeline in his hand but did not throw it to the child when he had the power to do so, we would certainly regard that person as a villain and accuse him of being morally responsible for the child's death.

If you translate this example up to the level of God's watching some poor human being floundering in the mire, you can see precisely why so many people who are obliged to go through some dreadful sufferings from time to time find it hard to believe in a compassionate, caring, and all-powerful God.

God, who 'sees the smallest sparrow fall,' ought to see the child in distress and do something about it. Most religious people grew up with the belief that God did wondrous deeds for His followers of old, even supplying an occasional miracle when one was needed. Then why doesn't He do it now?

## DOES GOD SEND WARNINGS?

Sometimes, people claim, God does influence the outcome of events by interfering with human consciousness. He uses the consciences of individuals, groups, and nations, to make them feel shame at not being active in putting matters aright when people are suffering abuse, maltreatment, or national disasters such as drought and famine or war.

Sometimes God appears to communicate with individuals through some kind of psychic faculty, perhaps sending premonitions or warnings or visions of things that later come to pass. People get uncomfortable feelings or vivid dreams about particular planes or trains, and avoid travelling on them. Then, when the planes or trains crash, they feel their hunches or premonitions were signs of divine intervention. Perhaps they were.

It would certainly be very nice to think that if we had enough faith, or prayed hard enough, or had lived good enough lives, then, when we got into a tricky situation, God would somehow or other fix things so that we were miraculously saved from whatever it was that was threatening us. But, as we all know only too well, God doesn't operate like that. And, as all ministers of religion know only too well, when people's prayers are not answered and their loved ones drown or die of cancer or crash their cars, all too often the result is that they lose their belief in God, for in their view, if God refuses to help those who have done nothing to 'deserve' suffering, then there is no sense or advantage in belief. To them, all religious fervour and promises of God's love and beneficence look like so many pious wishes, totally unjustified.

## DOES GOD CARE?

God is indeed Supreme, Omnipotent and Omniscient, but are we way off track in supposing that we are in any way special to Him? Out of all the millions of life forms that God has created, why should human beings suppose that they deserve any special attention from Him? Humans are always so self-centered; why, they even think, usually, that they are the chief inhabitants of this planet, and that if a space-ship landed from another planet, it would be the human beings with whom the aliens would communicate, and not the ants or the bees or the microbes.

Maybe all this searching for an answer in the realm of matter is on the wrong track. What is the relationship of God to our universe?

The Jewish philosopher Baruch Spinoza (1632-1677) believed that every part of the universe was inexorably determined by law, and thus, that every single thing follows its course by logical necessity; He did not believe there was any such thing as an accident. According to his system, it was therefore logically impossible for anything to be better than it already was, and if a thing seemed to be bad or evil, that was merely due to the fact that we are not in a position to understand the infinite perfection of the entire universe in its totality. He believed our notions of good and evil are simply subjective assessments of whether or not we considered a thing to be for our own benefit.

Spinoza argued that this subjectivity is misplaced; it is not true that everything is made just for our benefit. In order for a universe to be perfect, it would have to include the full range of experiences and beings, the lower as well as the higher; any universe that did not contain the full range would be less perfect than one that did.

Therefore, he argued, there must be room for the sinner as well as the saint.

Evolutionists discount the idea of humanity's falling from an original state of perfection into sin. The whole theory of evolution is based on the gradual progress of living things through countless changing forms in a steady upward trend toward complexity. According to this reasoning, maybe our moral awareness is no more than a part of that gradual progress, from rudimentary self-consciousness to a caring concern for the whole of humanity. Dogs and cats care for their families, but they do not regard dogs dying of starvation as an evil. The awareness that something could be thought of as evil has developed somewhere along the road as humans ceased to be just animals.

## FREEWILL MAKES IT INEVITABLE:

So far, all the theories under consideration have been based on the material universe as we know it. But what about the spiritual universe? Maybe it doesn't matter that much if we suffer pain or evil in this world of ours, because we will be compensated in the world to come for our suffering. The evil and the good - both will receive from the infinite justice of God the recompense of what they earned.

If human beings are to be permitted to have freewill, there has to exist the possibility of a range of choices, and inevitably some of the things we choose to do will be less good than others. Some of our choices will cause a great deal of pain and suffering to others; some will produce hatred, envy, greed, malice, fear, despair, contempt, pride, cruelty, cowardice, avarice and lust!

## PHYSICAL EVIL:

We have been speaking of evil as if we knew what it was. But what kinds of things are evil? It seems that there are two main sorts of evil, physical and moral. 'Physical evil' is suffering which arises from natural causes such as droughts, floods, earthquakes, diseases, and so on, and we can perhaps concede that although these may be unfortunate for the human beings affected by them, they are totally locked into the working-out of the natural law of cause-and-effect.

The many people who claim to feel a religious awareness through the beauties of nature - things like the blossoms of spring and glorious sunsets - are often taking rather a sentimental and one-sided view, for nature is also 'red in tooth and claw,' and is not really calm or gentle or peaceful at all. So often, we exist in spite of nature. Nature cares nothing for those it wipes out. There is there no element of 'justice' in natural disasters. A landslide can just as well fall on masses of innocent children as on one villain.

Nature is governed by rules which do not change to suit our needs or convenience. And the same rules apply when we humans act, for we are part of nature too. If we bomb people with napalm, they are burned. Bullets kill, drunken driving kills, carelessness in industry and in the home kills.

Are these things really God's fault? I mean, isn't it rather unfair and unreasonable to expect God to break the laws of nature on our behalf? If we ran for the bus and missed it, and then prayed to God to make the bus come back for our benefit, we would have started a chain reaction in which the bus would actually travel backwards and not forwards, and never reach its destination! If we were sitting under a falling rock and

God kindly altered the laws of gravity on our behalf so that we would not be crushed, it might result in countless millions of beings shooting off to their doom in space. And then, whose petition would God, if He chose to do so at all, respond to - yours, mine, someone else's? But what if each of us was praying for a different thing, one which would go counter to the requests of the other supplicants?

The three monotheistic faiths, Judaism, Christianity, and Islam, teach (and it seems a pretty reasonable demand anyway) that it's our business to live within the laws of nature and use them as best we can for the benefit of humanity and the planet. If we pollute our atmosphere, or destroy our oxygen-producing rain-forests, or wipe out endangered species, or eliminate wild plants whose medicinal properties might prove to be the very things we need as cures or antidotes, or eradicate our protective ozone layer, the responsibility is surely ours. How then can we blame God?

Mischief has appeared on land and sea because of (the corruption) wrought by the hands of men ( 30:41).

## MORAL EVIL:

But what about moral evil? Moral evil is the result of our own actions - not the bad things that we do through ignorance, but deliberately unkind and malicious deeds; it arises through international negligence, selfishness, hatred and spite. Spiritual evolution can only take place if there is freewill, and for freewill to exist there has to be the possibility of making wrong or immoral choices, or doing some things that are less good than others. This must mean,

inevitably, that in order to be free, we are bound to live in an environment full of dangers and challenges, an environment in which the results of our own free choices can damage ourselves and others.

In this century, people have had to live with the awful knowledge that they can completely destroy their entire environment and their whole species; the freewill exercised by a single person with a finger on a button could wipe out the whole of life as we know it. It is the existence of human freewill that allows individuals to be in such a position of authority. It was our tax money that paid the wages of the scientists who invented the bombs, our votes (or our negligence) that put the various tyrants in power over us.

In the story of Adam and Eve, the first human couple was created perfect, but like all subsequent humans, they were endowed with freewill. They chose to disobey God's command - that is, to sin. Before eating the forbidden fruit, Adam was neither good nor evil; in fact, he was not a moral being at all, since he had never exercised his freedom of choice. But after eating, along with his knowledge came responsibility.

This does not answer the criticism that if God had not given Adam (a) the command not to eat from it, and (b) the opportunity to do so, Adam would not have got himself into difficulties and upset his Maker.

If God were to remove the evil choices open to us, we could not justifiably be called 'good' at all, but would simply be mindless automatons and not free souls. Most of us would not be interested in that sort of existence. Could a life totally devoid of freedom be fulfilling in any way, let alone the conceived will of God for us?

# *File on Fate and Freewill*

We have noticed that everything in the universe is governed by the laws of cause and effect. This knowledge is the whole basis of science. If the universe did not follow laws, then we would never be able to reason things out, make predictions, and observe whether our theories were true or not. Nobody seriously doubts the statement that the principle of causation rules the whole of the realm of matter.

However, when we consider a human being, we begin to wonder whether we are dealing solely with the realm of matter, or whether there might not be something else involved as well. Is a human individual just a clever machine that must inevitably follow these natural laws, or is there another aspect - call it Mind or Soul - which is not necessarily obliged to be a 'prisoner' of those laws but might perhaps control them in order to mould that individual's own destiny?

Suppose we could acquire all the information about a person, all the bits of his parents' genetic patterns that he had inherited, all the influences acting on him through his background and education. Could we then predict exactly how he would behave in any given situation? Could we work out what he would do next in a crisis? Could we predict from such information how the adult character of a child would develop?

One who thinks such prediction is possible is termed a determinist. Those who would go even further than this and claim that all future events are already mapped out, and that nothing you could do in your life could alter your fate at all, are known as fatalists. They maintain that human activity is not free at all, but predetermined by all sorts of rules and motives acting on the will, and that anything we 'choose' to do is predetermined by the sort of persons we are.

The word 'fate' comes from the Latin 'fatum', meaning 'what has been spoken.' It presupposes some Entity which is in control, a Divine Mind or Order in the universe, the plan of which cannot be altered once it has been formalized. Once a thing has been 'spoken' or 'written', there is no escaping it; it must come to pass.

Fatalists do not necessarily think of this Entity as a personalized being or a God; many simply accept that the universe is governed by the abstract framework of the laws of nature, without any divine originator. It is the overall law itself which can never be altered or avoided, but each happening or observed phenomenon is the direct result of predetermined causes that have acted upon it. The plan, therefore, is inexorable and totally unavoidable.

Hence, fatalists believe that if one could be given full knowledge of all the facts and influences that were going to bear upon an individual's life, the details of that life could be inexorably predicted, even the time and condition of that individual's ultimate demise. All events are really results following causes which are laws fixed in advance, and human beings are powerless to change things, no matter how much they may desire or attempt to do so.

Other fatalists have a more personalized idea of the Divine Force and turn the whole process around. They take the point of view that God is Omniscient and therefore knows everything concerning everyone's past, present and future simultaneously, and that from the moment of a soul's conception or implantation in a body, He knows the exact moment when it will end. In other words, if the moment of your death has been fixed at 3:30 p.m. on a particular day, then, even though you may decide to stay in bed and not risk going out, you will not be able to escape your moment.

The problem of whether or not we have freewill is therefore twofold, based on the prior questions of whether or not it is true that God exists and has absolute knowledge of everything, and whether or not there is some part of a human being which is immaterial and not subject to the laws of nature.

Obviously, if there really is a God, He should know everything. If He is outside time, then while we are experiencing our present, He will know what our future will be. If He does know this, then what we are going to do in the future must, in some mysterious fashion outside our time, be predetermined and fixed. Therefore it seems that we are not actually free.

Thinkers from the earliest of times have struggled with this problem of whether human beings have freewill or are bound by fate. Socrates, for example, argued that it was nothing more than ignorance that made human beings the playthings of fate, and that education and knowledge would bring them freedom. Plotinus (24-270 C.F.) emphasized the difference between that which was spiritual and that which was governed by the laws of matter. He believed that the souls of human beings were free, but as soon as these immaterial souls entered material bodies, they became subject to physical laws.

Fatalism has moulded the belief and outlook of countless million of believers, although members of the different faiths tend to have somewhat divergent perspectives. Some people accept the notion of fortune-that their actions can be guided by the tossing of a coin or some other such method. Millions of people believe that their future is predetermined by the movement and position of the stars. A recent poll in the United States revealed that around sixty percent of the young people surveyed believed in astrology, and astrology is a key aspect of religion in China and Japan.

Hindus and Buddhists believe in karma, claiming that there are eternal laws of cause and effect that govern the lives of all people, and relying on the idea of reincarnation to provide answers for some of the problems raised. The doctrine of reincarnation puts forward belief in a multiplicity of lives in this world, a process of death and rebirth, in which the events and conditions of a person's present life are the direct result of his or her actions in a previous incarnation. Thus, some 'inexplicable' tragedies that appear to nullify the idea that God is gracious and kind are explained in terms of just punishment for something a person did in a previous life, and the sense of eternal justice is restored.

Jews, Christians and Muslims, on the other hand, reject the notion that human souls pass through long chains of lifetimes in various bodily forms. Instead, they believe that all human beings have but one lifetime here earth, which, they generally agree, is in some way a test or trial that determines their eternal fates in the life Hereafter.

Obviously, there is a problem here. If human beings face judgement concerning their earthly lives then they must be able to freely exercise a genuine and meaningful morality while on earth. This is particularly vital if human beings only get one chance at it-that is, are not reincarnated. In other words, if a God, karma, or anything else, is to attempt to make any sort of judgement on us, there has to be the possibility of our making genuine choices based on our own value judgements. Otherwise, judgement does not apply; if a person is not free to make a choice, then he or she cannot be held responsible for pursuing any course of action.

Believers in God insist that, while it may indeed be true that our personalities do depend to a great extent on our inherited characteristics - the physical bodies we have been given and our environment, particularly in our early years - we are not programmed robots. Not everyone reacts in the same way to a given situation; some of us are much more unselfish, generous, forgiving, helpful and able to cope than others. But we don't have to be. Although we are born with the ability to recognize and practice basic goodness, it is entirely up to us whether or not we use those abilities. If we see an old lady struggling up the road carrying heavy parcels, we can choose whether to go to help her, knock her down and steal her parcels, ignore her, or shout rude names at her and run away.

This leads on to an interesting thought. We can entertain ourselves by guessing what any particular individual might do to the old lady. But we all have a feeling of 'ought'; we think we know what course of action the good person, the religion person, the person of conscience, ought to take.

Whenever we say that a person ought to do something, we assume that the person is actually free and able to do it. Kant (1724-1804) clearly realized this when he insisted that human freedom was a moral necessity, for without it we cannot be considered responsible for the things we do. It is quite pointless to say that someone ought to help his sick mother, for example, if that person is locked up in jail or unconscious or living in a distant country. 'Ought' implies 'can'. However, say the fatalists, if God knows everything, then He must know in advance what any person is going to do at any time. And since actions are thus foreknown, they must be predestined. So where is the freedom of choice?

Against the notion of inevitable fate, however, the sacred scriptures of Judaism, Christianity and Islam maintain that people can influence what lies in store for them in the future. They are able to do this because aspects of their promised futures are conditional.

The key to understanding human freewill lies in distinguishing between the brain and the mind or soul-whether these are to be identified as a single entity or as two separate and distinct ones. The brain is a physical thing, part of the world of matter and subject to all its conditions; the mind and soul are not physical or material, but are able to exert the influence of will over the body. If human beings possess the freedom to choose various courses of action, the part that makes the choices is the mind, and God does not control anyone's mind by force.

Now, if God can do anything He wants, then it would obviously be perfectly possible for Him to control our minds and our choices. This is a matter that is within the capabilities of human beings themselves, and it would be only too easy for God.

However, the very fact that He allows people to choose not to believe in Him and not to do what He wants, demonstrates conclusively that God does not robotize peoples' minds.

Therefore, whereas we have to accept that nothing can happen without the knowledge of God, Who knows the present, past and future of all created beings, and whereas whether we are or are not going to obey or disobey Him is also known to Him, it nevertheless does not affect our freedom to make choices. We humans do not know what our destiny is, and therefore, whenever we choose what particular course we will take, we cannot be influenced by prior knowledge.

Each of the prophets, including Abraham, Moses, Jesus and Muhammad, taught that what people chose to do with respect to belief in God and obedience to His will makes a very great difference in the final outcome of their affairs. Simply because human beings have conscious souls, they have a tremendous ability to love and be kind, or to hate and be destructive. This means that although they may have all been born with souls of equal worth, they do not remain equal. Due to their inherent capability of bearing responsibility, the spiritual faculties of human beings raise them up above the level of the animal kingdom, although some individuals, of course, behave so badly that they in fact sink below the level of animals.

Another very important point to consider is that human beings have the power to kill - not only other creatures and other human beings, but also their own selves. There is a difference between death/ dying and killing/being killed. When a person dies, their soul or spirit departs according to God's will, and nothing the person can do will shorten or prolong their time. Once the soul has departed, the death and disintegration of the body follows shortly. When a person is killed (or kills), this is a matter of that human's freewill; they decide on the course of action - which is virtually always regarded as a criminal act. When they kill, they attack and fatally affect the body, following which the soul departs. It is a vital difference. A person can say: 'I will kill myself at three o'clock tomorrow', and do it; but a person cannot say: 'I will die at three o'clock tomorrow' with any real knowledge. (See also File on Death and Afterlife, p.149).

The sacred scriptures of all three of the monotheistic faiths-Judaism, Christianity and Islam-insist that God sent guidance to humanity from the very beginning of the human race. They hold that human freewill is a vital and decisive factor in our ultimate destinies, and is, in fact, the precise reason why God chose messengers, revealing Himself to them. What, it may be asked, was the main point of such revelations? To this the monotheistic faiths unanimously reply, 'Guidance, so individuals may be able to make the right choices and decisions to guide the actions of their lives.' If it had been impossible to do this because our actions and ultimate destinies were all predetermined, then there would have been no point whatsoever in such messengers and revelations.

According to Islam, if any part of humanity did not have the opportunity to hear the revealed words of God and His warnings, they would still be in a state of innocence, or ignorance, for which they could hardly be blamed. If it is humanity's duty to love and serve God and submit to His will, then obviously they have to be given the opportunity to know what that will is. Therefore the necessity of revelation is part and parcel of the notion of God's justice and mercy toward us.

Muslims believe that God revealed Himself to those whom He chose and trained, individuals who possessed the spirituality to understand. The messengers did not choose to do this work; on the contrary, God chose them, much to the surprise and reluctance of some of them. If it were impossible for people to choose to do God's will because their destinies were already immovably fixed, not only would God be unfair instead of just, but there would also seem to be very little point in making any attempt to live good lives. One of the very real dangers of fatalism is the despair and helplessness such an attitude engenders. Whether or not an individual actually is helpless, if he or she feels helpless that induces a passivity which becomes superstitious and does not promote the development of character and inner strength. On the contrary, it often leads to defeatism, hindering individuals from making any effort to improve either their own lot or the lot of those around them.

Those who believe absolutely in fate therefore run into the same problem as did the Greek philosopher Zeno of Citium, who lived in the third century B.C.E. He caught his slave stealing and proposed to beat him for it, but the slave retorted that he had no right to do so, since it was fated that he should steal.

If criminals were simply living out their destinies, then the responsibility for that would rest not with those poor humans, but with the one who fixed their actions, God Himself. In terms of God as First Cause, which we have been considering, this would also logically mean that God is the First Cause of all the wickedness, violence, oppression and evil ever committed by human beings, a concept that totally contradicts the Understanding of God which was presented by the prophets.

The whole ethos of the sacred scriptures of the monotheistic tradition is that there are alternative destinies for us, and that it is up to us to try to live in such a way that God may be pleased with us and admit us to His exalted Divine Presence in Paradise.

We must consider the possibility that God does indeed know everything, but that, at the same time, He leaves with us the choice of different courses of action. He must be able to see all the possible outcomes of whatever courses of action we choose, but in His Wisdom leave us free to make those choices.

'The inner span of Man is huge, almost infinite. He is capable of the most abominable crimes and the most noble sacrifices. The greatness of Man is not primarily in the doing of good deeds but in his ability to choose. Everyone who reduces or limits this choice debases Man. Good does not exist beyond one's will, nor can it be imposed by force. There is no force in faith.' See Islam Between East and West, Alija Ali Izetbegovie, American Trust Publications, 1993. pp.114-115. (See also 2:256).

# File on Prayer

Many people think that prayer is a complete waste of time, like talking to a brick wall. They cannot see any point in it. True believers take completely the opposite point of view - it's a bit like being in love. If you asked people in love why they spend time together, they'd probably say - 'Well, we just like being together. Prayer is like this - it is simply wanting to be with God. Those who pray draw great inner strength and peace of mind from prayer. God may not take away the storm, but He is with us in the midst of the storm.

It is not necessary to be in a special place, or go through special preparations for this sort of prayer. It is not like the special salah. Any place, any time - the presence of God and His angels is there.

This personal prayer, when we speak to God from our hearts, is called du'a. This is not the same thing as salah, but of course, people make du'a to God even while they are performing their salah - it is virtually impossible to separate the two.

## What are the types of Prayer?

Basically, there are five types - praise, confession, thanksgiving, requests, and silent adoration or love.

### Prayer involves:

saying - 'That's amazing!'
saying - 'I'm so sorry.'
saying - 'How can I ever thank you?'
saying - 'please can You help?'
saying - 'Just let me be in Your presence'.

### Praise:

Muslims spend a long time reflecting upon the nature of God and the wonderful universe we live in and realising that God is so much greater than we can ever really understand. When we are suddenly struck and moved in our hearts by the beauty of something we have seen or heard, or the intricacy, or the amazing attributes, or the complex interweave, or the all-embracing laws that are discovered day by day - we are seeing the 'Signs' intended for us. Sometimes people feel a tremendous joy welling up inside them; sometimes they are even moved to tears. (Although some

Muslims are against all expression of music or art, others argue that when art or music draws people near to awareness of God it is a good thing. This kind of art or music is quite different from the debased sexual type, or types that encourage wrong feelings such as hatred, lust, racism, etc).

## Confession:

Muslims, who try to be aware of God's presence with us in every second of the day, are deeply sorry when they do something wrong, or hurt someone. When they realise, they admit these wrongs or failures, and ask God to forgive them. This enables them to lay down any burden on their heart, and be at peace with God and themselves again. It is the reason why God gave us a conscience. Anyone who thinks they have never done anything wrong, or not hurt anybody or anything, is a fool, and simply not aware of their own actions.   A truly religious person is always humble. Muslims believe that so long as we are truly sorry, God will always forgive us (even if the person we have wronged does not forgive us); it does not mean that we can go straight out and do the wrong thing again. If any person is not sorry, they have until the time of their death to think again; after that, their book is closed and it is too late - they will have to face judgement.

## Thanksgiving:

Muslims are often humbled and surprised by the way God guides their lives, and shows them the right path if they ask to see it. They are aware of the many gifts God has granted them - for life itself, for all those who love us - good relatives and happy homes, loyal friends, for all those who help us in some way by word, deed or example - our teachers and guides, protectors, nurses, or anyone who just lifts our day. A true Muslim is not full of complaint, miserable and never satisfied, but rather is aware of the many blessings God has granted, even in the hard times.

## Requests:

Muslims always try to submit to the will of God, and sometimes this means accepting tests and trials that are very hard to bear. However, we believe that God would never put on us a burden that was really too hard for us. In tough times, we ask for strength, wisdom and Understanding, and the ability to see what is the right thing to do in any particular circumstance.   We pray for help - not because we think God has not noticed our problem, or because we think we know better than Him or are kinder than Him - but because in our closeness to God we realise what it is we should do to help or cope with it. For example, it would be

pointless to pray that a person should not die if it was their set time to die - but it would be excellent to pray for courage and tact to help that person, and to think through what would be the most practical and helpful way to be with that person in their time of suffering.

### Saying Nothing, Just Being There :

Sometimes people just need to sit and be still. Prayer doesn't always involve us in talking - it should involve listening as well as asking and thinking. Words are not always necessary, or possible. People in love often just silently enjoy being with each other, or knowing the other person loves them and is 'with them' in the heart, no matter where they are or what they are doing. People in love often just pause and think about the loved one, and feel deep joy and contentment. That is how it is with lovers of God.

Feeling the peaceful presence of God, or of His angels who watch over us, is actually quite a common experience for those who love Him. People can sense that peaceful presence as they pray, at home, at the mosque, out in the countryside, on the hills.

Sometimes this feeling only lasts a few seconds, but it is very intense. It could be like - 'a great relaxation came upon my mind and everything fitted together. I really felt that God was communicating with me'.

Sometimes this sense of presence can come from reading the Qur'an. You can start off just reading, and then suddenly realise that Someone as actually aware of you, and overlooking you with love, and that the message you are reading is speaking

straight to you. It may even show you the answer to the very problem or struggle you are going through. The realisation of God's presence has often reduced people to tears, and they are not ashamed and do not think they are 'soft' - they are just amazed and shaken and deeply moved.

'I can't find a phrase that really describes what went through me in that moment. It was a completely overwhelming sense of connection with God. The whole direction of my heart and life was swung completely around ... To try to convey it is like trying to describe what water tastes like when you're parched.'

# File on Death and Afterlife

## THE SANCTITY OF LIFE

The most precious of the responsibilities that Allah has granted to any living creature is the care of its own life. Muslims believe that no living thing has an automatic right to life; if Allah had not wished it to exist, it would simply never have done so. Every living creature receives its soul as a 'loan' from Allah, to take responsibility for it for as long as Allah wishes. The soul is not the same thing as the body; it 'inhabits' the body, and the body is its vehicle - but it is only a 'visitor', a 'guest'. The length of time a soul occupies a certain body is also Allah's gift, and therefore sacred. Every fresh breath you take is a gift - and could be your last! Once a life has been given, no human has any right to attempt to terminate it.

*'Allah fixes the time span for all things. It is He who causes both laughter and grief; it is He who causes people to die and to be born; it is He who causes male and female; it is He who will recreate us anew.'* (53:42-7)

*'Nor can a soul die accept by God's leave, the term being fixed as by writing.'* (3:145)

## DEATH

The decision about the moment for the ending of a life therefore belongs to Allah alone. It is a gross presumption for any human being to attempt to interfere with that decision, no matter how well-meaning.

Allah knows the exact length of any creature's lifetime even before their moment of conception. Some people develop a morbid preoccupation with trying to find out exactly when their moment of death will come-but the knowledge is hidden from them. It is not intended to be known. The ability to live each day as it comes, with grace and gratitude, and to be ready at any moment to return to Allah the soul He 'loaned' to earth, is part of the test of faith.

The Prophet's friend, Umm Sulaym, showed admirable faith and endurance when her little son died. She asked the members of her family not to tell Abu Talhah (the father) until she had spoken to him first. When he came home, she gave him his supper, made herself attractive, and even satisfied his sexual hunger. Then, when she saw that he was satisfied in every respect, she said to him: 'Abu Talhah, if some people borrow something from another family and then they ask for its return, should they resist its return? 'He said: 'No.' She said: '(Then)' I tell you about the death of your son.' Abu Talhah was actually annoyed that she had not told him before, and went to report everything to the Prophet, but he said: 'May Allah bless both of you in the night spent by you.' It so happened that she became pregnant that night, and they were blessed with a new baby. (Adapted from Muslim 6013; see also Muslim 5341).

It is easy to claim that you are a Muslim, submitted to Allah's will-but if you truly are, then you must be prepared to put Him first in every respect, to sacrifice anything you cherish if He demands it, and give Him ungrudgingly anything He asks. No human beings know the moment when their lives will be required by Allah and taken back, but they are all very well aware that the moment will certainly come.

*'Every soul will have a taste of death, and only on the Day of Judgement shall you be paid your full recompense.'* (3.185)

## AWARENESS

There are two odd things for us to consider about our awareness of our mortality. Firstly, it is precisely our awareness of death that makes us different from the other animals; they may see other dead creatures, but so far as we know, they are not aware that this is certain end for themselves too. Secondly, it is the only even in our own futures that we can be certain will happen-any other thing, success or failure, ambition or accident, we can have no idea about. Unfortunately for us, it is a certain event we rarely feel ready for, not even if we are old and ill and burdened heavily by the pains of this life. For most of us, death will confront us when we are not at all expecting or wanting it; we might be in the middle of unfinished business, or at an unsatisfactory moment in our personal relationships. We might be in perfect health, with all sorts of ongoing responsibilities.

Just like some people are obliged to retire from their lifetime's work just when they feel they are at last getting the hang of it and have it organised, and under control-so we are often obliged to hand back our lives just when we feel we are at last beginning to make sense of it, and are comfortable and secure.

There are so many different scenarios, including death from accidents, murder, warfare, natural disaster and so on. And

we have no idea when our final moment here will come.

Faithful Muslims will not fear that moment, but will try to live in such a way that if today was to be their last-they will be as ready as they can be to face Allah and answer to Him for the things they have done with their lives.

## NOTHING TO FEAR

Islam teaches that although you should fear the Day of Judgement if your life has been full of sins for which you never repented, death itself should not be feared. It is only human nature to shrink from pain and suffering, but Muslims are to do their best to bear all such trials with patience and fortitude. Death is the natural end of human life-it cannot be avoided, and no-one escapes it. Most very old people who are suffering will tell you that they do not wish to go tottering on for ever, especially when they have firm belief in something to follow in which they will be released from the pains of old age and ill health, and will become vigorous and active souls again, in the happy company of those they love.

It is when facing death that a believing person has such an enormous advantage over a non-believer, for the peace of mind and hope that it brings. It is quite pointless for people who assume (in the face of all the evidence otherwise) that the death of the human body is the end, to try to convince believers they are wrong, or to belittle their beliefs as weakness. Like the freewill to believe in God, the freewill to believe or not believe in Afterlife is one of the things granted to all humans during their time on earth. The moment they 'die' that freewill no longer exists, because they are at that stage either snuffed out into nothingness, or confronted with the reality of the situation of Afterlife and must cope with this new knowledge as best they can.

Even if a person has no belief whatsoever in the Afterlife, it is rather pointless and futile to resent the inevitable end of the human body, and a foolish gamble to assume that all religious teachers who have taught the life to come have been misled by God. Those who have gambled that they could get away with selfish, cruel and arrogant lives, abusing others, confident that death would be the end and there will be no justice or retribution to follow, will be in for a shock.

*'Do you think that We shall not re-assemble your bones? Yes, surely, yes-We are able to restore even your individual fingerprints!'* (75:3-4)

## DEATH CANNOT BE PREVENTED

When Allah requires us to move on, there is nothing we can do about it. It is very similar to a birth. Once a woman has conceived and a new life is growing within her, she cannot prevent a moment of birth. Similarly, we cannot prevent our moment of death-which will probably be far easier than birth. The soul can slip out of its own body with far less fuss than a new human struggling out of its mother's body. Some people are so fed up with their lives that they long to be done with it; others are desperately reluctant to let go- just as in childbirth some mothers really suffer in the last stages of pregnancy and long for the 'delivery,' whereas others are absolutely petrified of giving birth.

However, when the moment of death comes, just like the moment of birth, it can no longer be held back, and the individual concerned no longer has a choice but is confronted with an overwhelming personal event that over-rides everything else.

Death is beyond human control. No person can choose the time of their passing unless God sanctions it.

*'A soul cannot die except by Allah's*

*permission, the life-span being fixed as if by written contract' (3:145)*

Many people desperately try to prevent their deaths and pray for Allah to grant them some miracle that will keep them alive-but Nature runs its course and miracles are not granted. On the other hand, many people long to die, because they are so unhappy or in such pain, but Allah requires them to go on living.

*'If you think you control your own destiny, try to stop your own soul from leaving its body at your hour of death'. (56:81-87)*

*'When your time expires, you will not be able to delay the reckoning for a single hour, just as you cannot bring it forward by a single hour.' (16:61)*

(See also the comment on the difference between death and killing in the File on Fate and freewill, p.141).

## WHERE DO WE GO FROM HERE?

A belief in the survival of one's person after bodily death has been widespread since the earliest of times. Humans are instinctively aware that they have a 'self,' and they know that a time will inevitably come when their physical bodies will cease to function. So naturally, they are very interested to know what will happen to their 'selves' after that moment of death.

Obviously, if a person's 'self' is nothing more than a part of the brain-centre and the atomic construction of the human being, then the 'self,' like the body, will cease to be after the moment of death, breaking down and decomposing just like the rest of the body. If there is no soul, there is no life after death in the sense that a person continues to exist. Consequently, the only form of immortality you would be left with would be that of passing on some part of your

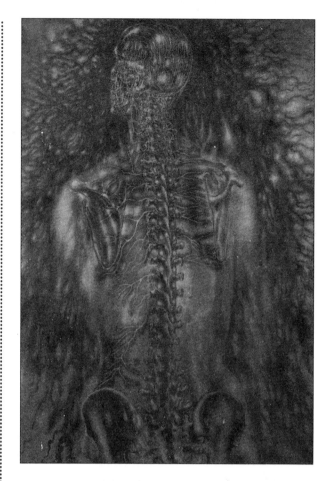

genetic structure to your children, whose material bodies and programs start off within your body. Most of us would not really regard that as immortality, however; this is not what we have in mind when we contemplate our hoped-for future survival as persons.

If we can accept the notion that a non-material soul inhabits the particular group of atoms belonging to us, despite the many changes taking place all the time in that group, then wouldn't it be possible for our souls to go on existing as separate entities apart from our physical bodies?

The earliest of people thought so, and left either real or symbolic food and drink and various useful objects in the graves of their dead, or set up shrines for them in their old homes, in order that their shades could continue to live happily alongside their families.

The ancient Greeks and Hebrews envisaged a rather gloomy afterlife for their beloved dead. They believed that there was a land for departed spirits somewhere beneath the earth, a miserable and desolate place to which no one would want to go. Naturally, if such was the lot of the 'departed,' then death was indeed to be regretted and feared. It would be far better not to 'survive' at all, but instead to abandon one's self to nothingness, or to a state of eternal sleep. It was probably fearful notions like these that led relatives to pray for their dead loved ones to 'rest in peace' and not be condemned to eternal wandering about in misery as unhappy shades.

## A BIT OF HOPE AND CHEER

Many religious thinkers were not at all happy to think that God could abandon in such an awful place individuals whom He had loved and cared for; it seemed totally unreasonable and out of keeping with thoughts of God as a Supreme Being of Love, who was also in control of everything, including life after death. And some, especially the Jewish Pharisees and early Christians, considered the possibility that the dead entered a state of sleep that would end on a great Day of Resurrection, when God would cause flesh to be miraculously restored to decayed bones and their souls would re-enter their former bodies.

Others believed that after death we would experience not a mere sleep, but our souls' journeying to somewhere else. And this 'somewhere' was not foreordained to be a grim place of dust and darkness, for surely a just God would establish varied consequences for our souls, depending on whether we warranted reward or punishment for our deeds in this life.

## WISHFUL THINKING?

It has been suggested, of course, that any kind of belief in the happy survival of the self after death is nothing more than wishful thinking. People naturally don't want to be 'snuffed out' and can't bear the thought that all their work and effort will come to nothing. They also have a strong desire to be reunited with deceased family and friends whom they had dearly loved.

If it could be proved that there was no life after death, a great many people would certainly give up bothering to be religious, since there would be no blessed reward or joyful reunion to come, no longer any point in trying to live a good, unselfish life to attain salvation in the Hereafter. Others might give up out of a sense of despair at the injustice of there being no future time or state in which wrongs would be put right and people compensated or punished for what they had done, frustrated that they obviously are not rewarded or punished during their present lifetime.

## BORDER-LINE CASES?

Now, while Heaven or Hell may be an extremely obvious fate for the real saints or villains, it surely does present a problem when it comes to borderline cases. Doesn't this make nonsense out of the whole notion? How will God decide for those of us who are neither very good nor very bad, but somewhere in the middle?

Some believe that though He doesn't consign us to Hell, in order to get into Heaven we will either have to be suddenly very much improved, or else there must be a process of gradual development that will continue after the death of our bodies. Roman Catholic doctrine suggests a place called Purgatory, a state in which souls not yet fit for Heaven might be purified and cleansed. However, other theologians, including many of the Jewish Pharisees at the time of the Blessed Jesus, believed that if our good deeds outweighed our bad ones by even the slightest amount, God would have mercy on us. The Qur'an presents the Day of Judgement as the culmination of God's mercy, when good and evil will finally be sorted out.

*'He has inscribed for Himself (the rule of) mercy. There is no doubt whatever that He will gather you together for the Day of Judgement'. (surah 6:12)*

*'We shall set up scales of justice for the Day of Judgement, so that not one soul will be dealt with unjustly in the least. And if there be (no more than) the weight of a mustard seed, We will bring it (to account)'. (surah 21:47).*

From the Islamic perspective it is interesting to note here that though good deeds are important, they are not in themselves sufficient for a person's salvation, which depends only on God's grace. The Prophet is reported to have said, 'None of you will enter Paradise on account of your good deeds alone.' The people asked him, 'Not even you, O Prophet of God?' He replied, 'No, not even me, unless God bestows His favour and mercy on me' (Bukhari).

## A LOGICAL PROBLEM

Belief in the Afterlife is the most decisive factor in human life. Acceptance or rejection of it determines the very course of a human being's living patterns and behaviour. Even though they may be good, unselfish individuals, people who believe that this world is all there are obviously only concerned with their success or failure in this world. But those who believe in the Afterlife are very well aware that it gives meaning and purpose to earthly life; they live, as it were, with their two feet in two worlds, and thoughts and concerns for the life Hereafter provide a very strong motivation in all they do.

The fact that many 'progressive' people doubt the reality of the Afterlife is not really due to science. It is the 'logic' of materialism which insists that, since after death a person is reduced to dust and since no person has ever witnessed a case of the revival of a decayed corpse, death and destruction must be the end of life and there is nothing after it. But is this truly scientific reasoning? Not to those who acknowledge that there are still unrecognised dimensions of reality. Even if not one single person has ever seen a case of revival, this only means that we can state with certainty that we do not know what will happen after death. It does not imply that nothing will happen. Science tells us nothing, either negative or positive, in this respect.

Just because no one has seen a thing does not mean that it has no existence or cannot occur. Honest scientists of real insight teach that there is a very great deal more even to physical existence and the material universe than that which we mortals can perceive with our limited senses. They admit that there may exist a realm which is not accessible to human awareness or bound by the limitations of the human intellect; it is utterly beyond human perception and remains Hidden or Unseen. The known material universe with which we are familiar is like only the tip of an iceberg, the bulk of which remains hidden from our eyes. Consequently, it should be admitted that the universe is full of all sorts of things that human beings have never seen and cannot imagine; the continued existence of the human soul after the death of the body is not a matter that any person is in a position to categorically deny.

## REWARDS AND PUNISHMENTS

No true Muslims should fear death, for they believe the Afterlife will be a time of great joy and reward for all their efforts on Earth, if Allah wills.

*'For those nearest to Allah, will come rest and satisfaction and a garden of delights, and ... peace; but if you are of those who have...gone wrong, then your entertainment will be boiling water and hell-fire. Truly, this is the absolute truth and certain.'* (56:88-95)

*'Those who believe and do deeds of righteousness. We shall admit to gardens with rivers flowing beneath-their eternal home; they shall have holy and pure companions there; We shall admit them to cool and deep shade.'* (4:57)

A blissful vision for a person used to the baking sands and blinding light of Arabia!

*'The true servants of Allah shall enjoy honour and dignity in gardens of delight, facing each other on thrones. A cup from a clear-flowing fountain will be passed round to them, crystal white, a taste delicious to those who drink it, free from headiness; they will not suffer intoxication from it. And beside them will be chaste women, keeping their glances modest, their large eyes full of wonder and beauty, as closely guarded as delicate eggs. They will turn to one another and ask questions-'I had an intimate companion on earth, who used to ask if I was really among those who bore witness to the truth, and when we died and became dust and bones, would we really receive rewards and punishments?' A voice said:- 'Would you like to look down?' He looked down and saw him, in the midst of the fire, and said... 'Had it not been for the grace of God, I should certainly have been there myself!'* (37:40-57)

Islam does not try to convince people that everything will be all right for everybody, and all people will be forgiven no matter what they have done. There is a condition attached-the one who has done evil and harm to others is obliged to face up to this and genuinely be sorry for it before their moment of death, and prepared to make reparation for their hurts and injustices as far as is possible for them.

For those who die still unrepentant, arrogantly abusive and damaging others to the last with no fleeting twinge of conscience, a punishing destruction is in store.

*'Those who reject our signs We shall cast into the fire; as often as their skins are roasted through We shall change them for fresh skins, that they may taste the penalty.'* (4:56)

There are a great many references to the Afterlife, and they are all very graphic; particularly the references to the punishments of hell (of which the idea of the fresh skins growing so that the punishment can continue and people not be just burnt up to oblivion is possibly the most harrowing!)

However, Allah Himself asks us to consider that these passages are to be taken symbolically and not literally.

*'In the Book are verses of fundamental meaning, and others which are allegorical.'* (3:7)

Since Allah has indicated that we cannot grasp with our limited human intellect what lies ahead of us, it is permissible to keep a very open mind on the subject, and just acknowledge that our Afterlife will be as inconceivably different as the butterfly's life is from the caterpillar, or the oak-tree from the acorn!

*'Now, no person knows what delights of the eye are kept hidden for them-as reward for their good deeds.'* (32:17)

Abu Hurayrah reported: 'Eye has not seen, and it has not entered into the human heart what things Allah has prepared for those who love Him.' Muslim (6780)

'In Paradise I [God] have prepared for the righteous believers what no eye has ever seen, no ear has ever heard, and what the keenest mind could never imagine.' (Hadith Qudsi).

We can easily point out the fallacy of supposing that restoring already created beings - ourselves - to life is in any way difficult for God. As the Qur'an puts it:

*'How can you disbelieve in God when you were dead and He gave you life? Then He will cause you to die and then will again bring you* to life. Then to Him you will return'. (surah 2:28).

*Is not He Who created the heavens and the earth able to create the life thereof?-Yes, indeed! For He is the Creator Supreme, of (infinite) skill and knowledge! (surah 36:81).*

People who believe in God are therefore obliged to regard 'mechanical' and 'materialistic' interpretations of the universe as actually being irrational, inferior, false and misleading.

# File on Marriage and Women's Issues, Polygamy, Feminism, etc.

## ON ATTEMPTED FORCED MARRIAGE:

### Press Report

The Independent, 8th June 1998.

## 'A hard lesson for the Asian Community to Learn'

*Yasmin Alibhai-Brown.*

Last Friday a Muslim couple were jailed for the unlawful kidnaping of their daughter Rehana.

She was a university-educated woman who refused a forced marriage and then (perhaps to punish her parents) went her own rebellious way, for a time even living with a drug dealer. They tried, but failed to persuade her to change her mind. In the end they spiked her drink at a funeral and attempted to smuggle her away to Pakistan. She realized what was going on and raised the alarm.

Each year there are over two-hundred cases of British girls being taken off to India, Pakistan or Bangladesh either under false pretexts or terrible duress and coerced into marriages. The Foreign Office has placed leaflets at airports giving these young women basic information about their rights in order to deal with this epidemic - which usually reaches a peak about now, just before the main school exams and the long summer vacation. In Bangladesh these girls can be put into prison if they raise objection and in Pakistan there is anecdotal evidence that a number of these young women have committed suicide.

Recently an Asian teacher of two 14-year-old girls at a British school told me how they had been imprisoned in a cellar for months and how the police and local council were worried about "interfering" in their culture.

Last week a white woman rang in tears to tell me about her daughter's best friend, who had cut her arms to shreds in protest against a marriage in Bangladesh.

So do I believe that the parents jailed last week are monsters, as the tabloid press would have us believe? Not at all.

They are, by all accounts, decent folk who love their children. They have a corner shop in Bradford which makes relentless demands on their time and energy. Like many other immigrants, they thought this sacrifice was all that was needed to make a good life. They also believed that the children would appreciate this and not be seduced by the ways of the West and that they would all carry on happy ever after as if they had never left that spot in the sub-continent which is still home in their hearts.

But the children changed; became more individualistic and self-aware. Most have not become westernised in any crude sense, but nor are they like their parents used to be.

Many Asian families accept and even rejoice in this. Others, however, have turned cruel, violent and as this case shows, even resorted to criminal means in order to recapture something that has long gone. Some religious and community leaders have encouraged these responses instead of enabling parents many of whom are illiterate and easily led, to manage and understand the inevitable changes in their lives.

What is even more disturbing is that because they are not getting supportive parenting, many of the young girls, especially the bright ones, are making choices which would alarm even libertarians.

Two things might provide an answer to these deep problems. One is the law and this is why the verdict is so important. As law abiding people with an over-developed sense of shame, such judgements will begin a process of education among the Asian community which is long overdue.

Those who claim such judgements are racist are now a minority. Secondly the laudable step taken by Labour to incorporate the European Human Rights Convention means that there is now a much more solid and fundamental framework to address these thorny issues.

The battle is no longer between their ways and ours. Protecting women is the enactment of a fundamental human right which we will all have to accept.

One can only hope that community leaders will use this opportunity to enlighten themselves and those in their flock so that we can stop this destruction of our own young ones.

## ON ABUSIVE MARRIAGE:

## Press Report

A letter quoted from Muslim News

Sir, My husband and I are Nigerian (Hausa). I have been married to him for 4 years and during these years I have suffered many troubles. I feel ashamed to say it but his type of behaviour is common in the men in my community. I experience neglect, not only myself, but also my children.

While my husband spends most of his time outside the house, I am all the time inside. He is the bread winner and determines how the money should be spent - mainly on himself. He buys himself expensive shoes to appear presentable around his male friends, while my children and I go without. Everyday I feel pain and hurt.

He is well educated and always undermines my Islamic knowledge, saying my knowledge is made by women for women only and bears no reference to him. This attitude is common - my friends, sister, mother, aunts face this daily.

As a woman, I cannot take an active part in my community. Needless to say I cannot be part in any decision-making in my own household - I merely exist. My husband insists this is the Nigerian way of life and we should not be contaminated by this society or the type of Islam practised in UK. Yet he came here to study and work and reap the benefit from this country.

Back home, women suffer daily. The house is like a guest house to entertain him and his friends. They take more than one wife - each one has one room where she has to be contented to live with all her children. There is no privacy. You are in a Catch 22 situation - if you decide to leave your husband, your father or brother will only send you back. They have all done the same thing. Women have no autonomy and must forever show their gratitude if husband, father or brother allows her to be educated further than secondary school. Even the religion is divided - a set of rules that applies only to women which is not taken seriously, after all we are just women.

Perhaps if you live in the west, it is easy to say 'leave your husband' - but it does not work that way for many women -where do you go? Where do you work to maintain yourself? And your children are never yours

- they belong to their father. If you are allowed to keep your children and return to your family you are caught in a poverty trap. Women don't own anything, not even themselves.

You may say teach your husband, but I feel angry teaching him about how to live, about his religion - this is not my job, yet I understand, how education is controlled and women moulded to accept their role - this is passed on from generation to generation and the problems go on. Our imams are like puppets playing a fool's game - they are not interested in our issues and our education system back home reinforces our lowly position. The problem is very complex. Hausa men are no where near to change - on a personal level, my husband is resistant to change and operates the 'follow the practice of his fathers' attitude.

Yours,
(name given)
London.

## ON WOMEN'S EQUALITY IN THE WEST

Equality of the sexes implies the abolition of all differences between men and women in education, electoral rights, the disposal of property, in opportunities for work and remuneration and as partners in marriage. It ought to imply the liability to the same duties (such as military service); but here the test of civilization is to make allowance for physical differences which only the least desirable male would regard as constituting unfair privilege. It certainly implies the same moral responsibilities, and the whole notion is indeed a moral one, based on the nature of human persons; it is a pity, indeed, that the term 'sexes' came to cloud the issue. The human male and human female cannot be regarded as equally endowed (in physical characteristics), so that the idea amounts largely to a social aspiration.

It is astonishing that the French revolutionaries, in their Declaration of the Rights of Man (1790) and their enlightened constitutions of 1791 and 1793, did not intend woman to benefit from any of their pronouncements. The challenge was taken up by the grandmother of feminism, Olympe de Gouges, who in her Declarations of the Rights of Woman and the Female Citizen (1791) declared that 'since women share the right to the guillotine, then they have the right to the hustings'.

The year after, in 1792, Mary Wollstonecraft published her Vindication of the Rights of Women. Her claims were modest enough, though firm: she was prepared to admit the superiority of the male in certain respects, and demanded reforms in education, legal status and, much too theoretically, a recognition of women's equality as persons; repeating many times that 'It is not empire, but equality and friendship which women want.'

Feminists have perhaps done more harm than good to the cause of emancipation, from Mme de Stael to Virginia Woolf and Winifred Holtby, by insisting rather loudly on historical grievances. Certainly the history of woman has been sordid. She has been held as unclean or bewitched in many primitive societies, she has been bought and sold until comparatively recent times. If she has been deified and sanctified in almost every religion, if she has held power in matriarchies, in temples and in palaces, she has been treated certainly as a minor throughout Europe until the twentieth century; her labour and her body have been exploited, she has always suffered from man.

Biologically there is no equality, and it is now plain that woman is the better endowed sex. More males than females are conceived; more males than females die before birth, more die from the age of one to five, and by the age of ten there are already more girls than boys. Women have a greater expectation of life. More men than women are victims of cancer, tuberculosis and insanity: women are both physically and mentally the more stable, though not necessarily stronger or more intelligent. On the other hand, though there have been distinguished women writers and thinkers in every age, they cannot be said to have excelled in creative work either in the arts or in the sciences. Since (in Britain) compulsory education for the masses, both male and female, was enforced only after 1870, it is too early perhaps to say whether this particular inferiority is natural or environmental.

The problem, then, is social. Perhaps the crudest statement ever made of the doctrine that woman's place is the home, was that of Euripides: 'A woman should be good for everything at home; but outside the home, good for nothing.' That is what many men secretly think and hope, and what many women are openly content with.

## COMMENTS ON SEXISM

Sexism - 'the opinion that one sex is not as good as the other, especially that women are less able in most ways than men'. (Longman's Dictionary)

Throughout most of human history, societies have been ruled by men. It is difficult to examine the, status of women because normally they have had none. Historical and religious writings over the last 3,000 years show us how many societies have viewed women.

'100 women are not worth a single testicle.' (Confucius)

'The female is a female by virtue of a certain lack of qualities.' (Aristotle)

'I permit no woman to teach or to have authority over men; she is to keep silent. (St. Paul's Epistle to Timothy, I Tim 2:12)

'Women must accept the authority of their husbands.' (I Peter 3:1)

'Every woman should be overwhelmed with shame at the thought that she is a woman.' (St. Clement of Alexandria, Ist century AD)

'Women should remain at home, sit still, keep house, and bear and bring up children.' (Martin Luther, 1483 - 1546)

'The souls of women are so small that some believe they've none at all. (Samuel Butler, 1612-80)

'What a misfortune to be a woman.' (Soren Kierkegaard, 1813-55)

'When I turned out to be a mathematical genius my mother said, "Put on some lipstick and see if you can find a boyfriend.".' (20th century American authoress)

## THE ATTITUDE OF THE PROPHET JESUS TO WOMEN:

The Christian Church has been guilty of sexism - but if we look at the life and teaching of Jesus, we find that he did not discriminate against people in a sexist way at all. He taught in the temple's Court of Women, showing that in his view women were just as intelligent as men. He included women among his disciples (see Luke 8:2). In his day, his attitude was revolutionary - for he lived in a very sexist society in which women were treated as second-class citizens.

## SOME UK MILESTONES

1857  Marriage and Divorce Act - women were given rights in marriage

1865  First woman doctor qualified

1900  National Union of Woman's Suffrage Society formed

1918  Women over 30 allowed to vote

1919  First woman MP elected

1928  Women allowed to vote at 21

1975  Sex Discrimination Act - 'equal pay for work of equal value'

1979  First woman prime minister elected.

## WOMEN IN THE THIRD WORLD

These facts are taken from a Christian Aid leaflet about the plight of women in the Third World.

- women are half of the world's population, do two-thirds of the world's work and produce half of the world's food. Yet women receive only one-tenth of the world's income, own only 1% of the world's property, and make up 70% of the world's refugees (with their children)

- two-thirds of the world's illiterates are women

- where women belong to a paid workforce they are often underpaid, have no job security and possess few rights

- women in Africa do up to three-quarters of all agricultural work in addition to their domestic duties.

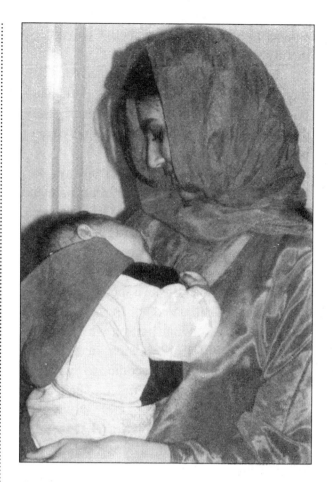

## ON POLYGAMY

**Press Report**

Sunday Telegraph, May 3rd, 1998.

# 'TWO'S COMPANY, THREE'S ALLOWED'

A suggestion that the Church should back polygamous marriages has a biblical precedent, says Ross Clark. It even finds favour with feminists

Devotees of exotic lifestyles will have been heartened by the suggestion of the new Archbishop of Cape Town, that the Church of England should turn its back on centuries of doctrine and embrace the practice of polygamy. "It has long been recognized in the Anglican Communion that polygamy in parts of Africa genuinely has features of both faithfulness and righteousness," he writes in a paper presented at the Lambeth Conference in July.

In our bare-legged, open-chested society, there are not too many taboos left, but polygamy is definitely one of them. For obscure reasons it has become the sin that the permissive age forgot.

And yet polygamy was not always so frowned upon. When, in 1909, the painter **Augustus John** camped on Grantchester Meadows outside Cambridge with an entourage described as "two wives and 10 naked children", he caused bemusement rather than condemnation - this in a society in which homosexuality still dared not speak its name.

There is an obvious reason why, during the following 90 years, homosexuality and adultery should have become so widely accepted, yet polygamy has failed to gain any followers - except perhaps for the legal implications. According to Dr.Patrick McGhee, a specialist in the psychology of relationships at Bolton Institute, the real reason society refuses to accept the practice is because it cannot stomach the legal mess which would be created if a multitude of spouses were each entitled to lay claim upon your estate.

'We like the law to be distinct," he says. 'We don't want one wife fighting over the property of the others. But the truth of the matter is that humans are slightly bigamous. They tend to have two to three partners over their lives."

Deep down, he says, far from feeling moral outrage at the idea of bigamists, we secretly admire them for the skill involved in their deception.

"People are fascinated by individuals who are able to sustain parallel lives in a society in which it is increasingly difficult to lead a private life. There is so much cross-referencing of data these days that the businessman who keeps one wife in Wimbledon and another in Aberdeen is bound to get caught in the end."

In tolerating adultery but not bigamy, western society appears to be completely out of step with the Old Testament. The commandments warn against adultery, but they do not say: "Thou shalt have no wives other than the one you've already got", and for good reason: at the time the Old Testament was written, polygamy was commonplace and perfectly accepted in Judea. You could have as many wives as you liked; the only thing that was frowned upon was having sex with another man's wife.

Polygamy died out in the Christian world for reasons which are not clear. But in some places it does appear to be enjoying a slow and steady rehabilitation. On the plains of Utah, a Mormon sect with the cumbersome title "True and Living Church of Jesus Christ of Saints of the Last Days" has revived the practice 100 years after the religion's fathers outlawed it as the price of avoiding a clash with the US Government, simply by not issuing marriage certificates.

One of the most interviewed practitioners, told reporters that he sleeps with his five wives on a strict rota: two nights with each, in the order in which they were married. 'When there's just two wives, it's hell," he said, excusing the arrangement. "But the more you add, the more it is balanced out".

It is not just Utah. The lower house of the Russian parliament, the Duma, recently debated the legalization of polygamy on the instigation of Sergei Semyonov, the twenty-two year old vice chairman of the parliament's committee for Family, Marital and Women's Issues, and himself the proud owner of a wife and three girlfriends. His argument, which was listened to with some sympathy from his fellow MPs, was that Russian men would be forced to take financial responsibility for their mistresses if they were allowed to marry them.

The Mormon polygamists have gained some unlikely backing from one of the most extreme feminist bodies, America's National Organization for Women. The idea is that by sharing childcare arrangements with their co-wives, women can have their cake and eat it: enjoy a family as well as a professional life. By living in a commune with a husband and six other "wives", avowed feminist Elizabeth Joseph told reporters, she was able "to go to law school knowing my husband had clean shorts in the morning and dinner at night".

With American radical feminists backing polygamy, it perhaps will not be very long before a breakaway group turns to polyandry, the practice in which a woman has more than one husband. It already happens among the Todas of southern India, where a woman will often marry two brothers, and among the Sherpas (no wonder the poor menfolk have become so good at running around carrying things). Polyandry has been forced upon Himalayan peoples by the high rate of female infanticide, which naturally results in a shortage of females in later life, but it is primarily seen by anthropologists as a means by which a society short of land can reduce its birth-rate.

Muslims tend to have fewer wives than they used to. One of the things about Muslim marriage is that you are supposed to treat all your wives equally, and that creates a problem for many men."

There is simply too much going on between the two partners psychologically for there to be room for more people.

Societies in which polygamy is institutionalised tend to be societies in which marriages are arranged, and in which having a large number of wives is taken to be a sign of wealth.

# File on Abortion

The U.K. Law on this issue is: The Human fertilisation and embryology act 1990.

## This Act allows abortion on the following conditions:

- that the pregnancy has not exceeded its twenty-fourth week and that the continuance of the pregnancy would involve risk, greater than if the pregnancy were terminated, of injury to the physical or mental health of the pregnant woman or any existing children of the family; or

- that the termination is necessary to prevent grave permanent injury to the physical or mental health of the pregnant woman; or

- that the continuance of the pregnancy would involve risk to the life of the pregnant woman greater than if the pregnancy were terminated; or

- that there is a substantial risk that if the child were born it would suffer from such physical or mental abnormalities as to be seriously handicapped.

## So, abortion is legal if two doctors agree on either of the following:

1. Continuing the pregnancy means that there is a risk to the woman's health, or that of her existing children greater than if the pregnancy was terminated, allowing up to 24 weeks of pregnancy; or

2. Continuing the pregnancy would involve severe damage to the woman's mental or physical health greater than if the pregnancy was terminated, or there is a strong risk of severe handicap in the expected child, or the woman's life is at risk if the pregnancy continues without time limit.

## Warnings:

- Abortion involves killing a living creature, by various methods. None are pleasant.
- Medical practioners often hate aborting unborn children, especially after the 10th week.
- Many women, in later life, bitterly regret that they had a child aborted, and never really get over it. They can feel (i) guilty (ii) immense sadness (iii) wonder what that child would have been.

Those who believe in life after death wonder if the unborn child and mother will one day meet.

## POINTS OF VIEW:

(i) That life is the gift of God from conception, and from that moment the child in the womb has the same rights as any other human.

(ii) Women have the right to control their own fertility, and should be able to choose whether or not to have children.

(iii) Abortion should only be done if the mother's life is in danger.

(iv) Abortion should not be done after the time the unborn child has developed the ability to feel pain.

## COMMENTS :

Modern ultrasound equipment can show the life, activity, and changes in the foetus from the very earliest moments. The body is developing, feeling and moving long before the mother is aware of it at around the 10th week.

It is certainly the case that a foetus has developed enough to be regarded as fully human by the sixth week, when its sensory and motor nerves are functioning, and it reacts to painful stimuli.

One hadith indicates six weeks as a highly important moment in the development of a foetus: 'When forty-two nights have passed over that which is conceived, Allah sends an angel to it, who shapes it, makes it ears, eyes, skin, flesh and bones; then the angel says: 'O Lord, is it male or female?' and your Lord decides what He wishes, and the angels record it.' (Muslim 6396).

In modern support of this, ultra-sound scanners can detect in the sixth week whether the foetus is male or female.

Most people who see the films taken by ultrasound of an abortion, and realise what is actually involved, very quickly realise how serious and terrible a matter abortion is. It is the taking of a life. Women who have abortion maybe adjust at the time, but the trauma of what they have done never leaves them for the rest of their lives.

Abortion is only lawful in Islam in a case where the life of the mother is genuinely at stake, on the principle that the life that already exists (the mother) takes precedence over the life that is still only potential (the unborn child). The tree trunk is saved at the expense of its branches.

*Extract from 'Living Islam',* Sr.Ruqaiyyah, Goodword Books, 1998.

Bereaved parents frequently find that people are uncomfortable about talking to them about their loss, and this does not help them resolve their grief. Sometimes family and friends are actually critical of their grief, and feel they are making a fuss about nothing.

It is important to realise that they have sustained a real death, and the loss should not be minimised.

Cases of abortion are highly sensitive, because inevitably the mother really is to blame for the death of her child, and the guilt is very real. Some get their guilt much delayed. As previously commented, many women who have not actually given birth to a full term baby do not have fully-developed awareness of the reality of the child, and push aside any feelings of guilt others try to engender in them. They may try to completely suppress and forget any incipient feelings. However, it is a fact that in almost every case, the guilt and grief will surface later on - perhaps when the woman has more knowledge-and she will have to face the torment of wondering what the child she destroyed might have been.

She may be quite unable to forgive herself; she may feel God will never forgive her. Allah expressed quite clearly that abortion is unacceptable to Him, and therefore it should not really be contemplated by a Muslim.

Many women in these circumstances try to convince themselves that the foetuses are not real 'beings', but just 'part of their bodies. This is not logical, and guilt feelings based on the reality of the unborn child will always surface later. Many women who have abortions are ashamed and in a state of panic, and once it is over often feel that the best way to deal with it is to put it out of their minds as quickly as possible-but by doing this, once again they rob themselves of the grieving process, and it will surface later.

The surface experience of many mothers who end a pregnancy they had not wished for is usually one of relief initially but a woman who does not mourn the loss may well experience great unresolved grief.

Sometimes the mother involved is only a young girl, and her parents are very angry with her; sometimes they also get angry not only because she got pregnant in the first place, but also because she then killed the baby, which, after all, would have been their grandchild. Grandparents should not be overlooked by those helping the bereaved.

However, censure and abuse of women and girls who have had abortions is unbecoming from those who are not in a position to know all the circumstances involved, as Allah is. Medical practitioners in most societies will terminate pregnancies for various reasons, interpreting the 'threat to life or sanity' of the mother involved quite widely. What they do not generally approve is the notion of abortion on demand, for casual social reasons.

Anyone who has seen tiny premature babies struggling for life in the same hospital where others of similar age and size are terminated, will tell you it is not a casual matter. Moreover, the women who have abortions usually do not do it casually at all, but suffer great anguish and distress and pain. So, people involved with cases of abortion should remember that very important hadith that those whose balance of mind is disturbed are not held responsible by Allah. They should take some consolation from that, if that was indeed the case.

In true Islam, no child should be born outside of marriage, and this is the ideal to be aimed at. In some societies, the harsh solution to the problem is to put the unwed mother to death. To be realistic in a western society, the best solution is to encourage a pregnant girl to have the baby and not abort it, and then see to it that the innocent child and the foolish mother are both properly cared for.

Even better is to solve the problem of unwanted pregnancies by encouraging menfolk to be honourable, responsible, kind and considerate in their sexual activity, and to make sure that their women-folk are adequately protected each time they have intercourse when a pregnancy is not desired.

Extract from 'After Death, Life', Sr.Ruqaiyyah. Goodword Books, 1998.

## THE CASE FOR ABORTION

- The decision to have an abortion is never easy, but no one is better suited than the woman concerned to make that decision.
- Taking control of their own fertility is every Woman's right, but there is no such thing as 100 per cent safe and certain contraception, so women still need abortion.
- Opinion differs as to when life begins. A minority has no right to impose its views on the rest of us.
- A foetus is only a potential human life, but there can be no argument about the humanity of the woman.
- Doctors have no special moral or ethical training which makes them fitter than pregnant women to make these sorts of decision.
- There will always be women who don't want children at all and we should respect that choice.

- No society has ever been known where abortion has not existed in some form, whatever the male secular and religious leaders have said.
- The argument is not whether abortion exists, but whether it should be legal, safe and dignified or illegal, unsafe and furtive.
- Every child has the right to be a wanted child. Abortion saves thousands of children from being unwanted and saves society from many problems.
- It is more of a trauma to give up a child for adoption than having an abortion.
- Even if abortion were made a crime thousand of women would still risk their lives and health in back-street abortion clinics.
- If a women is raped and becomes pregnant then offering an abortion is a humane and practical way of helping her.

In the UK, nearly 50% of women have an abortion during their lifetime-a huge increase on earlier times. It is particularly acceptable for girls under 16 and women over 40.

## THE CASE AGAINST ABORTION

- Modern science proves that the unborn child is a separate human being from conception. It is never just a part of his or her mother's body.
- By allowing abortion, society is taking the easy way out. It should concentrate on improving the quality of life in society.
- Even in the womb the unborn child has a right not to be killed.
- People with the most awful handicaps can lead happy, creative and fulfilled lives.

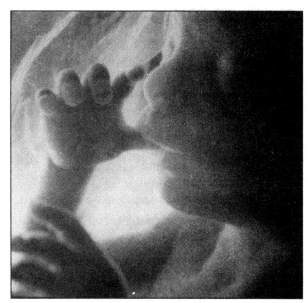

An unborn baby sucks its thumb.

- Abortion is discrimination against the weak.
- Abortion is not just a matter of 'religion'- it is about murder, injustice and the denial of human rights. The UN Declaration of the Rights of the Child states that children need protection before, as well as after, birth.
- Unborn babies are unique, different, they have potential personalities.
- Every aborted foetus was a potential human being, perhaps even a saint or a genius.
- Abortions can go wrong. They can leave terrible mental and physical 'scars' on a woman.
- If abortion is acceptable, where do we draw the line? Abortion is a form of infanticide.
- If society did more in the way of contraception and education, and helped single mothers by providing counselling and places where they could seek advice, abortion would not be necessary.
- Killing is killing, whether done in the back-streets or openly.

## ISLAM TEACHES

In the Afterlife, the 'unborn' child will ask why it was killed, and those who killed it must make amends.

## HADITHS

Abu Hurayrah recorded that two women of the Hudhayl tribe fought with each other, and one flung a stone at the other, killing both her and what was in her womb. The case was brought before the Prophet, and he gave judgement that the compensation to be paid by the woman who killed them, or her close relatives, was to provide a good quality servant of either sex for the unborn child, (and full compensation for the dead woman), the compensation to be paid to the dead woman's children and husband.

Hamal b. al-Nabigha of Hudhayl objected: ' Messenger of Allah, why should I pay compensation for one who neither drank, nor ate, nor spoke, nor made any noise? It is a nonentity.'

The Prophet rebuked him (Muslim 4168).

It was also recorded that if someone caused a woman to lose her unborn child the above compensation (of one servant) was due if the child was born dead; but if the child was born alive and then died, full compensation was due. (Imam Nawawi on Muslim 4166).

# File on Euthanasia

'Do not take life-which Allah has made sacred -except for just cause'. (17:33)

Sometimes life seems such a burden for someone that well-meaning people consider it would be better to end it, in as kind a way as possible. They give serious consideration to what is meant by the phrase 'just cause'. Are some conditions of life so unbearable, that a person would be justified in ending it - either their own or somebody else's? 'Euthanasia' means literally a 'good health' (usually thought of as being 'put to sleep' painlessly).

People who believe in euthanasia argue that sometimes we are kinder to our animals than we are to our people, for we would not stand by and see an animal suffer, but would kill it kindly.

They argue that putting a gentle and easy end to human life should be considered when an infant is born hopelessly deformed, or hopelessly mentally ill, when the prospective lifetime in front of it would be grim. It seems much kinder to the child, and to the family that cares for it and has no knowledge of what is to come. Nothing is more heartbreaking than watching a child face up to approaching death, usually with extraordinary courage.

Other people for whom euthanasia is seriously considered are the terminally ill. If a person of any age has become so riddled with pain through incurable disease that they feel they can not longer 'carry on', why should they be deprived of a 'good death'? Would it not be kinder to let them just slip away perhaps by a swift lethal injection?

Here, medical science has an enormous burden of decision, for sometimes the 'assistance' the doctors give to an individual actually prolongs a human life way beyond the moment when that person would have been allowed to 'go' in nature. Every doctor knows this dilemma-when 'not to strive to keep officiously alive'.

Should 'absence of medial care' be allowed? Many think that pneumonia (the 'old man's friend') really is as much easier way to die than to be repeatedly operated on and struggle on in great pain past the moment when that person would have died, if left to 'nature'. The whole business of when to give or not to give medical help is the dilemma faced by every doctor who is called upon daily to 'play God'. The doctor cannot avoid this situation-luckily for us, it is not usually something that ordinary people have to make decisions over.

## HELPING OLD PEOPLE TO DIE

What about the old people who have become 'vegetables' and no longer enjoy a real existence? Why should they be obliged to spend the last months and years of their lives sitting helplessly and bleakly in a kind of twilight existence? Often they feel they have nothing left to live for, and all their friends have gone before.

Quite frankly, such an attitude and such bleakness of existence is appailing. It is horrifying to those who have loved and cared for their ageing dear ones, and to all who are aware of their feelings and sensitivities.

## MAKING DECISIONS-'ACTING GOD'

But humans do have to give permission for medical help; they do sometimes have to consider switching off a life-support machine; they do have to accept the knowledge that their elderly relative, or one with an incurable disease, may be given the label NTBR-'not to be resuscilated'.

All these matters are very emotive. It is one thing for someone to sit down and think the issues through coldly and logically, and quite another matter for a person to be requested to end a loved one's life, for whatever reason. We are all aware of harrowing cases reported in the media where distraught relatives have taken such decision-making upon themselves, usually for the most noble of motives, and have remained traumatized by it thereafter.

Herein lies one of the problems of abuse of the whole matter-it would be all too easy to legalize euthanasia for social convenience reasons, resulting in the untimely deaths of all sorts of innocent people who might rather have stayed alive, in spite of their unhappy states. Unscrupulous people might cash in on the wealth and belongings of those they 'put to death'.

## MUSLIMS REJECT EUTHANASIA

Muslims reject euthanasia, because the reason for the disability or suffering will be known to Allah, and 'mercy' killing does not usually allow the person concerned any choice in the matter. They are appalled by the idea that any person should be put to death out of social convenience.

Muslims regard every soul as being perfect, even though the body it has been born in may be damaged for some reason. They also believe that Allah has decided how long anyone is to live, so it is not the personal choice of the individual anyway. It is Allah alone who knows the reasons for our sufferings and our tests. These tests may indeed seem very unfair to us when we do not know the reasons-but Muslims believe that all will be revealed in due course, and that Allah is never unfair.

The notion of killing somebody in order to give them 'the right to die with dignity' are understandable but misguided. It is quite wrong to suggest that a person struggling with pain or illness lacks dignity; to speak of euthanasia is really a condemnation of a modern society that is unwilling to help adequately.

It is better to pray for strength and courage, and to try to develop inner peace, and accept that Allah will grant death to an individual when it is 'better' for him or her.

Umm Salamah recorded that the Messenger said: 'If any Muslim who suffers some calamity says what Allah has commanded-'We belong to Allah and to Allah we shall return; O Allah, reward me for any affliction, give me something better in exchange for it'-then Allah will give something better in exchange: (Muslim 1999).

Anas recorded: 'None of you should wish for death for any calamity that befalls you, but should say: 'O Allah! Cause me to live so long as life is better for me; and cause me to die when death is better for me.' (Abu Dawud 3102, Bukhan 70.19.575).

A most important point to consider is that Islam teaches that when people bear their pains without losing faith, it is not pointless or useless and meaningless suffering, but it will be counted for them towards the forgiveness of their sins.

Umm al-Ala recorded that the Apostle visited her when she was sick. He said: 'Be glad, Umm al-Ala, for Allah removes the sins of a Muslim for his (or her) illness, as fire removes the dross from gold and silver.' (Abu Dawud 3086).

Aishah recorded that she told the Apostle of Allah that the most severe verse in the Qur'an was: 'If anyone does evil, he (or she) will be requited for it.' He said: 'But do you not know, Aishah, that when a believer is afflicted with a calamity or a thorn, it serves as an atonement for his (or her), evil deed.' (Abu Dawud 3087, Bukhan 70.1.544).

Abu Sa'id al-Khudri and Abu Hurayrah recorded: 'No fatique, nor disease, nor sorrow, nor sadness, nor hurt, nor distress befall a Muslim, even if it were (as small as) the prick of a thorn, but Allah expiates some of his (or her) sins for it.' (Bukhari 70.1.545).

## LIVING WILL

This is a written statement known as an 'advanced directive' or 'living will', which could be made if you do nor wish to be kept alive by artificial means in the event of a terminal illness or severe disablement.

It is up to you to ensure that the existence of your living will is made known to the doctors and nurses who will be responsible for complying with its instructions. For example, give copies to your nearest relative and your solicitor, and ask your GP to add a copy to your medical records. Also keep a copy in a place such as a handbag or wallet, where it is likely to be found immediately after an accident.

## MAKING A LIVING WILL

A living will should be drawn up when its author is clearly capable of making choices for himself or herself-doctors, or in some cases a court, might decide that a person suffering from a mental illness was not capable of judging the issues clearly enough to make such an important decision.

The statement should be in writing, signed by the person concerned and witnessed by an independent adult who is known to the person and who can vouch for the author's level of Understanding at the time of the signature. The witness should not have influence over the will's author - a person's spouse, child or doctor should not witness the document; a younger acquaintance or a doctor other than your own GP might make the most suitable witnesses.

If you wish to make a living will, discuss it fully with your doctor, who may be able to offer counselling. Once the will has been drawn up, it is a good idea to review it regularly in the light of changes in the law or in medical treatments.

When a patient declines medical treatment.

A person of sound mind who understands the possible consequences has the right to refuse medical treatment. The doctor must abide by the decision, even if it results in the person's death - a murder charge could not be brought against the doctor because he or she did not intend the death. However, treating a person in such circumstances could lead to the doctor facing a charge of assault.

A doctor or anyone else who assists someone in his or her wish to die could be charged with aiding, abetting, counselling or procuring a suicide - an offence carrying a maximum prison sentence of 14 years.

Provided that it is in their best interests, treatment may be given to people who are unable to make a rational decision about whether or nor to accept it - irrespective of anything they say. Relatives have no legal right to insist that treatment be stopped, although their views may be taken into account.

## PATIENTS WHO CANNOT EXPRESS THEIR WISHES

There is no absolute obligation upon doctors to prolong life regardless of the circumstances, as long as any decisions about treatment are made in the patient's best interests. There are instances when bringing about death by withholding or withdrawing medical treatment may not amount to a criminal offence.

Withholding artificial feeding or drugs from an unconscious patient who has no hope of recovery, in the knowledge that death will rapidly ensue, could be lawful, provided that reasonable and competent medical opinion indicates that the continuance of treatment would confer no benefit upon the patient, and that the necessary court consent has been obtained.

In the case of a patient suffering from brain death - irreversible brain damage causing an inability to function without life-support systems - it would be legal for the doctor, in conjunction with the family, to decide to withdraw treatment because the patient is already clinically dead. However, in the case of a person who is not classified as brain dead, prior court approval must be obtained before life-support systems may be switched off. This includes patients in a persistent vegetative state (PVS) - that is, unconscious and without prospect of improvement, although they are breathing without any artificial support.

The British Medical Association sets out four safeguards for doctors involved in decisions advising the withdrawal of treatment from PVS patients:

- Every effort should be made at rehabilitation for at least six months after injury.
- The diagnosis of irreversible PVS should not be considered confirmed until at least 12 months after the injury.
- The diagnosis should be agreed by at least two independent doctors.
- The wishes of the patient's immediate family should be given great weight. In cases of PVS where the medical decision is to discontinue feeding or treatment, the sanction of a High Court judge must be sought before taking any action.

A doctor who administers drugs in order to relieve the extreme suffering of a terminally ill patient is not guilty of any crime even if the drugs also hasten the patient's death. However, it is illegal to administer drugs with the intention of killing a patient, even if the patient has expressed a rational wish for this.

## THE CASE FOR VOLUNTARY EUTHANASIA

- It can quickly and humanely end a patient's suffering.
- It can help to shorten the grief and suffering of the patient's loved ones.
- Everyone has the right to decide how they should die.
- If the law in the UK was changed, doctors could legally act on a patient's desire to die without further suffering.
- It would help others to face death if they realized they could die with dignity.
- It would help others to face death if they realized they could die with dignity.

- It would help others to face death if they knew of their patient's intentions.
- The initial decision about euthanasia could be made when the individual was not under the stress of immediate suffering or anxiety.

## THE CASE AGAINST VOLUNTARY EUTHANASIA

- There are many pain-killing drugs which can help the patient die naturally with dignity.
- A patient might not be able to make a rational decision or might change their mind but be incapable of telling the doctors.
- Many people recover after being 'written off' by doctors.
- Old people might feel they are a nuisance to others and opt for euthanasia when in their hearts they want to continue living.
- Life is a gift from God and only God can take it away.
- Euthanasia devalues life by making it disposable - it could be the first step on to a slippery slope.

- The relationship of trust between doctors and patients could be destroyed. Under the Hippocratic Oath doctors must try to preserve life.
- If there were better facilities for caring for the dying, there would be less need for euthanasia.
- Doctors should not be executioners.

## THE VOLUNTARY EUTHANASIA SOCIETY [EXIT]

This society aims to bring about a change in the law so that:

'An adult person suffering from a severe illness, for which no relief is known, should be entitled by law to the mercy of a painless death, if and only if, that is their expressed wish.'

'Doctors should be allowed to help incurable patients to die peacefully at their own request. The patient must have signed, at least 30 days previously, a declaration making their request known.'

Voluntary Euthanasia Society
13, Prince of Wales Terrace
London W8 5PG
0171 937 7770

# *File on Drugs*

## DRUGS THAT CAN BE DANGEROUS

| Drug | What it looks like | How it's used | What it does | Risks |
|---|---|---|---|---|
| Amphetamines (Speed) | A white powder, or brown powder, may be in pill or capsule form | Usually sniffed or injected | Makes people lively, giggly, over-alert; depression and difficulty with sleep may follow | Heavy use can produce feelings of paranoia |
| Cannabis (pot, dope, hash, grass, ganga, weed) | Hard brown resinous material or herbal mixture | Smoked in a joint or pipe, sometimes with tobacco | Heightened appreciation of sensory experience; elevation of mood, talkativeness | Risks of accidents; can cause feelings of paranoia; sleepiness |
| Cocaine (coke) | A white powder | Usually sniffed | Makes people lively, over-alert, elevation of mood | Can lead to dependence; withdrawal can be very uncomfortable |
| Crack | Crystalline rocks | Smoked | Same as cocaine | Long-term use can cause deterioration in mental functioning, irritability, social withdrawal, loss of sexual desire |
| Ecstasy (E, Dove, Barney Rubble, XTC) | Tablets or capsules | Swallowed | Feelings of empathy with others at low doses, restlessness and anxiety at higher doses | Heavy use can cause psychological confusion, alienation and fear |
| Heroin (Skag, smack) | A brown or white speckled powder | Injected or smoked | Alertness at first, then drowsiness and drunken appearance | Overdose can cause unconsciousness; regular use leads to dependence; giving up becomes difficult |
| Magic mushrooms (Liberty cap) | Mushroom found growing wild | Swallowed raw, cooked or as a beverage | Heightened appreciation of sensory experiences; perceptual distortions | Mainly from eating other poisonous mushrooms by mistake |
| Other opiates (Dikes, 118s) | May include red or white tablets or ampoules | Swallowed or injected | Same as heroin | Same as heroin |
| LSD (acid) | Tiny coloured tablets; microspots on blotting paper; small absorbent stamps | Taken by mouth | Perceptual distortions can produce hallucinations; elevation of mood; sometimes causes severe panic or anxiety attacks | Heavy use can cause psychological confusion, paranoia. Risks of accidents while under influence |
| Tranquilizers | Prescribed tablets and capsules | Taken by mouth | Similar to alcohol, effect increased when taken with alcohol | May lead to dependence; withdrawal symptoms can include severe anxiety. |

## WHAT ARE THE DANGERS OF ILLEGAL DRUG TAKING?

### The main dangers

- Having an accident while under their influence.
- Some drugs may depress or stop breathing.
- Accidental overdose often leads to unconsciousness or even death.
- Regular use leads to addiction or dependence. Drugs can also have nasty side-effects.
- They can bring on confusion and frightening hallucinations.
- They can cause unbalanced emotions or more serious mental disorders.
- First time heroin users are sometimes violently sick. Habitual users are very ill on withdrawal.
- Users become anti-social, frequently dirty, sick, and wetting the bed.
- Later still, there may be more serious mental and physical effects and illness.
- If a drug user starts to inject, infections leading to sores, abscesses, jaundice, blood poisoning and even the AIDS virus may follow.

## HOW ABUSING DRUGS CAN HARM SOCIETY

### Personal problems

- Relationships may become strained, especially with friends and family.
- Rather than helping you to face up to life, drugs may simply become one more problem in addition to the ones you already have.

### Money problems:

- It costs money to take drugs - they are expensive. A heavy user may end up spending all their money on 'feeding the habit'. Many addicts become thieves.

## Press Report

The Daily Mail, April 28, 1998.

*By Professor Heather Ashton*

A psychopharmacist at Newcastle University who has spent more than 20 years studying the effect of drugs on the human mind.

There are literally millions of people of all ages and all classes in this country who have tried cannabis and claim to have had no ill effects.

Indeed, as the Government launches its drugs White Paper - a document that maintains the strict official ban on cannabis - it is probably fair to say that the weight of liberal opinion is in favour of its legalization.

There are MPs who argue that its use is harmless. At countless dinner parties the law is derided. One serious broadsheet newspaper has campaigned openly for cannabis to be made legal.

Why not, so the argument goes, when the drug is not nearly as dangerous as heroin, nor as addictive as cocaine, nor as unpredictable in its consequences as LSD or Ecstasy?

Why not, when the anti-cannabis laws are flouted so openly, when half the students at universities have tried it and when the drug is said to pose fewer dangers than either alcohol or and tobacco?

Well, there are good reasons why not. As someone who, since the Seventies, has studied the impact on the human brain of various drugs - including cannabis - it seems to me that the 'legalize pot' campaigners are jumping ahead of the evidence in a cause that owes more to fashion than to hard science.

During my research I have come into contact with many different types of cannabis user, from students who consume it on a casual basis to habitual users.

I must stress that I'm not speaking as an anti-cannabis campaigner. I'm an academic, not a pundit or a politician keen on promoting a particular policy.

But as the pressure grows to legalize cannabis, it seems to me increasingly important that the facts should be understood, particularly by those who argue that cannabis isn't really harmful. anyway. It is time we took a long, dispassionate view of the evidence.

Take the claim that cannabis isn't addictive. Research demonstrates that this simply isn't true. My own experience with student users shows that they can and do suffer severe withdrawal symptoms when they try to come off the drug.

Once I was unable to complete my study of one group of chronic cannabis smokers in a commune because they could not keep their appointments.

They lost their academic edge, and their studies suffered badly. And, crucially, those who stopped smoking the drug exhibited no great improvement.

A study in the U.S. conducted about ten years ago, underlined the point. A group of regular cannabis users was given oral doses of the drug under strict laboratory conditions. Later, unknown to them, the drugs were replaced by harmless placebos.

Without their regular genuine 'fixes', they ended up suffering tremors, stomach pains, nausea, headaches and a range of other unpleasant side-effects. One of the reasons is the way cannabis is absorbed by the body. It isn't like alcohol, which can be sweated out within 24 hours. The narcotic effects of a single joint last 48 hours.

But the various chemical residues in the drug find their way into the body fat, where they remain for as long as a month. And of course regular users keep on absorbing more and more.

Contrary to claims by the 'legalize pot' campaign, it definitely affects the brain function. A Department of Transport study in the late Eighties confirmed that cannabis impairs the ability to drive. Another study showed that, after alcohol, cannabis is the most common drug involved in road deaths.

Research into airline pilots who had smoked one moderate dose of the drug not only found that it had a marked impact on performance, but that the impairment lasted up to 48 hours.

Just as disturbing was the finding that, after 24 hours, those pilots were unaware that their abilities were still affected. But they continued to make potentially disastrous mistakes when they were tested on a flight simulator.

Now all this may seem somewhat overstated to the people who smoked the odd joint back in the Sixties and Seventies without seeming to suffer any great harm. Indeed, the legalization campaigners point to the experience of those years as evidence that the drug is relatively safe.

But I fear they are missing a crucial point. Over the years, the strength of the average cannabis joint has increased dramatically because of careful plant-breeding and hydroponic farming to produce more potent varieties, such as Silver Pearl and Skunkweed. The old reefer of the Sixties offered a relatively mild dose. A modern joint can be as much as 30 times stronger. And of course the very fact of that increase in strength adds to the chemical deposits in the body and stimulates the desire for another strong buzz.

Whether or not this leads on to experimentation with harder drugs may be open to debate. But I think there is an analogy with alcohol abuse. Most people like a drink, but relatively few go on to become alcoholics. It must be true, however, that the more drinkers there are, the more alcoholics there will be. I suspect that the same pattern applies to cannabis. The more users there are, the more will be tempted to try something stronger.

This, after all, is what is suggested by the experience in Holland, where cannabis has been legal for years. The use of hard drugs has risen noticeably.

It is interesting to note that the Dutch authorities have now reduced the amount of cannabis that can be sold for personal consumption.

There is one other point that the legalizers tend to overlook: the risk of cancer.

It took decades before the carcinogenic effects of tobacco smoke were fully understood. How long will it be before it dawns on cannabis users that they risk very nasty cancers of the throat, tongue and mouth, not to mention emphysema and other chest troubles?

In fact, in some respects a joint can be more dangerous than a cigarette because it has no filter and a higher igniting temperature.

If any future government is tempted to lift the ban on cannabis, it will have to do so despite the evidence that it creates dependency, that it impairs the cognitive function of the brain and that it poses a risk of cancer.

The only argument that is left concerns the undoubted fact that the present law is so widely flouted as to be virtually unenforceable. But wouldn't the law be equally unenforceable if the ban were lifted? After all, since cannabis clearly has a deleterious long-term effect, many groups in society would still be forbidden from using it, no matter how liberal the Government wanted to appear.

Could we ever contemplate pilots, bus drivers or surgeons using the drug? How could we ever police a law that allowed some people to use the drug but forbade others?

There has been plenty of emotion in the drugs debate, plenty of passion and commitment. Am I alone in wishing for a more considered approach? And for a climate if in which science and rational analysis can take the place of tub-thumping zealotry?

# File on Shi'ism

## ALI

Ali was the son of Abu Talib, Muhammad's uncle and guardian. He was a lot younger than Muhammad, but had grown up in Muhammad's household, and there was a close, relationship between the two. He was the next person after Khadijah to believe in Muhammad's prophethood, although only a boy of 10 or 12 at the time. He remained a loyal supporter of Islam ever after. At the Hijrah he risked his life for Muhammad: he slept in the Prophet's bed to fool his enemies into thinking that he was still there, so giving Muhammad a head start on his pursuers. In Madinah he was a close friend and confidant of the Prophet. He married Muhammad's youngest daughter, Fatimah; their two sons were the grandchildren of the Prophet. There are many stories which show Muhammad's fondness for these two boys.

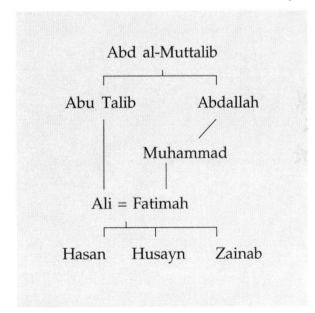

Shi'ites who believe that Ali was the rightful successor of Muhammad. They refuse to call him the fourth caliph, but the first Imam, therefore dismissing the first three caliphates as invalid. Although they look back on this period as a Golden Age, Ali in fact had a difficult time of it. Members of Uthman's family had been made governors all over the empire, and they blamed Ali's supporters for his death. Several powerful relatives of the Prophet refused to recognize Ali as caliph until the assassins had been brought to justice.

Civil war broke out, but it came to arbitration, and Ali eventually made peace. Some of Ali's followers took this as a sign of weakness, and Ali wasted valuable time and resources dealing with them. They became known as the Kharijites (the 'Seceders') because they were the first to withdraw formally from the other Muslims, forming a separate group within Islam. This puritanical group still exists today, but they never grew into a major movement like the Shi'i.

It is thought to have been a Kharijite who assassinated Ali in the mosque at Kufa, Iraq in 661. There is some question as to where his remains are buried, but the traditional site is at Najaf in Iraq, which has since become an important religious centre. Among other things, it can boast the world's largest cemetery, surrounding Ali's shrine. The corpses of many Shi'ites from all over the world are brought here, to be taken inside the sanctuary and then carried three times round the outside of Ali's mausoleum, before being buried near to the tombs of Ali and some of the other Imams.

## SHI'ITE ISLAM

The Shi'i are named after the Shi'a of Ali - the Party of Ali. They can be called Shi'is or Shi'ites; and you can talk of Shi'i Islam, Shi'ism or the Shi'a. The Shi'ites have always been a minority in Islam, and despite all the times their extremists grab the headlines, today they still make up only about 15% of all Muslims. The largest group of Shi'ites (about 48 million) is in Iran, where they form over 96% of the population. Iran is the only country to make Shi'ism the official religion. The Shi'is also form the largest religious group in Iraq. There are also Shi'ite minorities in India, Pakistan, the Gulf States, the USSR and East Africa.

Virtually all of the remaining 85% of Muslims are Sunnis - those who claim to follow the 'path' or the example or Sunnah of the Prophet. They claim the Shi'ites have brought changes or innovations (bida) into the religion; whereas the Shi'ites insist they are the true faith and everyone else has it wrong - hence the disturbances between the two.

Reasons why Shi'ite Muslims believe Ali should have been the first Khalifah.

- He was the first male Muslim (after the Prophet, of course), and the first of the Companions to believe in Islam.
- When the Banu Abd al-Muttalib gathered at the Prophet's invitation, he asked them to make a solemn pledge: 'Whoever helps me in this matter will be my brother, my trustee (wali), my helper (wazir), and my heir and successor after me.'

None of his relatives responded except Ali, who stepped forward and said 'O Messenger, I will be your helper'. The Prophet then blessed him and said clearly: 'Sit down; you are my brother, my trustee, my helper, my inheritor and successor after me.'

- The Shi'ites interpret surah 5:55 as being the nomination (nass) of his authority (wilaya) by Allah: 'Your authority is Allah and His Messenger, and those believers who perform the prayer and pay alms while they are bowing in prayer'.

Shi'ites claim that only Ali had paid alms whilst bowing in prayer.

(Wali = the most appropriate for authority).

- At the Gathering of Ghadir Khumm, the Prophet concluded his speech with the words: 'Whomsoever I am the authority over, Ali is also the authority over.'
- At the time the Prophet set out on the Tabuk expedition, he said to Ali: 'You are in the same position with respect to me as Harun (Aaron) was to Musa (Moses), except that there is no prophet after me.'

Thus he required of him the duties of helping, administering and deputizing for him both during his life and after his death. (See Surah 20:29-36).

- Musa told of Harun deputizing for him in delivering the message, supporting and strengthening him when he said: 'Deputize for me among the people. Act for their benefit and do not follow the path of corrupters.' (Surah 7:142).

Shi'ites therefore believe that Ali's succession was confirmed by the precise statement of revelation.

- His Shi'a included the Banu Hashim, Salman, Ammar, Abu Dharr, al-Miqdad, Khuzayma b.Thabit, Abu

Ayyub al-Ansari, Jabir b. Abdallah, Abu Sa'id al-Khudri.

- Shi'ites reckon his Caliphate to have been for 30 years after the death of the Prophet; for 24 years and 6 months he was prevented from administering the laws of his office, and for 5 years and 6 months of these he was involved in warfare against other Muslims. He died on 21 Ramadan, 40 AH.

## SOME WAYS IN WHICH SHI'ITE ISLAM DIFFERS FROM SUNNI ISLAM

### Leadership:

- Shi'ites believe that Muhammad chose Ali as his successor. He should therefore have been accepted by all Muslims as the first caliph - or Imam, as they call their leaders.

- The only caliph that both Shi'ites and Sunnis accept is Ali. In particular, Shi'ites reject the caliphates of Abu Bakr, Umar and Uthman, and they do not accept any changes implemented by them. (A minority of Shi'ites, the Zaydis, do accept the first three caliphs as well as Ali. These represent the most moderate form of Shi'ism.)

- Shi'ites believe that each new leader of the Muslim community should be chosen by the previous Imam, by divine inspiration (so that it is really Allah's choice). They also think he should be a descendant of Muhammad, and thus of Ali.

- The Sunni caliphs held mainly political power. For the Shi'ites, their leader's religious authority is far more important. (They could therefore regard Hasan as their Imam, even when he had no political influence.)

### The Scriptures

- Sunnis believe that Muhammad's role in revealing Allah's laws (in the Qur'an) and guiding people to Allah (in the Sunnah) ended with him. Shi'ites cannot believe that Allah would ever leave them without guidance, and therefore maintain that their leaders have the right to interpret the Qur'an for them. It follows that their Imams must be sinless and unable to make mistakes because Allah would not lead his people astray.

- Sunnis interpret the Qur'an literally, but Shi'ites claim that its hidden meaning was given by Muhammad to Ali.

- Sunnis accept six books of hadiths which they call 'The Accurate Six'. Shi'ites have their own collection of books of hadiths, mostly passed on through the Imams.

### Beliefs

- The Shi'ites expect the Madhi (the 'divinely guided' one) to appear before the Day of Judgement, and bring in a reign of justice and peace. This is a popular belief among Sunnis as well; but the Shi'ites expect the Mahdi to be their Hidden Imam (i.e. their last Imam, whom they believe to have disappeared rather than died).

### Ritual Practices

- All Muslims accept the Five Pillars, but Shi'ites are permitted to combine the five prayers into three sessions.

- Shi'ites have many saints. The Twelvers, for instance, venerate the Fourteen Pure Ones (Muhammad, his daughter Fatimah and the Twelve Imams). They perform elaborate rituals at their shrines, and commemorate their births and deaths annually.

## Sects:

The main branch of Shi'ism, the Twelvers, or Imamis, are found mostly in Iran today. Their name comes from their belief that their twelfth Imam, called Muhammad, did not die but disappeared. While they await his return, they rely on his representatives to lead them, like the Ayatollahs (meaning 'Sign of Allah').

The next largest group of Shi'ites is in Lebanon and Syria, and scattered throughout Africa and Asia. They are the Seveners, or Isma'ilis, so called because they accept only seven Imams and believe that their seventh Imam, called Isma'il, is the Hidden Imam. Their present leader is the Aga Khan.

A famous Sevener group of the twelfth and thirteenth centuries was known as the Assassins (or Hashishi). They doped themselves with hashish, and then committed acts of terrorism against Sunni Muslim statesmen.

The Seveners look for the hidden meaning of the Qur'an in even greater depth than other Shi'ites, and they have given birth to a number of secretive sects, like the Druze.

The Alawi form another small Shi'ite sect. Their name means 'followers of Ali'. They are found in Syria and have combined Islamic beliefs with many others from different religions.

# File on The Ideal Islamic State

The Islamic State is an ideal - it does not and has not ever yet existed, even though the Prophet spent his later years establishing the foundations of this ideal in Madinah. It means a state actually up and running, according to the will of God, an active Theocracy.

Muslims believe that no just kingdom can operate if it is run by unjust people, who have not first created the Kingdom of God in their own hearts. However, it is not enough for Muslims just to accept God as Ruler in their hearts - the aim is for the whole of society to be able to run according to the just and compassionate will of Allah, with the people at peace, content, successful and thriving.

What a wonderful state this would be! These aims are the real point - it is not just a question of politics, Muslims wishing to be led by Muslim leaders. To create an Islamic State is not an end in itself, but a means to an end. The real aim is the development of a community of people who stand up for right against wrong, for equality and justice. In other words, it is the creation of such conditions as would enable the greatest possible number of human beings to live to the best of their ability - spiritually, morally and physically in accordance with the will of God.

It is in this sense alone that Islam is a theocracy (a community of people accepting the rule of God, as opposed to monarchy (rule by a royal family), aristocracy (rule of the people by the people), or meritocracy (rule by people of special merit). The merits or defects of each system are often based on personal preferences. A Muslim can accept any of these systems, so long as the rule is according to God's laws.

## ABUSE OF POWER

An Islamic State is only pretending to be a 'theocracy' if it is really a case of the rule of an individual leader, who is granted such exaggerated reverence and power that his own will becomes law. Too much power in the hands of one person is always dangerous - even the noblest of people make mistakes, and power corrupts. Such a rule may start well, but develop into the worst type of tyranny if a clever ruler manages to convince himself and his unfortunate subjects that his tyranny is God's will, and then if they oppose him they would be opposing God. Thus he can impose his own unchecked domination upon them. Islam teaches: 'Follow the revelation sent to you from your Lord, and do not follow guardians other than Him' when they divert from that will. (surah 7:3).

A Muslim ruler should only, ever, rule on those terms.

## EVERY MUSLIM IS RESPONSIBLE

So, the theocracy encouraged in Islam is not a case of handing over all responsibility to one ruler, or a class of particular religious 'experts', but the whole community of Muslims, including the rank and file. Allah did not appoint any particular individual, group, race or class to represent Him on earth, but the whole community. In this sense, all believers have been granted the caliphate, and all are responsible and answerable to God.

## THE ISLAMIC RULER'S CHARACTER AND ABILITIES

The first and most important thing is to choose the right leader.

- An Islamic ruler should be personally beyond reproach, both morally and spiritually. It is his job to 'enjoin good and prevent evil' in others (surah 22:41). This involves unswerving justice tempered with compassion and wisdom; and the leader must be beyond hyprocrisy or corruption.

- He should be of outstanding intelligence and mentally sound, so as to have the ability and wisdom to rule.

- He should have good organizational and managerial talents, so that his subjects do not end up suffering because of his mistakes.

- He should have robust physical health, for the role is so stressful, strenuous and demanding that an infirm person would not be able to cope.

- He should not be politically ambitious, or out to seek that position. If he was, he would be quite unsuitable for office, as he would either be ignorant of its grave responsibilities, or he would be wishing to take advantage of his official power.

- He should not seek to publicize or promote himself, but should be able to rely on the good opinion of others of his known and proved suitability. (Someone who goes out canvassing or making his own speeches in order to influence the masses really ought to be disqualified! Bought votes, and pressure for group votes, are in direct opposition to the spirit of Islam).

## SHOULD THE RULER BE A MAN?

There is a hadith that no good would come to a nation ruled by a woman. However, that tradition is not a strong one, and is countered by the fact that the Qur'an gives the example of a female ruler who was requested to become Muslim but not to give up her throne. The Muslim world is actually in the unique position of having had more female leaders in this century than any other society. However, although female Muslims have equality with males in the eyes of Allah by nature of their own virtue, Muslims accept that women have particular physical problems, with attendant hormonal and emotional difficulties from time to time, and Muslim women are expected to accept a man as the head of their household; therefore Muslims generally place more confidence in male leadership.

## RULE BY CONSENT OF THE PEOPLE

If the leadership is granted to an individual, it must be with the consent of the people. There is no concept of the 'divine right of kings' or the 'infallibility of priests' in Islam. Every Muslim stands on equal level with other Muslims as Allah's vice-regent on earth. None has preference by virtue of high birth, or belonging to a special religious group. Muslim history is full of examples of ruling Caliphs being publicly called to the right path by ordinary men and women. The lowliest villager has the right to tell the Commander of the Faithful if he deviates in any way from the path of righteousness.

In other words, the rulers and officials in an Islamic State are answerable both to God and to those they rule for their actions, and the people have every right to criticize not only their public behaviour but also their private behaviour.

## RULE BY THE NASS, AND NOT NECESSARILY FIQH

A State truly established on the basis of God's Law cannot enforce any ruling that contradicts the spirit of the Qur'an and Sunnah, even if every singly citizen asks for it. However, if the citizens are also Muslim, a ruler is not sharply marked off from the rest of the population, they are all working towards the same goal.

Islam covers every aspect of life, and fiqh (the study of Islamic Law) attempts to provide detailed legislation for every possible situation. This law is based on the Qur'an and Sunnah established fourteen centuries ago. The major part of it lies in using deductive reasoning (qiyas), which includes the personal wisdom and judgement of the authorities, based on the social and intellectual environment of their time, and their own approach to interpretation of the legal sources (which do not go back to the Prophet's own time in their written form).

That environment was vastly different from that of today. For this reason, many conclusions if made now might differ radically from conclusions made then. This has led to conflict of opinion amongst today's Islamic scholars.

Some regard the ancient rulings as having a validity of their own, as law. They claim that explicit statements, commands and prohibitions in the Qur'an and Sunnah are quite sufficient to cover all possible modern legal situations.

Other scholars disagree - and point out that any matter not specifically covered by Qur'an and Sunnah was not because God forgot to mention it, or did not know it would come up in the future; the nusus (plural of nass) laws of Islam were intended to mark out the boundaries within which any community could develop, leaving specific examples to be worked out case by case.

The true and eternally valid Shari'ah (the nass rulings) is therefore much more concise than the mass of legal minutiaea evolved over the centuries. The True and Eternal Divine Law was laid down entire: 'Do this'; 'Don't do that'; 'This is right, and therefore desirable'; 'That is wrong and therefore to be shunned'.

These are the self-contained and unambiguous nass rulings. They are not subject to various interpretations but are universals, and can be applied to every stage of human social and intellectual development, in any place, in any circumstance. (For example, the nass rulings are 'Be honest', or 'Be modest', or 'Be compassionate'- how these rulings are worked out in practice in specific circumstances is that which is open to human judgement).

All the rest of Islamic jurisprudence, the fiqh, reflects specific talented people, times and mentalities, and should not be regarded as having eternal validity, no matter how much the authorities behind them were (or are) respected.

'Do not ask about matters I have left unspoken; behold, there were many before you who went to their doom because they put too many questions to their prophets, and disagreed thereupon. Therefore, if I command you to do anything, do as much as you are able to do; and if I forbid you anything, abstain from it.' (Muslim).

A modern Islamic State need not, therefore, conform to any particular historical precedent. It must run acording to the nass, the main principles leaving the widest possible scope for interpreting laws in accordance to the needs of any particular time or social condition.

## RIGHTS AND DUTIES

An Islamic state should be able to claim full loyalty from all its citizens, wholehearted co-operation in all sectors of life, and complete obedience to the law of the land and the commands of the rulers, so long as they are in keeping with the will of God.

- Where the will of God is being broken, the citizens would have the right not only to withdraw co-operation, but also to stop the offending ruler from acting in that way.

- The citizens would be required to pay their contributions to a fairly-agreed tax-plan willingly, and not to misappropriate its funds.

- The citizens would be expected to participate in striving for God's will to be free to be done (jihad) in any capacity for which they are deemed fit. If the State came under attack, this would then include military defence - 'Permission to fight is given to those against whom war is being wrongfully waged' (surah 22:39). On no account should it be a war of aggression or conquest - 'Fight in the way of God those who fight against you, but do not yourselves commit aggression; for behold, God does not love aggresors' (2:190).

- The Islamic State has the duty to protect the life, property and honour of every citizen, no matter what their status, class, caste, colour or creed (ie. even if they are not Muslims).

- It has the duty to protect the freedom and individual liberty of every citizen, so long as there is no valid reason to prevent it. If prevention becomes necessary, it should not just be arbitrary or based on one person's whim or opinion or grievance - it must follow the due process of law (ie. you cannot just rush out and attack or intimidate people you think are doing wrong).

- It has the duty to respect freedom of expression (You can hold whatever opinion you like - but you have not got the right to deliberately abuse or hurt or cause trouble with it. That impinges upon the rights of others).

- It has the duty to see that no citizen remains unprovided for as regards the basic necessities of life - food, clothing, shelter, medical aid, education, employment. The Prophet made it clear that 'the government is the guardian of those who have no guardian.' 'The leader is a shield from behind which the people fight, and by which they protect themselves' (Bukhari and Muslim).

- The State should strive at all times to create conditions in which goodness can be regarded as normal, and badness be suppressed and got rid of, as far as possible. This does not mean forcing people to pray and fast, or beating them up for not wearing Muslim clothes; it means striving for honesty and justice and compassion and unselfishness - which may sometimes involve being forced to take action over a person who is abusing others in some way.

## A FEW RELEVANT HADITHS

'Muslims should pay attention to the ruler appointed over them, and obey them whether they like it or not, except when they are ordered to do a sinful thing. If ordered to do a sinful thing, a Muslim should neither listen nor obey.' (Muslim 4533).

This sometimes involves having the courage to risk your own safety by standing up to an unjust ruler. To raise one's voice against wrong is a foremost duty of a Muslim.

'The highest kind of jihad is to speak up for truth in the face of a government that deviates from the right path' (Abu Dawud, Tirmidhi, Ibn Majah).

Muslims should not have a slavish, laissez-faire mentality.

The Prophet sent an expedition and appointed a man over the people, and ordered that he should be listened to and obeyed. The people made him angry over something. He said: 'Fetch dry wood for me.' They did so. Then he said: 'Light the fire', and they did so. Then he said: 'Did the Messenger of Allah order you to listen to me and obey my orders?' They said: 'Yes.' He said: 'Then get into the fire.' At this they began to look at one another, and said:

'We fled from the Fire (ie the path to Hell) to find refuge with the Prophet, and now you ask us to enter it?' They (did not obey, but) stood quiet until his anger cooled down and the fire went out. When the expedition was over, they related the incident to the Prophet, who said: 'If you had gone into the fire, you would not have come out. Obedience to a commander is only an obligation if he commands what is good (ie. in keeping with the will of God). (Muslim 4536).

## WHAT SHOULD A MUSLIM DO ABOUT AN UNJUST RULER?

In what circumstances is one justified to rise up against an unjust ruler?

Firstly, Muslims should be very careful not to elect to high office any person for his administrative qualities while ignoring his moral and spiritual qualities. It is the moral and religious quality of that Muslim which should be kept in mind when trusting him as a ruler. If someone manages to get himself appointed despite being a wrongdoer, obedience to him is not binding on the people. No obedience is due to the created which involves disobedience to the Creator.

Should one rise up against a tyrant after he has assumed power? Some Muslims (eg Ahl-i-hadith) say this should not be done in any circumstances, but he should only be criticised and brought to the right path by persuasion. Others (eg. the Hanafi madhdhab) say his tyranny not only makes him invalid, but revolt can be raised against him if circumstances permit and it would become possible to install a just ruler in his place.

Muslims must remember that it is physically impossible to ensure full justice and absolutely fair treatment to everyone under all conditions and circumstances. When individuals are under the impression an injustice has been done, and feel wronged, they have the right to air their feelings and seek the protection of the law, but should not revolt against the government simply on the basis of their feeling wronged. A great deal of unjust harm to other innocent parties has frequently resulted over people zealously leaping to defend their principles. Muslims should exercise patience.

This does not mean weakly submitting to tyranny and raising no voice against it -

but that a Muslim should avoid fretting and fuming, or flouting the authority of the person at whose hand he is suffering. Administrators are not infallible - they can make mistakes, and there is every likelihood that from time to time injustices will be committed. It is the duty of the aggrieved to get their wrongs redressed by legitimate and legal means, but not by disrupting the order of society. If they show patience, God will surely reward them in the Life to Come.

## WHEN A RULER'S AUTHORITY CEASES

So long as the ruler has been properly elected by a legally established system, all citizens owe him their allegiance, however much an individual may dislike his person. If his government then involves committing something against the will of God, a Muslim's duty of obedience ceases as regards those laws. If an Islamic government sets itself openly and deliberately against God's will, it ceases to be Muslim, and its authority should certainly be withdrawn - but this cannot be left to the discretion of individual citizens to decide. It can only be taken by the community as a whole, or its properly appointed representatives. The ruler can be impeached through a tribunal, or a referendum can be held on the question of his deposition from office. The citizen's duty is to watch over the activities of government, and they have the right to criticise, and in the last resort, depose.

However, no one person, or peer-group, or section of the community, has the right to use disruption and rebellion to impose its will on everyone else. A leader's overthrow should only be by the open verdict of the majority within that community.

On the other hand, an Islamic leader or government can give severe punishment for those who rebel and undermine its solidarity or disrupt its unity - the punishment should not be the will of one person, or one group in power, or one section of the community. Offenders (complainants) should be properly tried in a court of law, and all facilities provided for their defence and the right of appeal.

## CONCLUSION

The keynote of an Islamic State should be its fairness and justice. There is no happiness or strength in a society that permits some to suffer undeserved want while others have undeserved luxury.

If it is a case of the whole community suffering privation, that is quite a different matter; the communal feeling can lead to spiritual strength.

However, if resources are so unevenly distributed that some live in affluence while the majority are being exploited, and are using all their energy in search for their daily bread, poverty becomes a real enemy, and may drive the whole community away from God-consciousness into the arms of materialism.

### In an Islamic State,

- There should be no soul-grinding poverty side by side with affluence.

- All resources should be harnessed to the task of providing adequate means of livelihood and welfare for all the citizens.

- All opportunities should be open to all citizens equally, and no-one should enjoy a high standard of living gained at the expenses of others.

## THE BEST RULER

'The best of your rulers are those whom you love and who love you, who invoke God's blessings upon you, and you invoke His blessings upon them. And the worst are those whom you hate and who hate you, and whom you curse and who curse you.' Someone asked: 'Shouldn't we overthrow them by the sword?' He said: 'No, as long as they establish prayer among you. If you have a ruler over you, and you find that the ruler has indulged in an act of disobedience to God, you should condemn the ruler's act, but not withdraw yourself from keeping them as ruler.' (Muslim).

## A NEW POLITICAL IDEOLOGY

Several new Islamic political-cum-cultural organisations and leaders have sprung up. Some of the more important of these are:

- Hasan al-Banna set up Ikhwanul Muslimeen (Muslim Brotherhood), whose intellectual spokesman was Syed Qutb. Its influence is still widespread throughout the Arab world.

- Maulana Abul Ala Mawdudi set up Jamaat-i-Islami, which operates in Pakistan, India and Bangladesh. Its theorist was Maulana Mawdudi himself.

- ABIM was set up in Malaysia. It is the most influential organisation among young Muslims both politically and intellectually.

- The most practially successful authority was Ayatullah Khomeini in Iran, whose book Vilayat-e-Faqih suggested the new way of running a Muslim state.

The most important idea they preached was that only with a genuine Islamic authority in power can Muslims retain, preserve and propagate Islam; have an opportunity of replying to western secularist thought in theory and in practice; and succeed in proving to the world that the Islamic alternative is the only correct process for humanity, if humanity is to be saved from moral degeneration and total destruction.

The common elements in the theories of these organisations and political movements are:

- The assertion that sovereignty belongs to God alone.

- The Qur'an and the Sunnah are the basis of the entire legal structure, and no law shall be passed that would be contrary to these two authorities.

- Freedom and justice for all are ensured.

- Law-making authorities should be elected, but there should be a law-validating body through election or selection from the existing 'ulama of the land.

- The executive authority must be an elected body or a person selected from among the most pious and righteous of the country. According to Ayatollah Khomeini the authority should be a jurist (faqih). The process of election may vary.

- Dictatorships or hereditary kingships are not regarded as Islamic in origin.

- There must be peace among Muslim groups and among Muslim and non-Muslim groups.

- Jihad is obligatory for all Muslims when they are wrongly attacked or when Islam is under threat.

- Private ownership is permitted along

with public ownership and state ownership.

- Wealth is a trust and gift from God, hence poor people have rights over that wealth - rights to be fulfilled by the wealthy through obligatory 'poor due' (zakah), through personal, voluntary, charity (sadaqah), in the form of donations to charities, organisations or individuals, and through the equitable distribution of wealth.

- Charging interest (riba) on loans and hoarding are sins and hence forbidden.

- Equitable distribution of wealth is ensured through the law of inheritance and through other means prescribed in the Qur'an and the Hadith.

- Wealth must be utilised for the welfare of the people in order that 'it [wealth] be not a thing taken in turns among the rich of you' (Qur'an, 59:7).

# File on Some 'ISMS' and Islam

## IMPERIALISM

The practice of a country which has become a nation and embarked on commercial and industrial expansion, of acquiring and administering territories inhabited by peoples usually at a lower stage of development.

## CONSERVATISM (TORYISM)

Originally the party of the aristocracy and landed gentry. Conservatism has been supported since the end of the nineteenth century by large business interests. Industrial policy seeks to reconcile the need for central direction with encouragement of individual enterprise - ie. 'welfare capitalism'.

Its main characteristics are:
-   fear of social progress - it likes people to 'know their place', keep in it, and be good at it.
-   exaggerated respect for authority.
-   exaggerated respect for nationalism.
-   reactionary and dogmatic tendencies.

## HUMANISM

The struggle for release from religious authority. The main features are:
-   liberty of the intellect
-   faith in human progress
-   the belief that people can improve their own conditions without any supernatural help, and indeed, have a duty to do so.

-   the belief that religion is only an evolutionary process, and expression of yearning to understand the world. We grow out of it as we become mature.
-   the belief that science is evolutionary too, and gradually reveals the truth.

## CAPITALISM

An economic system in which the means of production and distribution are owned by a relatively small section of the society, which runs them at its own discretion for private profit. It arose towards the end of the eighteenth century in the UK, where the factory owners approved of free enterprise and free trade.

The main characteristics are:
-   it leads to economic inequality, the exploitation of the labour force, and the exploitation of the consuming public;
-   the system is motivated by private profit rather than public welfare;
-   it leads to recurrent economic crises - boom and bust - and instability; people can be ruined.

It does bring about efficient production and gives the strongest incentive to enterprise and good service.

## CHRISTIAN SOCIALISM

This movement was launched in 1848 (The Year of Revolutions). The main moving force was compassion because of the wretched conditions of workers.

The main characteristics are:

– disapproval of sweatshop industries, and 'sweated labour'

– disapproval of the consequences of unrestrained capitalism

– disapproval of the evils of the enclosure system

– encouraging co-operative workshops, working men's colleges, elementary education and the trade union movement.

## SOCIALISM

A society in which men and women are not divided into opposing economic classes, but live together under conditions of equality of opportunity, economic security, and a fair distribution of national wealth, using in common the means that lie in their hands of promoting social welfare and the Brotherhood of Man. Socialists aim to reorganize society by creating intelligent public opinion by education and legislation. They believe in:

– a planned economy

– public ownership of vital industries and services

– reforms in social justice and industrial efficiency.

Socialism can lead to:

– a regimentation of all social life;

– laziness, and couldn't care-less attitudes because of a generous welfare system and State ownership of industry;

– trades unions being able to disrupt other people's employment;

– economics coming before ethics, and

– individuals being reduced to mere economic units.

## LIBERALISM (THE WHIGS)

A progressive party in the sense that they appreciate all the humanistic aspects of Socialism, while strongly disapproving of State control.

Their chief characteristics are:

– dislike all monopolies, state or otherwise;

– belief in co-ownership of industry;

– Electoral reform to proportional representation

– tax reform and

– pro-Common Market/Europe policies.

## COMMUNISM

An extreme expression of socialism. In this system, all property belongs to the community, and social life is based on the principle 'from each according to his ability, to each according to his needs'.

It sounds good, but no such society yet exists. Communists attempt to overthrow existing systems and establish dictatorships of the proletariat.

Their first task is to establish socialism under which there remain class distinctions and private property, and differences between 'blue' and 'white' collar - (management and workers). In time, the system is supposed to give way to Communism through rising dissatisfaction.

There is no belief in a Divine Power, and all religious systems are condemned as delusions that have been used to keep the 'masses' from questioning or challenging the social order. All religion should be banned. All loyalty should go to the Party. The Party will organize co-operative farming and factories, and organize men and women as 'work units' with state care for their children.

This system can lead to highly corrupt

power struggles, and people at the bottom living in terror of those at the top.

## MATERIALISM

The belief that there is no supernatural order of things, no life after death or Judgement; the only things that have real meaning and value are therefore material, physical things.  Therefore progress is sought and measured through material comforts, successes and acquisitions.

## RELATIVISM

This system stresses that no single, universal criterion can be used to determine whether an action is ethical or not.  Each person uses his or her own criterion, and this criterion may vary from culture to culture - hence the ethical character of different social values and behaviours are seen within specific cultural contexts.

Businessmen engaging in activities in another country are bound by its norms and values.

## UTILITARIANISM

This system holds that the moral worth of personal conduct can be determined solely by the consequences of that behaviour.  An action is ethical if it results in the greatest benefit or 'good' for the largest number of people.  Hence, it is very income-orientated, and making as much money as possible becomes the main activity.

It ignores the basic question of what is wealth, pleasure or health, and what happens to the minorities? (For example, if the majority decide to legalize hard drugs, or accept sex without marriage, who will protect the interests of those who think otherwise?

# File on Muslim Welfare Organizations

## ISLAMIC RELIEF - IN PARTNERSHIP WITH THE NEEDY

Established in 1984, Islamic Relief is an independent relief and development organization providing humanitarian aid during emergencies and working for the long term development of the world's poorest nations. The aim is to alleviate poverty and suffering wherever and whenever it occurs.

Through working in partnership with the needy, Islamic Relief's work directly benefits an estimated 25 million people each year.

Since 1984, Islamic Relief has established its reputation as a pioneer in the provision of emergency aid for the victims of conflict or natural disasters, its work spanning across Africa, Asia and Europe. Islamic Relief was one of the first aid agencies to provide emergency relief to Bosnia and Chechnya.

Alongside its emergency relief programmes, Islamic Relief also invests in several long-term development projects such as the provision of clean water. The lack of access to clean and safe water accounts for 80% of the world's curable diseases. 25,000 children die every day from water-related diseases. Islamic Relief provides tubewells, piped water systems and wells serving whole communities.

From Bosnia to Bangladesh, from Albania to Pakistan, Islamic Relief's community-based health projects include the provision of vaccinations, nutritional foods, medical equipment, feeding centres, outpatient clinics, training for health workers and programmes for the disabled, mothers and children.

A decent education and vocational skills can help break the cycle of poverty. It can also potentially help people to become more self-sufficient by earning their own livelihoods. Today, over 800 million children still do not attend school. In South Asia alone, around 420 million people are illiterate.

Islamic Relief's education and vocational training projects provide school materials, classes in adult literacy, computers, sewing, tailoring, food processing and languages. Islamic Relief also recognizes the specific needs of women in this area of its work.

The fine example left behind by the Prophet Muhammad forms the basis of Islamic Relief's Orphan Welfare Programme. The programme is designed to provide sustained support to thousands of needy children worldwide and the benefits are intended to reach their families and communities too, insha'Allah.

At Islamic Relief, Ramadan provides a welcome opportunity to reflect on our work. Ramadan is not only about fasting, but also forgiveness and feeding the needy. Islamic Relief provides poor and vulnerable people with food packets containing essential food items like flour, sugar, oil and other essential ingredients. 'Id-ul-Fitr for children is made extra special with 'Id Gifts, bringing smiles to their faces!

The Sunnah of Prophet Ibrahim recommends the performance of Qurbani where the meat of an animal is offered in the name of Allah. This is associated with 'Id-ul-Adha, a major celebration in the Islamic calendar. It is also a time to remember the less fortunate for whom meat would be a luxury item in their diets. Islamic Relief offers Qurbanis on behalf of its donors and around 150,000 people benefit from an average 15,000 that we offer annually. Islamic Relief was also a pioneering force in the canning of Qurbani meat.

In the UK, Islamic Relief's Community Support Scheme extends financial assistance to organizations offering a service to the community such as Schools, Women's Groups, Service Providers for Refugees etc.

None of Islamic Relief's work could have been achieved alone without the blessings of Allah and the generosity and valued support of many committed individuals from all over the world.

There is still much more that needs to be done and many more people to reach, but together with your help we can go from strength to strength.

*'The likeness of those who spend their wealth in the Way of Allah, is as the likeness of a grain (of corn); it grows seven ears, and each ear has a hundred grains. Allah gives manifold increase to whom He pleases. And Allah is all-Sufficient for His creatures' needs, All-Knower.'(2:261).*

## ISLAMIC RELIEF IN BiH

Islamic Relief started its activities in Bosnia in April 1992 and has remained active in the area since then. Activities were co-ordinated from Sarajevo and in the early years from Zagreb (Croatia). Offices are now established in Sarajevo, Tuzla and Zenica.

The years up to 1995 were dominated with relief and emergency projects due to the ongoing war and destruction in the country. The war caused hunger, homelessness and destruction of services and infrastructure which affected every aspect of peoples' lives. The displaced people who had forcibly been uprooted from their homes in areas like Srebrenica and Zepa also had to be supported. The activities during this period included:

- Food distribution (including Ramadan and Qurbani)
- Medicine distribution
- Refugee Camps
- Orphan sponsorship
- Cultural Activities
- Providing heating sources to residents through provision of gas, coal and wood.
- Supporting women victims of the war through various activities including counselling
- Small local projects which focused on local production of food. This included bread, milk, eggs, tomato sauce etc.

One of largest projects that was embarked upon was in Gunya in Croatia supporting refugees from BiH with income generating and livestock restocking projects. All of these were much needed, yet Islamic Relief also realized that a time would come when the country would need to be rehabilitated and developed through more long term projects. Hence in 1995 it was decided to embark on some development projects while still continuing various relief activities. As the war subsided more emphasis was given to the given to the long term projects as this would lay the foundation for Bosnia being able to stand upon its own feet in the future.

## WATER & SANITATION PROGRAMME (WSP)

Water is a natural, but often scarce resource, essential for human life and all other bio systems. Islamic Relief Worldwide recognizes this, hence it has initiated a water and sanitation Programme.

Many countries in North Africa suffer from inadequate water supply. In areas like South Asia although water as a whole is not scarce the water network and the quality of water is very poor. A significant amount of children and adults lose their lives due to diarrhoea related diseases. In fact more than 2 million deaths from diarrhoea alone could be avoided each year if all people had reasonable water and sanitation services.

The shortage of water very often affects the agricultural capacity of a country. This is of extra importance in the developing countries where a large amount of the population are involved in agriculture. By far the majority of the water used by man goes into growing of crops. Most of this water is from rain falling directly on fields and the farmer is the passive recipient. In arid or semi-arid areas the low or erratic rainfall can be the cause of crop failure and the resulting food shortages affect more people on a regular basis than any other disaster.

- 25,000 children die every day from water related diseases.
- 80% of the sickness in the world is due to unsafe water and poor sanitation.

    Many people in the world suffer from either water shortages or the lack of access to safe water. It is estimated that at least 30% of the world's population still does not have access to safe water. Water is, of course, an essential resource and one that is taken for granted in the developed world.

- A family of six needs over 90 litres (20 gallons) of water a day, just for basic drinking, cooking, and keeping clean.
- Outpatient Centre, Bangladesh

    Islamic Relief Worldwide Outpatient Centre in Rangpur was established in 1993 and offers health services such as vaccination and the diagnosis of illnesses, as well as providing general health education. Thousands of people have received help to date.

- Harelip/Clef Palate Operations, Pakistan

    This is an initiative undertaken by IRW in conjunction with Child Care International (CCI), a Birmingham based charity. This was in response to the harrowing plight of those children suffering from a facial deformity known as Harelip and/or Cleft Palate. Simple plastic surgery can, insha'Allah, rectify this disorder. The actual surgery can be done quite cheaply because volunteer doctors are willing to offer their services for free.

- Supplementary Feeding, Sudan

    Islamic Relief with the help of UNICEF in Sudan is running a feeding centre in the Al-Shareel area of El-Obeid to treat cases of malnutrition and diarrhoea, which is a big killer in poor countries. The number of diarrhoea cases in the area has risen dramatically and already 548 children and 290 women have received help from the centre. Plans are being made to extend the same facilities to the Allah-Karim area of the town.

- School for Impaired hearing, Sudan

    IRW's school for deaf and hearing impaired children in El-Obeid, Sudan has increased greatly in size. It has grown from one class with twelve students to four classes with twelve students each. After essential refurbishment the school opened in September 1995. The school is a unique institution in the area and provides a stimulating, happy environment in which children are able to gain a sense of self-worth. Both pupils and teachers are extremely proud of their school

• Ophthalmic Visits, Sudan

Islamic Relief Worldwide (IRW) has sent volunteers to several of our development projects around the world. Dr.Ahmed Sadiq, a registrar in Ophthalmology, pointed out that although the clinical work done is very good, it is significantly hampered by the lack of equipment, facilities instruments and medication.

## INCOME GENERATION

Islamic Relief Worldwide (IRW) recognizes the need for poor people to initiate their own enterprises so that they may endeavour to provide for themselves and their families.

## RURAL POVERTY

Rural poverty is often characterized by a lack of assets as well as income. Land is an important source of income and status, some of the poorest people have no land holdings and therefore have to resort to finding employment, which is not always easy to come by and is usually very poorly paid. Studies have shown that there is a definite link between landlessness and poverty. The lack of landholdings also makes it difficult for the poor to secure loans because they have no collateral. The rural poor find themselves having to resort to money lenders for loans instead, this

means having to pay very high interest rates which leads to increasing debts. Self-employment thus becomes a desirable option but is hard to achieve if access to credit cannot be obtained.

## LIVESTOCK PROJECTS

Not only is the lack of landholding a major problem for the rural poor, but so is the lack of any livestock holdings. Animals are often the mainstay of any rural household providing an ongoing source of food such as milk, by providing meat, or even manure for fertilization of crops. Livestock, therefore, become an important asset to a rural family. This is especially so in areas of malnutrition.

## THE COMMUNITY ACTION PROGRAMME, BANGALADESH

The Community Action Programme (CAP), formerly known as Islamic Relief Rural Aid Programme (IRRAP), is located in the districts of Rangpur, Bangladesh. Through the establishment of local groups (shomities) it aims to initiate income generating activities by developing local savings and credit schemes. Local people save a certain amount of money each week and this is (along with Islamic Relief's support) then used to finance such activities.

The need for poor people to be involved in income generating activities is so that they can be free from the constraints of poverty. This becomes easier to understand when you become familiar with the conditions that poor people in the developing world have to face. Knowledge about these conditions is important in knowing how to help.

## SADAQA JARIYYA (CONTINUOUS CHARITY)

This is usually a Deed of Covenant for the most efficient and tax effective form for helping the poor and needy.

The most valuable way you can support Islamic Relief is to give regular donations by completing a covenant form. This is the easiest and most cost effective way to administer your gift to the poorest people around the world. Your Gift will be increased by 33% at no extra cost to you, as each time your donation is received, they can reclaim from the Income Tax you have already paid to the Inland Revenue.

Anybody who pays Income Tax in the United Kingdom can make a covenant.

When signing a Deed of Covenant, you should intend if to last for a minimum of 4 years. But in cases of financial difficulties, it is possible to cancel before then.

If you don't pay income tax, you can still make a regular gift to Islamic Relief by filling out the Banker's Order form only. Alternatively, one off donations can be made at any time by cheque or postal order.

## THE ORPHAN WELFARE PROGRAMME

The aim of this project is to help needy orphans world wide by supplying them with assistance in the form of health care, education, nutrition and income. Over 4,000 orphans have been supported since 1986.

As Muslims we are aware of the great rewards of helping orphans. The prophet, peace be upon him said: 'I and the person who looks after an orphan and provides for him, will be in paradise like this.' (As he placed his index and middle fingers together.)

All humans have basic needs. We take these needs for granted. Many people around the world are deprived of the basic necessities such as education, health services, shelter, safe and clean water. Children and especially orphans are most vulnerable and as a result suffer the most. Islamic Relief seeks to address the problem through the Orphan Welfare Programme (OWP). The programme aims at pooling the funds of contributors in order to provide support and services not only to the child but also to the family and the community as a whole.

*Section Four*

# THE SET PASSAGES

# On what Muslims believe about the nature of God

Surah 1, Surah 2: 115-117, Surah 6: 95-99, Surah 30 : 20-25,

Surah 112

The set passages are taken from Yusuf Ali's translation.

(This does not necessarily indicate that his is the best translation, but it is the most widely available. In my own opinion, that of Muhammad Asad is the best).

If you know any other relevant passages, that's fine - but these passages are specifically mentioned by the GCSE Syllabus, and are required reading.

## SURAH 1

| 1:1 | In the name of God, Most Gracious, Most Merciful |
|-----|--------------------------------------------------|
| 1:2 | Praise be to God, The Cherisher and Sustainer of the Worlds; |
| 1:3 | Most Gracious, Most Merciful; |
| 1:4 | Master of the Day of Judgement. |
| 1:5 | You alone do we worship, and we seek aid from You alone. |
| 1:6 | Show us the straight way, |
| 1:7 | The way of those on whom Thou hast bestowed Thy grace, those whose (portion) Is not wrath, and who go not astray. |

This surah is often called al-Fatihah - the Opener; Umm al-Kitab - the 'Mother of Books' - the essence of Divine Revelation; Surat al-Hamd - the Surah of Praise; Asas al-Qur'an - the Foundation of the Qur'an; and as-Sab al-Mathani - the Seven Oft-Repeated verses (because it is repeated so often in the daily salat).

The Prophet himself called it 'Umm al-Kitab' (Bukhari).

It contains, in condensed form, all the fundamental teachings laid down in the Qur'an about Allah:

- His Oneness and Uniqueness
- that He is Creator and the Power sustaining the worlds/universes
- that He cares for all the worlds/universes
- that He gives blessings and is merciful, and is the source of all life-giving grace.
- that He is the One to whom we are ultimately responsible
- that He is the Judge of all His created beings, and that judgement will take place at a particular time
- that He is the only power that can really guide and help us in our lives
- that He is the motivation for righteous action in this life

- that He is worshipped and adored, once He is 'realised'
- that He is the One Who can grant blessings, and is aware of those going wrong
- that there will be Life after Death, and a consequence for our actions
- that He can and has shown us the right path through message-bearers (the prophets)

In fact, God needs no praise; for He is above all praise. He does not need to be told the things we ask for; He knows our needs better than we do ourselves. His generous compassion and blessings are open, without asking, to the righteous person and the sinner alike. This prayer is for our own spiritual education, consolation and encouragement.

That is why the words in this surah are given in the form in which we should say them.

'The Most Gracious (or Compassionate)' in Arabic is 'ar-Rahman'.

'The Most Merciful' in Arabic is 'ar-Rahim'. Both these words stem from the same root - 'loving tenderness'

(Note: in Arabic, the word 'the' is 'al'. When this is followed by certain letters of the alphabet, the 'l' is dropped, and the first letter of the next word replaces it; so, al-Rahman is pronounced ar-Rahman; al-Dar is pronounced ad-Dar; al-Salaam is pronounced as-Salaam; al-Shahadah is pronounced ash-Shahadah; al-Nur is pronounced an-Nur.)

In the English language, the meaning is not quite as it is in Arabic. If we say 'the most' anything, it implies a comparison (good, better, best); in Arabic, it means that there is no being that can compare to God.

'Mercy' implies pity, long-suffering patience and forgiveness, all of which we need, and which always flow from God

towards us. There is a mercy which goes before the need for them arises, the grace which is ever-watchful, giving guidance and protection. For this reason, the term ar-Rahman is not applied to any other than God, and means the quality of abounding grace inseparable from the concept of God's Being; the quality of ar-Rahim is a term which expresses the action of God in delivering that grace and mercy, and its effects upon us. The term could apply to human beings too, if they were compassionate.

This phrase is placed before every surah except surah 9 (which may originally have been a continuation of surah 8), and is said at the beginning of every act undertaken by a devout Muslim.

The word 'Rabb' is often translated as 'Lord', the one with authority over everything. It also means Cherisher, Sustainer, and Bringer of everything started to its final completion. God cares for all He has created.

(For example; Nasut, the physical world

knowable by our senses; Malakut, the invisible world of angels; and Lahut, the divine world of Reality).

When we become aware of God's love and care, mercy and grace, power and justice, we also become aware of our own shortcomings and His all-sufficient power. We worship Him, and ask Him for His help, and realise there is no point in asking any other for help.

God is the True Guide. We may be wandering aimlessly, and in the dark. Our first step is to find the Way, and the second step to keep on it. Our own wisdom may not be enough to do this. The Straight Path is often 'the narrow way' or 'the steep path' which most people turn away from, because it is hard. It is an irony that in our society the Straight Way is often stigmatized and laughed at, whereas the Crooked Way is praised by the masses. We can only judge correctly with the help of God's guidance.

As regards God's grace, it flows towards all people way beyond what they deserve. As regards His anger, our own actions are responsible for this, as a result of our falling for temptations or becoming careless. It applies to the evil consequences we bring upon ourselves by wilfully rejecting God's guidance, and acting against His laws.

## SURAH 2: 115-117

2:115 To God belong the East and the West: whithersoever ye turn, there is the Presence of God. For God is All-Pervading, All-Knowing.

2:116 They say: "God hath begotten a son": Glory be to Him. - Nay, to Him belongs all that is in the heavens and on earth: everything renders worship to Him.

2:117 To Him is due the primal origin of the heavens and the earth: when He decreeth a matter, He saith to it: "Be'" and it is.

It is utter nonsense, in fact a blasphemy, to believe that God could procreate in a human or animal way, and have sons or daughters.

God does not have a material nature. The expression 'subhana' (glory) applied exclusively to God, implies His utter remoteness from any imperfection, or any likeness to any created being or thing.

God certainly does not have a physical body, and is not involved in the processes of the physical body, such as sex, eating or excretion.

That which is purely spiritual lies beyond that which is physical.

These verses therefore repudiate the Christian doctrine of Jesus being the Son of God. Muslims believe that Jesus was indeed specially created from a virgin mother, but although this was miraculous, it did not make him in any way divine - he was a prophet like all the other messengers/ prophets.

In the spiritual sense, we are all the children of God, and can completely agree with Jesus when he prayed: 'Our Father, who is in Heaven'.

Heaven and earth are not in themselves eternal; they were caused to be, and created. They need not necessarily have ever existed. The fact that they do exist means that they were caused to do so. Muslims (and Jews and Christians) believe that God was the ultimate Cause.

If there was a particular method of creation, such as a Big Bang, it does not mean that God does not exist, but that He caused those conditions to be or take place.

Materialists may say that matter is eternal; there is no proof whatsoever. Things as we know them now came into being (and once did not exist) and will perish.

God's 'amr (His Command, Direction, Design) is unrelated to Time.

6:95 'It is God Who causeth the seed-grain and the date-stone to split and sprout. He causeth the living to issue from the dead, and He is the One to cause the dead to issue from the living. That is God: then how are ye deluded away from the truth?

6:96 He it is that cleaveth the day-break (from the dark): He makes the night for rest and tranquillity, and the sun and moon for the reckoning (of time): such is the judgement and ordering of (Him), the Exalted in Power, the Omniscient.

6:97 It is He Who maketh the stars (as beacons) for you, that ye may guide yourselves, with their help, through the dark spaces of land and sea: We detail Our Signs for people who know.

6:98 It is He Who hath produced you from a single soul (nafs) Here is a place of departure: We detail Our signs For people who understand.

6:99 It is He Who sendeth down rain from the skies: with it We produce vegetation of all kinds: from some We produce green (crops), out of which We produce grain, heaped up (at harvest); out of the date-palm and its sheaths (or spathes) (come) clusters of dates hanging low and near:

And (then there are) gardens of grapes, and olives, and pomegranates, each similar (in kind) yet different (in variety): when they begin to bear fruit, feast your eyes with the fruit and the ripeness thereof. Behold! in these things there are Signs for people who believe.'

This is a beautiful passage concerning God's wonders of creation, and the Signs we are to find in it.

The first thought is of the wonders involved even in our simple animal needs - the seedgrain and datestone splitting in order to sprout and provide us with food.

This leads to a contemplation of the interaction of the living and the dead. In the realm of nature as we know it, the borders between living and non-living, organic and non-organic, are mysteries. For example, iron is a 'dead' thing, and yet we can make it alive by eating vegetation that has absorbed it through its roots; once we have eaten it, it becomes part of our physical body-matter - and once anything has become living, it goes on being living through the cycle of reproduction and also of decay and return to the 'humus' which makes us 'human'. The Prophet Jesus also used the image of a seed, which seems to be dead, but yet if it is buried (planted) it sprouts up to become one of life's forms. And this is also a mystery - for who could guess without knowing in advance, that a particular seed would turn into wheat, or a huge tree, or a human being with all its genetic possibilities?

We have the daily miracle of morning, noon and night, and the concept of Time, measured by us through reference to astronomical features - sun, moon and stars. Beyond this, we have the Theory of Relativity (Einstein's theory), and the awareness that Time is only relative to where we are and the speed at which we are travelling. In the realm of Eternity and Infinity, there is no Time.

We think about the sign that we can actually put astronomical creations to practical use - like using the stars for navigation; to us, they seem to remain in the same relative position - yet astronomers have proved they (and we) are moving at incredible speeds according to the laws of the universe.

We think about the mystery of the origin of the human soul, and the countless millions of individuals who have sprung from that one original soul, and its division into male and female. The word given in verse 98 as 'person' is 'nafs' in Arabic; this does not mean a first human being, but soul or self in the sphere beyond the human/ physical. Therefore, the implication is that human beings, male and female, all derived from an original single soul - and not that

woman derived from man. Therefore it follows, of course, that male and female are part of the same whole, and equal.

We are to think about the 'sojourn' or 'stay' of our particular soul on this earth, and the ultimate destiny towards which we are progressing.

We are to think about the physical blessings God grants us in our universe, and the spiritual fruits for those who understand the Signs, with the aid of God's mercy.

There is a refrain in this passage, which develops as it goes along:

v.97 - 'We detail Our signs for people who know';

v.98 - 'We detail Our signs for people who understand';

v.99 - 'In these things are signs for people who believe'.

The passage has an allegorical meaning of coming from nothingness into life through the seed; our daily life passes through the realm of Time; the spiritual experience of passing into the vast reaches of the spiritual world guided through our faith; our growth and development, and the final harvest when we reap the fruits of our faith.

So many different kinds and species of fruits - how like the different kinds of human beings, who might be completely different, yet of equal value.

30:18 Yea, to Him be praise, in the heavens and on earth; and in the late afternoon and when the day begins to decline.

30:19 It is He Who brings out the living from the dead, And brings out the dead from the living, and Who gives life to the earth after it is dead: And thus shall ye be brought out (from the dead).

30:20 Among His Signs is this, that He created you from dust; and then - behold, ye are men scattered (far and wide)!

30:21 And among His Signs is this, that He created for you mates from among yourselves, that ye may dwell in tranquility with them. And He has put love and mercy between your (hearts); verily in that are Signs for those who reflect.

30:22 And among His Signs is the creation of the heavens and the earth, and the variations in your languages and your colours: verily in that are signs for those who know.

30:23 And among His Signs is the sleep that ye take by night and by day, and the quest that ye (make for livelihood) out of His bounty : verily in that are Signs for those who hearken.

30:24 And among His Signs, He shows you the lightning, by way both of fear and hope, and He sends down rain from the sky and with it gives life to the earth after it is dead: verily in that are Signs for those who are wise.

30:25 And among His Signs is this, that heaven and earth stand by His command: then when He calls you, by a single call, from the earth, behold, ye (straightway) come forth.'

Although human beings are created 'from dust' - (the word 'Adam' comes from 'admah' meaning 'dust' or 'mud'; the word 'human' comes from the living part of that dust - the 'humus') - they have a mind and soul which can in part understand the farthest reaches of Time and Space. This is, in itself, a sign for us.

The simplest of living cell-structures, once in existence, are in a way eternal - because they endlessly grow and divide and produce identical copies of themselves. At some stage in our evolution, a stage still in the realms of mystery, came the origin of sex. At some point the living cells stopped being just 'carbon copies', but became male and female. This then led to sexual reproduction, with children arising out of the union of the sexes. Moreover, it is the male that sends forth seed, and the female that produces eggs to fertilise, and then carries and brings forth the child, whether that child is male or female.

All the genetic possibilities for the future child originate in the bodies of two separate people, a male and female; the future characteristics and character of the child-to-be are all programmed into the moment of fusion between seed and egg.

One of God's special signs is the flowering of love between men and women, and the growth of special relationships between them in marriage. The love and mercy felt by family members for each other is different in kind from that felt towards other people.

Another sign is the variety of God's creations; all humans are human, yet there is enormous variety in type, race, colour, language, etc. No one kind is more beloved by God than any other - they are all God's creations.

Another sign is the gift of sleep; it is full

of wonders. It brings refreshment and healing, it gives us an altered state of consciousness and the possibility of experiences we cannot have whilst waking (eg flying), it gives us all kinds of experiences through dreams. The Qur'an suggests that during sleep our souls may leave our bodies, and in this way, experience for brief spells an existence that is outside the human body.

Thus, we have here a series of signs to awaken our souls and lead us to Reality:

- our origin and destiny

- the first beginnings of social life through sex and love

- to understand our diversities through differences of climate and external conditions

- the awareness of unity in our diversity

- our psychological conditions leading to insight into our higher reaches of spiritual hopes and fears.

We are asked to think about the subtle forces of nature such as lightning or electricity, which may kill or bring prosperity; the rain cycle, which can bring deserts or abundant fertility.

We are asked to think about the whole of creation standing or falling by His command - it could disappear in the twinkling of an eye.

We are asked to think about our own souls; even if we believe that when we die that is the end of it, and we will not be answerable at all for our actions in some mysterious place in an Afterlife - that is not the case at all; when God summons us, we will be unable not to be brought before Him.

## SURAH 40: 61-68.

40:61 'It is God Who has made the Night for you, that ye may rest therein, and the Day, as that which helps (you) to see. Verily God is full of grace and bounty to men: yet most men give no thanks.

40:62 Such is God, your Lord, the Creator of all things, There is no God but He; then how ye are deluded away from the Truth!

40:63 Thus are deluded those who are wont to reject the Signs of God.

40:64 It is God Who has made for you the earth as a resting place, and the sky as a canopy, and has given you shape-and made your shapes beautiful, -and has provided for you sustenance, of things pure and good; - such is God your Lord. So glory to God, The Lord of the Worlds!

40:65 He is the Living (One): there is no God but He: call upon Him, giving Him sincere devotion. Praise be to God, Lord of the Worlds!

40:66 Say: "I have been forbidden to invoke those whom ye invoke besides God, -seeing that the Clear Signs have come to me from my Lord; and I have been commanded to bow (in Islam) to the Lord of the Worlds."

40:67 It is He Who has created you from dust, then from a sperm-drop, then from a leech-like clot; then does He get you out (into the light) as a child: then lets you (grow and) reach your age of full strength; then lets you become old,- though of you there are some who die before;-and lets you reach a term appointed; in order that ye may learn wisdom.

40:68 It is He Who gives Life And Death; and when He decides upon an affair, He says to it, "Be", and it is.'

The phases of night and day are often used as a symbol to draw attention to God's mercy and blessing. It is all part of His mystery - another thing for us to ponder; did we evolve with bodies needing to rest and recuperate because God had organized the astronomical features of our particular world so that the motion of sun, moon and earth gave us Night and Day? Which came first, the chicken or the egg?

If we are deluded and led astray by false and superstitious beliefs, we must be ignoring the signs God has given us in His created universe, and not grasping the deep principles.

The earth on which we live is only a temporary resting-place for us; our real and eternal lives are the lives of our souls, which come from outside the physical universe, and will return to a realm outside the physical universe.

God, when we begin to understand Him, is the Only Reality; we must take our standard and inspiration from Him - we must bring our own will and actions into unison with His Reality. This is the meaning and aim of Islam. When we do bow to the Real and Everlasting, we are saved from falling victims to that which is false and will swiftly pass away.

Verse 67 deals with the stages of human physical life and development;

- firstly, simple matter (dust)
- the minute individual sperm in the father
- the fertilized ovum in the mother's womb
- the birth as a human child
- youth and full maturity
- decay and old age
- death.

In some cases, the later stages apart from death are never reached, but for each individual God has allocated a set time, and in that set time he or she is to seek for wisdom.

Life and death are in God's 'hands'. Whatever He wills, comes to pass - whether this is to create or to annihilate. it will come to pass, no matter what the individual human being is doing, or wants, or begs for. We have to live in order to be ready for that moment when we will give up our life; but we need to know that we never will be ready. A good rule of thumb is to live every day as if it was to be your last; live, as though you were going to die tomorrow, love, as though you were going to live forever.

## SURAH 112

> In the name of God,
> Most Gracious, Most Merciful.
> 112:1 'Say: He is God, the One and Only;
> 112:2 God, the Eternal, Absolute;
> 112:3 He begetteth not, nor is He begotten;
> 112:4 And there is none like unto Him.'

The Prophet used to describe this surah as 'equivalent to one third of the whole Qur'an (Bukhari,Muslim, etc). It was revealed in the early Makkah period.

Allah is One, and Unique in every

respect, without beginning and without end. He is so sublime, so far beyond our limited Understanding, that the feeling that He is a Personality is only our best way to try to think about Him.

We call God 'He', but 'He' is not a 'he'. 'He' is beyond any notion of humanity or sexuality.

There is nothing that can be compared to God, therefore we can never adequately describe or define Him.

The quality of His Being is beyond the range of human comprehension or imagination. Anything that we can think of is based on His creation, and cannot be in any way comparable to Him.

Any attempt at making artistic or figurative representations of God, or even abstract symbols to 'describe' Him, cannot possibly come anywhere near the truth, and are illusions.

However, we feel that He is near us, He cares for us, and we owe our existence to Him.

He is Eternal, not limited by time or place or circumstance.

We must not think of him as having a father, or a son; His qualities and nature are unique.

In verse 2, the word translated as 'Absolute' is 'Samad' in Arabic. This is the only place in the Qur'an where this word is used, and it is very difficult to translate. It is a concept applied to God Alone - that God is the Primary Cause, the Eternal and independent Being, and that everything existing or conceivable goes ultimately back to Him as its source, and is therefore dependent on Him for its beginning as well as for its continued existence. All other existence is temporal and conditional. He is dependent on nothing, but all other persons and things are dependent on Him.

These verses teach the falseness of any belief in many gods (polytheism) or that God is part of Nature (pantheism) or that God could have physical or incarnate offspring (a common feature in many ancient religions, and in Christianity).

# On the roles and status of women and men

Surah 16: 97
Surah 2: 228
Surah 3: 34

If you know any other relevant passages, that's fine - but the ones given above are the required passages.

## SURAH 16: 97

> 16:97 'Whoever works righteousness, man or woman, and has faith, verily, to him will We give a new life, a life that is good and pure, and We will bestow on such their reward according to the best of their actions'.

In Arabic, whenever it mentions 'he' or 'him', it really implies both 'he and she', or 'him and her'. It is a characteristic of the language that when both sexes are being referred to, usually only 'he' is written, instead of the more modern 'they' - which correctly does not imply either sex, but both.

This is one of the Qur'an passages that emphasizes 'man or woman', so that it is crystal clear that both are included.

Both sexes have spiritual as well as human rights and duties to an equal degree, and the future reward is to both equally.

The important things in Islam are to have faith in God, and to live good lives. Faith, if sincere, means right living - when faith and right living go hand in hand, our lives are transformed by God's grace. Instead of being troubled and worried, we enjoy calm and gain purity and contentment. The transformation is visible in this life, but the reward in the Life to Come will be far beyond what we have earned or deserved

We will be rewarded in the Afterlife according to the best of our actions.

## SURAH 33 : 35

> 33:35 'For Muslim men and women, for believing men and women, for devout men and women, for true men and women, for men and women who are patient and constant, for men and women who humble themselves, for men and women who give in charity, for men and women who fast (and deny themselves), for men and women who guard their chastity, and for men and women who engage much in God's praise,-for them has God prepared forgiveness and great reward.'

Once again, both men and women are specifically referred to. This verse was given in response to a question posed by the Prophet's wife Umm Salamah. She knew that the revelations always seemed to refer to 'he' and asked about it. The Prophet was granted this specific revelation as a direct reply to her question.

The virtues to be rewarded are:
-   faith, hope, and trust in God, and in His benevolent government of the world;
-   devotion and service to Him in our

practical daily lives,

- love and practice of truth, in thought, intention, word and deed.
- patience and constancy, in suffering and in our right efforts.
- humility, and the avoidance of an attitude of arrogance or supremacy.
- charity - help to the poor and unfortunate.
- the duty of service in His name.
- self-denial, not only in food but in all appetites.
- chastity and purity in our sexual relationships and in thought, word and deed.
- constant attention to God's message.
- Encouragement of the desire to get nearer to God.

For people who build up these virtues, there will be a great reward in the Life to Come.

## SURAH 2: 228

> 2:228 'Divorced women shall wait concerning themselves for three monthly periods. Nor is it lawful for them to hide what God hath created in their wombs, if they have faith in God and the Last Day. And their husbands have the better right to take them back in that period, if they wish for reconciliation. And women shall have rights similar to the rights against them, according to what is equitable; but men have a degree (Of advantage) over them. And God is Exalted in Power, Wise.'

Of all the things permitted by God, divorce is the thing He most dislikes. In the circumstances, God will forgive those who feel that they must divorce, for He knows the real grievances of both parties, and hears the cry of all who suffer.

Islam tries to maintain and preserve the married state as far as possible, especially when there are children involved, but it does not insist that people are condemned to suffer unhappy lives together if they really cannot find peace between themselves.

So, hasty action is checked, to leave the door of reconciliation open at several stages. Even after a divorce, a suggestion of reconciliation is made, subject to certain precautions.

A period of waiting (iddah - pl.iddat) for three months is ordained, in order to see whether or not the marriage just set aside is still likely to result in the birth of a child. This is not necessary where the divorced woman has not consummated her marriage and is still a virgin, or when a divorced woman has actually been delivered of a child. Her iddat ends with the birth of the child.

The differences in the economic situation of men and women in most Muslim societies is what makes the man's rights and liabilities a little greater than the woman's. It does not mean that the man is superior, or has greater rights. The man has the duty to maintain the woman, and the weaker sex is entitled to special protection in Islamic law. The word 'but' has the meaning here of 'since' or 'because'.

## SURAH 4 : 34-35

> 4:34 'Men are the protectors and maintainers of women, because God has given the one more (strength) than the other, and because they support them from their means. Therefore the righteous women are devoutly

obedient, and guard in (the husband's) absence what God would have them guard.

As to those women on whose part ye fear disloyalty and ill-conduct, admonish them (first), (next), refuse to share their beds, (and last) beat them (lightly); but if they return to obedience, seek not against them means (of annoyance):

For God is Most High, Great (above you all).

4:35 If ye fear a breach between them twain, appoint (two) arbiters, one from his family, and the other from hers; If they wish for peace, God will cause their reconciliation: for God hath full knowledge, and is acquainted With all things.'

This verse also deals with the subject of divorce, and the relationship between men and women; it is probably the most controversial verse in the Qur'an, because it appears at first sight to give Muslim men permission to beat their wives, and enemies of Islam are quick to seize this verse to point out the 'cruelties' of Islam, and the subordinate position of women. This is not a fair criticism at all, as will be explained.

Firstly, the verse states that men are intended to be the protectors and maintainers of women, and this is something that Muslims accept. The word 'qawwam' does not imply a domineering boss or master, but rather means 'one who stands firm in the business of others, protects their interests, and looks after their affairs'. Some translations of the Qur'an have used the word 'guardians' which has a somewhat different - meaning, as if the women were indeed inferior. This is not what the word implies. Protectors and supporters is the true Islamic sense - the men are to take care of their women. (Muhammad Asad's translation is : 'Men shall take full care of women with the bounties which God has bestowed more abundantly on the former than on the latter, and with what they may spend out of their possessions').

Why should men protect and support women? The reason given is because they have the ability to earn income. At the time the Qur'an was revealed, that was certainly the case for the vast majority; moreover, women had virtually no access to birth control, and so were unable to do much more than child-rearing for a large part of their married lives. However, the Qur'an was not intended just for those times, but for all people, in all times. Those who believe in a modernistic approach to the teachings always look to the spirit and principles taught; it could easily be argued that in this day and age the women are often the breadwinners while the men are unemployed. As situations change, so one has to look into the spirit and meaning of the Qur'anic text to see Allah's intention. It was that women should be given full support and assistance, and should be able to rely on a man to look after them. Men do not suffer the physical problems involved with menstruation, pregnancy, childbirth and breastfeeding, with all the hormonal upheavals that go along with these things.

It does not mean that a woman should not go out to work, but that in a Muslim marriage, she should not be obliged to do so, in order to make ends meet. It is the husband's duty to provide, and the wife's to provide the comfort and safe haven of a loving home.

(It is perhaps worth mentioning that the Prophet's first wife Khadijah had already produced at least four children before she married him, and ran a successful trading business. She was the Prophet's employer before she became his wife. She then went on to have six children by him, when she was over forty. Of the Prophet's later wives, it is known that Zaynab bint Jahsh earned her own income in the leather trade, and Umm Salamah and Safiyyah also earned their own incomes.)

A good wife can always be trusted. While her husband is there with her, she should strive to be cheerful and encouraging towards him; when he is absent, she should take care of his household, his property and his reputation - by guarding her own virtue. If she has accepted a position sheltered by him, she should for her part justify that position by the way she lives and loves.

It is vitally important that a woman should always take care to marry a man that she does respect, and whose wishes she can obey with content. If her husband is unreasonable, or selfish, or abusive, she will never be content. This is a good reason why marriages are arranged with such care, often without the seducing atmosphere of emotional love. If a woman does not respect her husband, perhaps because he is inferior mentally or morally, how can she obey him?

If a man expects his wife to do anything contrary to the will of God - in other words, any nasty, selfish, dishonest or cruel action, etc - she has the right to refuse him. Her husband is not her master; a Muslim woman has only one Master, and that is Allah. So long as her husband represents Allah's will in the home, well and good. If he does not, how can she obey?

If a husband finds that his wife has become disloyal to him, and is conducting herself to his shame, then he may not just ignore this, but it is his duty to do something about it. Yusuf Ali's translation of 'disloyalty and misconduct' refer to the Arabic term 'nushuz' (Lit. 'rebellion'). This really means ill-will, every kind of deliberate bad behaviour of a wife towards a husband (or vice versa), including what is today called 'mental cruelty'. With reference to the husband, it also denotes physical ill-treatment of his wife; in this context, it seems that a wife's ill-will implies a deliberate and persistent breach of her marital obligations.

With luck, it may be enough just to point something out verbally. Communication is everything in a relationship, especially in a marriage. However, the text implies that things have gone beyond this point.

If she takes no notice, then the relationship is starting to break down. A husband could then find it difficult to sleep with his wife, and might begin the separation. This is usually such a serious step in a marriage that it clarifies the mind, and the couple are brought to the stage of talking things through and reaching some agreement.

If that fails, a Muslim man has the right in the last resort to try physical assertion. Every translation of the Qur'an makes it clear that a brutal beating is not what is allowed. (One scholarly commentator thought that the phrase meant to overwhelm one's wife and woo her into bed!). This is one place in which the sunnah of the Prophet is so vital in making meanings clear - the Prophet insisted that a man should never beat a woman, and most certainly never hit her about the face or head. He could hardly expect to hit his wife and then expect her to calmly share his bed later that night. No Muslim man should ever hit 'one of Allah's handmaidens'. All these things were clear statements of the Prophet, and make it quite evident that to rebuke a woman physically for her misconduct in marriage was definitely only to be a last resort, when all else had failed. It is pretty obvious that very few marriages can possibly be mended by a man starting to hit his wife!

There is also no suggestion that a man should ever hit his wife out of anger, frustration, irritation, annoyance or disappointment, or just as the result of losing his temper. All those things are totally unIslamic, and the man would be ultimately held to account for them if he did them, at the Day of Judgement. If a Muslim man foolishly uses this text to grant himself the right to beat his wife, he has completely misunderstood the principles of Islam, in which one Muslim should never seek to hurt another, especially not his closest neighbour and friend, his wife. The only allowed context is out of love for a wife guilty of real misconduct in the marriage, whom it is still possible to bring back to a contented marital relationship.

In his famous Farewell Sermon, the Prophet referred to this issue again, and said that physical punishment should only be considered if the wife was guilty of obvious and blatant physical immoral conduct, and that the beating should be symbolic, and not done in a way that would cause pain.

Once the man and wife are in harmony again, no more continued ill-feeling should continue. No nagging, or continually bringing matters up again and again.

The next verse, (v.35) gives the excellent advice that if the relationship looks like really breaking up, then they should call in the help of two supporters, one for each side in the dispute, and listen to everything that needs saying with witnesses who can help calm things down. If they really wish for peace, deep down, then God will cause their reconciliation.

# On Racial Harmony

Surah 30:22

Surah 49:13

If you know any other relevant passages, that's fine - but the ones given above are the set passages required.

## SURAH 30:22

> 30:22 'And among His Signs is the creation of the heavens and the earth, and the variations in your languages and your colours; verily in that are Signs for those who know.'

The fact that there are so many different kinds of varieties and species, all created by God, is one of His Signs. Why should He make so many different types of things? If He was going to create a horse, why should He make huge carthorses and sleek racehorses and pretty little Shetland ponies and miniature horses? Which type does God like best? Which sort of horse is better than the other sorts?

These questions are ridiculous, of course. All the species are perfect, each in their different ways. They are beloved by their Creator equally, since He made all of them.

If God was going to create human beings, why did He make them of so many different types and nationalities and colours and characteristics? Which does He like best? Tall white ones, curly-haired black ones, those with slanted eyes? Does He prefer those who can speak Arabic, or

English, perhaps? These questions are equally ridiculous.

We were all made different. In this is an important Sign. God accepts, loves, and encourages variety, and values all varieties. So should we. There is no nationality, or race, or colour better than any other.

## SURAH 49:13

> 49:13 'O mankind! We created You from a single (pair) of a male and a female, and made you into nations and tribes, that ye may know each other (not that ye may despise (each other). Verily the most honoured of you in the sight of God is (he who is) the most righteous of you. And God has full knowledge and is well acquainted (with all things).'

This verse picks up the idea of the creation of human beings from an original couple (Adam and Hawwah/Eve). We have no scientific evidence whatsoever for how human beings originated. The theory of evolution from the ape or monkey line remains a theory and has not yet been proved; although it may be accepted as a working hypothesis, it is no more than that.

The Qur'an teaches that what was more important than the physical origins of humanity was the spiritual origin, and that there should be a real sense of unity between all peoples because all have descended from the one original couple.

Surah 4:1 makes it clear that humanity was created from a single 'nafs' - a word meaning soul or self as well as living person. From that single soul came male and female, two equal partners.

God wills that nations and tribes should appreciate and feel fellowship with each other, and not despise each other.

The most honoured of all humans was not the richest, or most powerful, but the one who was the most righteous and virtuous. Honour in the sight of God should be the human being's prime aim, not power over others, or conquest, or feeling that one tribe or class or group is superior to any other.

Muhammad Asad's translation of this verse is that 'We have created you all out of a male and a female', meaning 'every one of you came from a father and a mother' - in other words, you are all biologically equal and of equal dignity and worth.

The only form of superiority, in God's eyes, was in the amount of our striving to do His will; and any teacher will tell you that the pupil who gets 'A' for effort is not necessarily the cleverest, but the one who tries hardest to overcome his or her difficulties.

*Section Five*

# OFFICIAL INFORMATION

*The London Board (Edexcel) Examination GCSE*

# Religious Studies (1478/1479) Syllabus

Edexcel is offering two syllabi for GCSE Islam. They are Syllabus 1478 and Syllabus 1479. These replace the old Syllabus 1477 which is no longer valid.

The student working outside school conditions is advised to opt for Syllabus 1478.

The work for Syllabus 1478 and 1479 is the same, but with Syllabus 1478 a student may go to the examination centre and sit two papers which will count for 100% of the GCSE marks. They answer five questions of equal value, instead of four.

For Syllabus 1479, the examination papers only count for 80% of the marks, and the other 20% are gained by students doing two pieces of coursework outside the examination room, which have to be marked and assessed by accredited teachers during the academic year. Usually this is not possible outside a school situation. They choose one option from alternative A and one from alternative B, and both essays should be around 1500 words in length, (c5 sides of A4 paper, at 6-8 words per line). The advantage - they do those bits in advance. The disadvantages - it is much longer, you have to apply for the current subject titles each year, and you have to have them marked by an accredited teacher and sent in by an accredited centre).

Therefore, we will assume that most students taking on this course will opt for Syllabus 1478.

This syllabus provides a coherent full course balanced in terms of breadth and depth and offers all candidates, of any religious persuasion or none, the opportunity to demonstrate their attainment irrespective of their gender, ethnic or social background.

The syllabus consists of 13 Units divided into Alternative A and Alternative B.

## These are: Alternative A

Unit A1   Religion and Life from the viewpoint of Christianity and at least one other religion

Unit A2   Religion and Life from a Christian Perspective

Unit A3   Religion and Life from a Catholic Perspective

*Unit A4   Religion and Life from a Muslim Perspective

Unit A5   Religion and Life from a Jewish Perspective

## Alternative B

Unit B1   Buddhism
Unit B2   Christianity
Unit B3   Catholicism
Unit B4   Mark's Gospel
Unit B5   Hinduism
*Unit B6   Islam
Unit B7   Judaism
Unit B8   Sikhism

Candidates are required to study one Unit from Alternative A plus one Unit from Alternative B. For the full GCSE in Islam, we therefore choose units A4 and B6.

# The Syllabus for Unit A4

## UNIT A4: RELIGION AND LIFE FROM A MUSLIM PERSPECTIVE

This Unit is divided into four sections, examined by written paper only, and a fifth section, examined either by written paper (course 1478) or by coursework to be handed in and marked in advance (course 1479).

**Those doing syllabus 1478** should look at the three options given for the questions, and choose ONE of them, for this alternative. They should then make a study of that subject, according to the suggestions. In the exam, they will be asked a question about that subject, which they will answer in the normal way. As for the other questions, they will not know in advance what the wording is going to be - to avoid cheating. The only bit you are given in advance is the subject area - and you may choose right at the start which option you wish to do, and ignore the others. The answer required will be of the same length as the other answers on the paper, and will carry equal marks.

**Those doing syllabus 1479** will be set a specific title, and are required to write an essay of around 1500 words (c5 sides of A4 paper, for writing of 6-8 words per line). These are handed in and marked in advance by accredited teachers at accredited centres. TITLES NEED TO BE CHECKED EACH YEAR by contacting the Board for details. Be very careful not to do old titles, and therefore get disqualified.

## SPECIFICS:

In order to meet the evaluation assessment objective, candidates need to be aware of non-religious, as well as religious, responses to religious and moral issues.

Candidates will be required to demonstrate knowledge and Understanding, and the ability to evaluate alternative points of view, in respect of:

### Section 1 Believing in Allah

- How religious upbringing and experience in a Muslim home and community can lead people to believe in Allah.

- The nature of religious experience as seen in the Night of Power for Muhammad, a greater awareness of Allah in observing the five pillars.
- The evidence of design and order in nature and how these provide evidence for Allah's existence.
- What Muslims believe about Allah's nature as shown in Surahs 1; 2:115-117; 6:95-99; 30:20-25; 40:61-68; and 112 (all verse references in this text are from 'The Holy Qur'an' translated by Yusuf Ali).
- Why some people do not believe in Allah or are unsure about belief in Allah.
- How Islam responds to the problem of evil and suffering.

## Section 2 Matters of Life and Death.

- Arguments about life after death.
- Islamic teachings and interpretations about life after death (akhirah).
- Islamic teachings on life as created by Allah and sacred to Allah. The social context of abortion, including current legislation in the UK, and non-religious arguments about abortion.
- Muslim attitudes to abortion and contraception and the reasons for them.
- The social context of euthanasia, including current legislation in the UK, the different forms of euthanasia and non-religious arguments.
- Muslim attitudes to euthanasia.

## Section 3 Marriage and Family Life

- Changing attitudes to cohabitation, marriage and divorce in Britain.
- Islamic teaching on relationships between the sexes, the nature and purpose of marriage, choice of partner, cohabitation, adultery, homo-sexuality, and the reasons for these teachings.

- Differences among Muslims in their attitudes to divorce and the reasons for them.
- Changing attitudes to the nature of the family in Britain.
- Islamic teachings on the family and how the mosque and madrassah help with family life.

## Section 4 Social Harmony

- The growth in equal rights for women in Britain.
- Differences among Muslims on the roles and status of women and men, and the reasons for them (Surahs 16:97; 2:228; 4:34).
- Prejudice and discrimination and the nature of Britain as a multi-ethnic society.
- Islamic teachings on racial harmony (Surahs 30:22; 49:13; the last sermon of the prophet Muhammad).
- The contribution of one Muslim person or organization to racial harmony.
- The quality, variety and richness of life in Britain as a multi-faith society and the problems related to this.
- Islamic teachings about relationships with other religions.

## Section 5 Options

(For syllabus 1478, you choose in advance from either option 1 or 2 or 3. Option 4 is for Syllabus 1479 only).

## OPTION1: Religion and the Media

The variety and range of specifically religious programmes on the four terrestrial TV channels (including an in depth knowledge of one such programme and the reasons for its popularity/unpopularity);

- How one religious or moral issue of

concern to Muslims has been dealt with in either a TV soap opera, or the national daily press;

- A religious theme or themes as explored in one film or TV drama.

## OPTION 2: Religion and wealth and poverty

- Islamic teachings on: possession, uses and dangers of wealth: stewardship; charitable giving, compassion and justice, the relationship between rich and poor;

- The relief of poverty and suffering in Great Britain by Muslims. Detailed knowledge of the work of ONE Muslim person, community or organization.

- An outline of the need for world development in response to the causes, extent and effects of poverty in the world; the work of Muslim agencies in world development. Detailed knowledge of ONE such agency will be required.

## OPTION 3: Religion and the Environment

- The religious and moral issues concerning care for the environment, the dangers of pollution, proper use and conservation of resources.

- Islamic teachings on creation and stewardship which could have an effect on attitudes to the environment, and on animal welfare.

- The work of Muslims in support of conservation of the planet and its resources. Detailed knowledge of the work of ONE Muslim person, community or organization will be required.

## OPTION 4 - SYLLABUS 1479 ONLY

Religion as expressed in art, music or literature

This option is only available as a coursework option.

## UNIT B6: ISLAM

This Unit is divided into four sections, examined by written paper only, and a fifth section, examined either by written paper (course 1478) or by coursework to be handed in and marked in advance (course 1479).

In order to meet the evaluation assessment objective, candidates need to be aware of non-religious, as well as religious, responses to religious and moral issues.

Candidates will be required to demonstrate knowledge and understanding, and the ability to evaluate alternative points of view, in respect of:

### Section 1 The Beliefs of Islam

The Muslim beliefs of -
- Tawhid (the oneness of Allah and the unity of his creation);
- Risalah ( the belief in Allah's prophets and holy books especially the belief in Muhammad as the seal of the Prophets and the Qur'an as the final word of Allah);
- Akhirah (the belief in the Last Day and life after death).
- The concept of al'Qadr (Allah's foreknowledge).
- The meaning of Islam as submission to the will of Allah.

### Section 2 Authority and Values

- The nature and authority of the Qur'an. Detailed knowledge of the contents will not be required.

- Differences between the authority of the Qur'an and Sunnah and their relationship to the Shari'ah. The principles of the Shari'ah as law of Allah and the way of life for Muslims. Although this will require awareness of an outline of Muhammad's life, specific questions will only be asked on Muhammad as the perfect exemplar.
- Different attitudes to authority, leadership and traditions between Sunni and Shi'ah Muslims and the reasons for them.
- The concept of the ummah and the importance of unity in Islam.

## Section 3 Serving Allah

- The concept of ibadah (life as worship of Allah), as expressed in the five pillars: shahadah, salah, zakah, sawm and hajj.
- Practical ways in which Muslims submit themselves to the will of Allah; the broad contents of the Shari'ah with more specific reference to laws on food, dress and separation of the sexes.

## Section 4 Being a Muslim in Great Britain

Ways in which British Muslims live out their faith in a non-Muslim society, and problems they face with reference to education, work, mosques and madrassahs, marriage and funeral rituals, food and dress, alcohol and gambling, riba (charging interest).

## Section 5 Options (You choose in advance - either option 1 or option 2).

## OPTION 1: The Mosque

- The architectural and other main features of a mosque and the reasons for them.
- The role and function of an imam in Sunni mosques.
- British organizations of mosques and the reasons for the differences between them.
- The role and function of the mosque in the local Muslim community.

## OPTION 2: Jihad

- The Muslim belief in jihad as a struggle in the service of Allah; interpretations of greater and lesser jihad; practical implications.
- The conditions for a holy war; the attitude of British Muslims towards war and conflict, including any differences of opinion.

*Please note : Candidates entering for this syllabus may not enter for any other GCSE Religious Studies Syllabus or GCSE (Short Course) Religious Education syllabus in the same May/June examination.

Please note : This syllabus is available at the May/June examination only. Centres will be required to indicate the approximate number of candidates they intend to enter for the May/June examination on the Early Notification of Entries Form which is sent to centres in the early summer of each year.

# GRADE DESCRIPTIONS

Grade descriptions are provided to give a general indication of the standards of achievement likely to have been shown by candidates awarded particular grades. The descriptions must be interpreted in relation to the content specified by the syllabus; they are not designed to define that content. The grade awarded will depend in practice upon the extent to which the candidate has met the assessment objectives overall. Shortcomings in some aspects of the examination may be balanced by better performances in others.

*In relation to the religion or religions studied:*

## Grade F (the bottom grade : score 25-30%)

Candidates demonstrate elementary knowledge and Understanding of beliefs, values and traditions studied and their impact on adherents and others. They do this through limited use of specialist vocabulary and knowledge, sometimes correctly but not often systematically, and by making simple connections between religion and people's lives. They support and evaluate responses to issues studied by giving a reason in support of an opinion.

## Grade C ( Above average: score around 50% +)

Candidates demonstrate, generally with accuracy, a knowledge and Understanding of beliefs, values and traditions and their impact on individuals, societies and cultures. They do this by using correct specialist vocabulary when questions specifically demand it and describing accurately and explaining the importance of the key elements of the religions(s) studied. They identify, support, interpret and evaluate different responses to issues studied by presenting relevant evidence to support arguments, incorporating reference to different points of view and using arguments to make reasoned judgements.

## Grade A ( the top grade: Score around 70% +).

Candidates demonstrate detailed and comprehensive knowledge and Understanding of beliefs, values and traditions and their impact on the lives of individuals, societies and cultures. They do this by consistently using and interpreting a range of specialist vocabulary, drawing out and explaining the meaning and religious significance of the key elements of the religion(s) studied and explaining, where appropriate, how differences in belief lead to differences of religious response. They support, interpret and evaluate a variety of responses recognizing the complexity of issues, weighing up opinions and making reasoned judgements supported by a range of evidence and well-developed arguments.

This syllabus meets the requirements of both the GCSE criteria for Religious Studies and the GCSE/Key Stage 4 General Criteria. Each Alternative of this syllabus also separately meets the requirements of the GCSE (Short Course) Religious Education criteria. Consequently, this syllabus provides the opportunity for Short Course and full course candidates to be taught together.

# The Syllabus Analyzed

THE SYLLABUS ANALYZED, SO THAT YOU CAN GET A GOOD OVERALL PICTURE OF WHAT YOU NEED TO KNOW, FIND OUT, AND DO.

You need quite a lot of specific knowledge, and all of the topics you can look up and study well in advance.

The most vital aspect in this section is the logical presentation of your own thoughts and opinions, based on that knowledge, and an ability to present - and if necessary argue against - at least one other point of view.

## UNIT A4

### Section 1  Believing in God

Religious experience - You need to be able to explain, and if possible describe, what a religious experience is.

- family and mosque upbringing. (influence and background encouragement)
- the Prophet's Night of Power (personal experience of God, angelic presence)
- The Five Pillars (personal worship through faith, prayer, fasting, giving and pilgrimage)
- Sufism (dhikr and trances)
- Miracles

Have you got a personal example or experience?  Do you know of someone else's experience, that you could talk about?

Can you define what a miracle is, and

give an example? (Could you give an example concerning the Prophet Jesus?  Or one concerning the Prophet Muhammad?) Do miracles still happen today?  Can you give an example?  Consider whether religious faith should be based on the miracles, or on reason and discipline and love.  Why did both Jesus and Muhammad refuse to 'do' miracles to order?

The Argument from Design.  Can you explain this argument, and other arguments that attempt to prove the existence of God?

The set Qur'an passages: You have been set 1; 2:115-117; 6:95-99; 30:20-25; 40:61-68; 112.  Go through these, and see what they teach.

Why do people reject belief in God? Can you present some of their arguments?

The origin of evil and suffering, and the

problem of God's attitude towards these topics. Why does God allow evil and suffering? Is He responsible for them? Is there any purpose to them? Can we avoid evil? What about the arguments for freewill and predestination - al-Qadr?

## Section 2 Matters of Life and Death

- Arguments and proofs for life after death.
- Muslim teachings on Barzakh, Resurrection and Judgement, Heaven and Hell.
- The sacredness of life: people may not end it; people cannot end it before their time.
- The arguments concerning abortion.
  - none at all, from conception;
  - yes, up to week six (40 days), but not later;
  - never, except when the mother's life is in real danger.
- The arguments concerning contraception
  - Yes, with the full agreement of both parties;
  - never, because it is going against the will of Allah for a new child to be born;
  - yes, the Prophet allowed the withdrawal method;
  - yes, if it prevents pregnancy, provided it is with the consent of both parents;
  - no, if it is contraception that aborts a pregnancy (eg coil, morning after pill).
- The arguments concerning euthanasia.
  - never, as it goes against the will of Allah;
  - yes, on the principle of kindness and removal of suffering;
  - no euthanasia, but one should not prolong life artificially.

- can one die before one's allotted time anyway?
- Merits of not using euthanasia
  - sufferings counted to the person's credit in Akhirah.
  - We can learn through suffering.
  - We may need the tests; it may be God's will for us to give an example to others.
- Muslim rulings on those three subjects, giving two points of view for each.

## Section 3 Marriage and Family Life

- Attitudes to living together, marriage and divorce:
  - Marriage 'not safe', 'not necessary'
  - marriage penalized by tax system
  - it's easier to separate if you're not married
  - you want to keep your independence
  - 'divorced' children fear future commitment
  - experiments find suitable partners
  - Who cares? It's nobody else's business
  - Should you keep virginity until marriage?
- Muslim teachings:
  - No sex before or outside marriage (including homosexuality and sexual variants)
  - 'love' makes you vulnerable and clouds judgement
  - fall in love after not before marriage
  - parents should help choose good husband/bride, and carefully check if they are sound and suitable.
  - Muslim women have to accept authority of husband, so must take care to choose a man whose authority they CAN accept.
- Purpose of marriage?

- for people to learn caring and tolerance
- more financial and home security;
- stability to bring up better balanced next generation
- to provide a loving, halal environment.

■ Know the basics of what happens at a Muslim wedding:
  - dowry (mahr) payable to woman
  - contract/promises conditions
  - agreed witnesses to the free agreement of the bride (who does not have to be present in person)
  - signing of forms in front of witnesses
  - declared publicly (not done in secret) - the point of the walimah party

■ Know which things are cultural and not Islamic:
  - henna painting
  - expensive dress- whether red/gold or white and traditional dress (in Islam the bride may not be present if she doesn't wish it)
  - 'fancy' dress for husband
  - huge parties with all the expense
  - paying any dowry money to husband's business, to father, etc. It is for the bride to keep for personal use, and a 'guarantee' for her welfare should divorce follow.

■ Purpose of wedding ceremony:
  - to gain public agreement from husband and wife to their various rights and duties:
  - a contract both agree not to break, and if they do, the offended party may seek divorce.

■ Divorce: different Muslim attitudes:
  - marriage should be for life
  - divorced women are treated as second-class citizens in some

societies, and find remarriage very difficult.
  - if one has married a cousin, divorce becomes almost impossible because of family pressure.
  - Islam does not teach that a couple should be chained together for life if their marriage is not working.
  - Islam does allow taking a second wife rather than divorcing the first. (Wives don't get this privilege in Islam, as they don't anywhere else).

■ Problems concerning divorce :
  - some Muslims abuse Islam - too easy divorce for men
  - some women are set aside because of age or some trivial reason.
  - some women not even warned, but told to move out.
  - some men make polygamous marriages in spite of the feelings of previous wives (forbidden in Islam)

■ Muslim attitude:
  - should never divorce lightly, (most hated thing which Allah has allowed)
  - should always do everything to prevent divorce, especially discussion of grievances and counselling with two representatives for each side.
  - should think carefully about future of any children

■ The family in the UK:
  - extended families decreasing
  - western-type 'nuclear' families increasing
  - no wide family 'help' network
  - many new and multiple partnerships
  - children lose one parent and gain a stranger
  - many children live in one-parent households

- some people accept homosexual relationships and variant relationships as normal, and children are brought up in these households.
- unemployment problems: many men not bread-winners
- old people problems; what to do with elderly relatives?

## Section 4 Social Harmony

- Know something of the history in general of the equal rights for women movement.
- Understand the status and roles of men and women in Islam:
- set passages 16:97, 2:228, 4:34.
- Muslim teachings :
  - all Muslims have the same potential worth and equal duties
  - women should be granted consideration because of their biology: menstruation/hormonal upsets linked with this
  - pregnancy/childbirth/feeding/hormonal upsets linked with these
  - women physically weaker not expected to do man's labour
  - men should not expect to capitalize on women's wealth and property; they should be able to support their families, even if the woman is more wealthy. Her money etc. is hers.
  - the man's role is to lead, guide, provide, and protect
  - the woman is expected to accept her husband as head of the household, and not go against his wishes unless he asks her to do something contrary to Islam.
  - the woman's role is to love and care for, and run a halal home; some schools of thought do not

require her to do housework or breastfeed children without financial help. If she does those things out of love, it is to her credit.
- Neither must compromise the home by being unfaithful.
- Neither should compromise the home through neglect, cruelty, etc.
- You need to be able to explain what is meant by:
- prejudice
- discrimination
- sexism/ageism
- multi-ethnic/multi-faith
- racialism/racial harmony
- second-class citizens
- the 'Third World'
- Know what is meant by a multi-faith society; what are the chief faiths practiced in the UK? What are the chief sects within Islam? What are the problems caused by multi-faith society?
  - intolerance
  - culture clash
  - mixed marriages
  - rejection of those who marry 'outside'
- You need to know the details of one Muslim person or organization involved in promoting racial harmony. Some suggestion are given in Unit Sixty.
- Be aware of at least two points of view about Muslim relations with other world faiths
  - The People of the Book (Ahl al-Kitab) are accepted, men can intermarry with their women and Muslims can eat their food.
  - Why? People of One God, One Revelation, same chain of prophets, all against paganism, polytheism and atheism. (Know what those words mean and be able to explain them).

- Against world faiths based on polytheism and idolatry
- All Muslims against Zionism
- Some Muslims misguidedly anti-Jewish because of the behaviour of some Jews of Medinah at the time of the Prophet.

## THE SPECIAL OPTION QUESTIONS

In the section 5 for Unit A4, there is a choice of three questions.

You only have to answer ONE question. Therefore you may choose your subject in advance, and forget all about the other topics. For the topics you choose, you need to do a fair amount of personal research. You would not have time to study more than one topic.

As you can choose your subject in advance, choose right at the start, forget the others, and stick to your choice.

Find out as much as you can about your chosen subject; keep a file on it.

Do some letter-writing, and seek help from Muslims in the know.

### These are the Topics

A4..1.....Religion and the Media
A4..2.....Religion and wealth and poverty
A4..3.....Religion and the Environment

You will have to write an essay on ONE of the A4 topics. You will not know in advance exactly what they will ask, only the area of study. Look at the specimen questions and see the SORT of question asked; but remember you will not be asked the same question!

## A1.....RELIGION AND THE MEDIA

You need to know what the specifically religious programmes are, on BBC 1,2, ITV and Channel 4.

You need to know roughly what these programmes are like, what do they seek to do, what sort of things are included? eg. Worship - Songs of Praise, First Light, This is the Day. Heart to Heart, Sunday Service. Magazine - News reviews and interviews. This Sunday. Religious Documentaries - Everyman, Heart of the Matter, Witness.

You need to know ONE of these programmes in detail, and the reasons why it is popular or unpopular.

You need to know how one religious or moral issue has been dealt with either in a TV soap opera (eg. Neighbours, Eastenders, Coronation St., Brookside), or in the national daily press.

It could be an issue like abortion, homosexuality, drugs, racism, etc. Be able to describe the moral issue, explain why it is an issue, show how the programme deals with it. Would any other way be better?

You need to know a religious theme or themes in ONE film or TV drama (eg Ghost, Flatliners, Touched by an Angel etc.).

## A2.....RELIGION AND WEALTH AND POVERTY

You need to know general Muslim teachings on money and its uses and dangers; charitable giving in zakah and sadaqah; and issues concerning rich and poor, compassion and justice.

You need to have clear opinions of what is wrong about exploitation, greed, selfishness, ignoring suffering and distress.

You need to look up facts on the work of ONE Muslim person, community or organisation dealing with poverty or suffering. This could involve writing a few letters, gaining some facts.

You need to have clear opinions and general knowledge on the causes, extent and effects of poverty in various parts of the world.

You need to look up facts on ONE Muslim agency dealing with the environment or world development.

Some examples are given in UNIT SIXTY.

## A3..... RELIGION AND THE ENVIRONMENT

You need to look up facts on the care of the environment, pollution, proper use of resources and conservation.

You need to have clear opinions on creation and stewardship, the meaning of khilafah - especially with regard to the environment and animal and species welfare.

Maybe you could consider such things as - factory farming, chemical farming and weed killing, zoos, animal experimentation, killing for 'fashion', killing for 'sport' - eg foxes, badgers, hawking. You need detailed knowledge of ONE Muslim person, community or organisation involved in conservation work. You could consider such areas as World Wildlife, bear-training, gardens and water-supply in the desert, work in famine regions, flood prevention, work in earthquake zones, etc.

## UNIT B6

### Section 1 Beliefs of Islam

- You need a clear Understanding of what is meant by Tawhid, Risalah, Akhirah, al-Qadr, and submission to the Will of God.

### Tawhid:

- nature of God; the Beautiful Names;
- the concept of Transcendence (God infinite and eternal and beyond human knowledge)
- the concept of Immanence (God nearer than jugular vein)
- know the meanings of Omnipotent, Omniscient, Omnipresent, Eternal, Absolute, Infinite.
- Be able to explain the meaning of Shirk (dividing God's unity, considering Him to have 'relatives' or partners in power; superstition).
- the Creation of the Universe (scientific and religious)
- the Big Bang, Expanding Universe, No-beginning

### The main arguments for the existence of God:

- the argument from First Cause/First Motion
- the argument from Contingency
- God the Necessary Being
- the argument from the evidence of Design in the universe
- the argument from Teleology - that things are evolving towards a planned 'end' or 'goal'.
- Origin of Evil and the effects of Evil

### Risalah:

- the revelation and nature of the Qur'an/its 'history'
- what is meant by prophecy and prophets?
- a basic outline of the life of the Prophet Muhammad
- a basic knowledge of other prophets - especially Ibrahim, Ismail, Nuh, Yusuf, Musa and Isa.
- a basic awareness of what the Bible is, and Muslim opinions about it.
- Muhammad as the Seal of the Prophets. What does this mean?
- the Qur'an as the final revelation for all humanity and all time.

## Akhirah:

- knowledge of what the Qur'an teaches. Are the passages about Heaven/Paradise and Hell meant literally, or are they allegorical? Qur'an states these things beyond human knowledge.
- basic outline of Islamic beliefs:
  - death of body
  - release of soul
  - the role of angels, especially Azrail and Recorders
  - the Barzakh period
  - the fates of good and evil whilst in the grave
  - the resurrection (even to our fingerprints)
- the Day of Judgement
  - future fate in either Heaven/Paradise or Hell.
  - knowledge of what it is on which our judgement is based:
    - □ our beliefs,
    - □ our actual lives
    - □ our attitudes
    - □ our intentions (niyyah)

## Al-Qadr: this includes

- expression of the freewill versus determinism problem
  - Is everything foreknown and therefore predetermined?
  - Is our judgement based on revelation to us, and our choice or response to it?
  - Is God like a computer? He knows every possibility and what will happen to us if we choose any particular course of action, but He leaves that choice to us?
  - does Judgement make sense without freewill?
- Islam as submission:
  - the definition of Ibadah, or service

- every aspect of life, not just the Five Pillars
- our Noble Character - honesty, courage, generosity, compassion, etc.
- the belief that God knows and sees everything you do, and knows your motives, influences and circumstances, and it is all recorded.

## Section 2  Authority and Values

- the revelation and nature of the Qur'an; the basic principles of how the Prophet received his revelations
  - the Night of Power
  - receiving revelations under various conditions
  - the Makkah period - facing persecution
  - the Madinah period - general rules for life and society
- The main principles of the Qur'an:
  - tawhid, risalah, akhirah, human rights, human life-style.
- Be able to define what is meant by Sunnah, hadith, hadith qudsi and Shari'ah.
- Some examples taken from the Prophet's life story - try to get one good example of each:
  - his kindness to women, children, animals, nervous young warriors, the elderly, loyalty to his friends.
  - Collect and learn a few good hadiths
  - Be able to explain the difference between an ordinary hadith and a hadith qudsi
- Be aware of different Muslim attitudes towards the hadiths:
  - all hadiths equally important
  - some hadiths not reliable, and why

- the Prophet given the same authority as the Qur'an, and why
- the Qur'an always superior to anything not actually revealed in it
- only that revealed in the Qur'an necessary?

■ Be able to explain what is meant by a Madhdhab.
  - Know the names of the four chief Sunni Madhdhabs and the main Shi'ite one.

■ Know the main differences between Sunni and Shi'ite:
  - leadership; family of Prophet ( ie. descent) v.elected leader (ie. merit).
  - Imam = learned, noble person; or 'shadow of God', ayatollah.
  - the Shi'ite loyalty to the '12 Imams'
  - the 'Hidden Imam'
  - Seveners or Twelvers?
  - the Imam to come, or Mahdi
  - rules for marriage v. mutah marriage
  - orthodox prayer v. inclusion of prayers for Ali, his descendants and Imams.
  - heroes v.saints (Shi'ite tendency to pray at tombs/shrines)

■ Define what is meant by Ummah
  - equality of sex and race
  - the 'family' of past, present and future Muslims
  - that Muslims should feel for each other in practical terms - help, honour, protection and support.

## Section 3 Serving God

Get detailed knowledge of:
■ the Five Pillars
■ the Basic Beliefs - the Seven Articles (including tawhid, risalah, akhirah, angels, jinn and Shaytan)
■ Prayer

- the call to prayer
- preparation for prayer
- the performance of salah
- the differences between salah and du'a

■ Zakah
  - reasons for the tax on wealth
  - who may benefit from zakah

■ Sawm - fasting, especially in Ramadan (rules and reasons for, especially spiritual aims)

■ Hajj
  - rules for ihram
  - the main rituals (circling, wuquf, stoning, sacrifice)
  - the places visited and what happens at each
  - the emotional feelings of hajj
  - the spiritual benefits of hajj
  - who is excused (the poor, sick, those prevented)
  - who is forbidden (the dishonest, debtors, wrong-minded)

■ Basic knowledge of halal and haram
  - the principle of harmful and beneficial in all walks of life
  - the actual foods forbidden (pork and pork products, meat killed wrongfully or cruelly - must be killed with a sharp or piercing implement (eg. knife, arrow, bullet), not a blunt one, (eg club), meat dedicated to another 'god', meat that 'died of itself', meat with undrained blood)
  - foods allowed - Jewish kosher and Christian
  - debate over 'Christian' meat; some Muslims extreme and will not accept it; are western slaughterhouses really 'Christian'? Does 'Christian' mean acceptable to the RSPCA (which DOES accept halal slaughter, of course); what

about a Hindu butcher if he kills humanely?

- halal and haram ways of life
- forbidden ways of earning a living - cheating, dishonesty, exploitation, pornography.
- halal and haram ways of dressing
- modesty for men
- minimum dress for men
- modesty for women
- debate over what is meant by awrah
- types of clothing not accepted - transparent, tight, low-cut, short, etc.
- discussion on hijab - what it really means, is the headscarf compulsory? Different forms of hijab. Hijab rejected in various Muslim places. Do women have to cover their faces? The Qur'an asks for lowered eyes and bosoms covered. Tolerance - Muslims should not force others, or ridicule or humiliate

■ the separation of the sexes: reasons why this is advised (protects innocence; avoids temptations; safeguards from abuse; can concentrate on studies); advantages and disadvantages (poor education for women? all-male education can become crude and ignorant of women and their needs). Advisability of not being alone with men - use a chaperone who is not going to abuse you. Be aware of male relatives who sometimes abuse.

## Section 4 Being a Muslim in Great Britain

■ Be aware of what the main problems are:
(a) for 'ethnic' Muslims - Asians, Arabs, Turks, Indians, Bangladeshis,

Malaysians, etc.
- problems of mixed schools
- should women see male doctors and vice versa?
- too many dogs.
- not enough organization or unity
- culture 'too heavy'
- problems with mixed marriages, half-caste children
(b) for 'white' Muslims-
- cannot access 'race laws'
- no Islamic cultural background
- may be disapproved or persecuted by own families
- may be rejected by 'ethnic' mosques
- dress difficulties - don't wish to call attention to themselves, or be accused of 'fancy dress'.
- loss of previous community and friends - eg Church congregation, social life dependent on alcohol.

■ What are the problems in schools?
- mixed sexes
- modest uniform?
- use of showers? Muslims don't even like same-sex nakedness.
- should girls be allowed to wear hijab? At what age?
- should boys be allowed to grow beards or wear caps?
- sport and swimming. What to wear?
- RE lessons - are other faiths presented as superior? Is Islam being taught incorrectly? What to do about assemblies? What to do about Christmas and Easter
- immorality condoned - what to do about unIslamic people and practices taught in sex education lessons, or in literature?
- some Muslims disapprove of all art or music, some allow two-dimensional art on paper or fabric,

and allow music which is not sexual or nationalistic.

- no facilities in toilets for washing private parts
- no private facilities for prayer
■ What are the problems at work?
  - many of the same problems as at school
  - halal and haram jobs
  - discrimination and abuse in he workplace
  - lack of facilities for wudu and prayer
  - dishonesty and exploitation from both bosses and workers
  - mixed sex working society. Does this matter if not left alone?
■ Mosque and madrassah problems:
  - local mosques too concentrated on one race/culture
  - no opportunities for women?
  - how do local mosques cope with converts?
  - language problems - some Imams don't speak fluent English.
  - no sermons be in English, for those who don't speak 'ethnic' languages?
  - are 'village imams from 'the old country' useful in UK society?
  - do the madrassahs bore the children/waste their time?
  - How could madrassahs be better used?
  - How can mosques gain qualified helpers?
■ Marriage and funeral rituals:
  - know the general format of a Muslim marriage, and which bits are cultural only and not Muslim.
  - know the format of the washing of the dead, the salat ul-janazah, funeral arrangements, burial facilities.

■ Leisure pursuits:
  - Islamic teaching on alcohol, drugs, gambling. Know why they are haram.
■ Riba: have a clear definition of what this involves
  - as regards making money interest
  - as regards exploitation through property and goods,
  - trade as regards exploitation through monopolies
  - Islamic banking: the bank should not capitalize on a borrower's loss, thereby increasing the debt. The bank should not do its own trade in haram spheres of business. The discussion concerning whether Muslims should have mortgages or insurance policies.

## B1....THE MOSQUE

You need to know all the features of a typical mosque, and what they are for - eg. minaret, mihrab, minbar, dome, prayer hall, qiblah niche, clocks showing prayer-times, facilities for wudu, rooms for social use.

You need to know what an Imam does, in Sunni mosques. Could you construct a typical day? eg. regular prayers, problems, visits, lectures, entertaining groups, funerals, etc.

You should find out a list of mosque organisations and the differences between them - eg UK Islamic Mission, Jamaat-i-Islami; Hizb ut-Tahrir, Barelvis, Deobandis, Ahl-i-Hadith, etc.

You need to know how the mosque is involved in the local community - 'Id parties, lectures, education, women's groups, study groups, youth clubs, welfare work, charity sales etc.

## B2....JIHAD

You need to be able to define the difference between the usual use of the word jihad in military terms, and the more important meaning of the Greater Jihad - personal striving to live a good Muslim life.

How do you as a Muslim make a personal jihad? It could be at home, at school, at work, or in caring for someone. How do you struggle for Allah through helping people, being courageous, patient, etc?

You need to know the set conditions for a military jihad or holy war.

You need clear opinions on the situations in which war is justified; you must present at least two points of view. eg. tyranny or conquering the territory of others is wrong; defence is right.

# Specimen Exam Papers and Marking Schemes

## SPECIMEN EXAMINATION PAPERS

In this section, you will see what the examination papers actually look like.

It is very important that you study these carefully.

It will give you some confidence in advance, for you will no doubt recognize many of the items asked, and could probably answer many of these questions already, even before you start your study.

If you can't answer anything, don't worry - that is what this course is for - to teach you the material you will need.

Studying these specimen papers will rehearse for you that horrid first moment when you turn over YOUR exam paper, and see what you will have to do.

So many people get into a panic, and fail to follow the instructions correctly. Studying these specimen papers in advance gives you the chance to see how the questions are laid out, what sort of things are asked, how much you are expected to do.

## THIS IS THE KEY TO SUCCESS:

It will give you the opportunity to take careful note of how the questions are marked. Notice how the marks allotted for each question are given at the end of each section of the question.

- A section could have 2,4,6 or 8 marks.

- Sections with 2 marks only expect an answer of one sentence or so.

- Sections with 6 or 8 marks are Very Important. You have to realize that if they have 8 marks to give, they must be looking for 8 facts or statements, and to score 8, your facts must be right. If you only write 2 lines, it is impossible to score 8 marks, even if what you said was right.

## YOU DON'T GET THE SAME QUESTIONS

If you use these questions to get in some practice, that is fine! But you will not be asked exactly the same questions in your exam, although many of them may be similar.

Your questions will be kept sealed and secret until you actually enter the exam room. But they will be subjects chosen from the set Syllabus.

## SPECIMEN PAPER FOR UNIT A4: RELIGION AND LIFE FROM A MUSLIM PERSPECTIVE

LONDON EXAMINATIONS GCSE
Religious Studies (1478)
Specimen Paper 1 (100% examination)

Time: 1 Hour 45 minutes

**These Instructions are given to Candidates.**

Answer Five questions, One question from Each section, from the unit you have studied.

In the boxes on the Answer Book, write your centre number, candidate number, the syllabus title and number, paper number, your surname and initials, signature and date.

Answer All questions in the Answer Book.

Supplementary Answer Sheets may be used.

Information for Candidates

The marks for the various parts of questions are shown in round brackets: eg. (4 marks).

## SECTION 1 BELIEVING IN GOD

You must answer One question from this section

**EITHER**

A4.1. (a) Describe a religious experience (2 marks)

(b) Explain how it might lead someone to believe in God (6 marks)

(c) Explain the teachings of the Qur'an on God as creator and all-seeing. (8 marks)

(d) "The world is designed, so there must be designer who must be God." Do you agree? Give reasons for your answer, showing that you have considered another point of view. (4 marks) (total 20 marks)

**OR**

A4.2 (a) What is a miracle? (2 marks)

(b) Describe how a religious upbringing in Islam might lead someone to believe in God. (6 marks)

(c) Explain Muslim responses to the problem of evil and suffering (8 marks)

(d) "Miracles don't happen nowadays."
Do you agree? Give reasons for your answer showing that you have considered another point of view. (4 marks) (total 20 marks)

## SECTION 2 MATTERS OF LIFE AND DEATH

You must answer One question from this Section

**EITHER**

A4.3 (a) What does abortion mean? (2 marks)

(b) Describe two different Muslim attitudes to abortion. (6 marks)

(c) Explain Muslim beliefs about life after death (akhirah). (8 marks)

(d) "No Muslim could ever use contraception."
Do you agree?
Give your reasons, showing that you have considered another point of view. (4 marks) (total 20 marks).

**OR**

A4.4 (a) What does euthanasia mean? (2 marks)

(b) What is Muslim teaching on euthanasia? (6 marks)

(c) Explain Muslim beliefs about life after death. (8 marks)

(d) "Once you're dead, you're dead. There can be no life after death."

Do you agree?

Give reasons for your answer, showing that you have considered another point of view. (4 marks) (total 20 marks).

## SECTION 3 MARRIAGE AND FAMILY LIFE

You must answer One question from this section

**EITHER**

A4.5 (a) Describe one thing which must happen in a Muslim wedding ceremony. (2 marks)

(b) Give an account of Muslim teaching on sex outside marriage. (6 marks)

(c) Explain how being a Muslim might help a couple in bringing up their children. (8 marks)

(d) "Having a religious wedding ceremony makes no difference to how the marriage works out."

Do you agree?

Give reasons for your answer, showing that you have considered another point of view (4 marks) (total 20 marks).

**OR**

A4.6 (a) What is adultery? (2 marks)

(b) What is the purpose of marriage in Islam? (6 marks)

(c) Explain why there are different attitudes to divorce among Muslims. (8 marks)

(d) "It is better for children to live with both parents even if they are unhappy together, than for the parents to separate."

Do you agree?

Give reasons for your answer, showing that you have considered another point of view. (4 marks) (total 20 marks).

## SECTION 4 SOCIAL HARMONY

You must answer One question from this Section

**EITHER**

A4.7 (a) What is sexism? (2 marks)

(b) Give an outline of Muslim teachings on the roles of women and men (6 marks)

(c) What benefits does living in a multi-faith society bring to religious believers? (8 marks)

(d) "In a multi-faith society there should be no attempt to convert people."

Do you agree? Give reasons for your answer, showing that you have considered another point of view. (4 marks) (total 20 marks).

**OR**

A 4.8 (a) What is racial discrimination? (2 marks)

(b) Give an outline of Muslim teachings on racial harmony. (6 marks)

(c) Explain Muslim teachings on human rights (8 marks)

(d) "All religions treat women as second-class citizens."

Do you agree? Give reasons for your

answer, showing that you have considered another point of view. (4 marks) (total 20 marks).

## SECTION 5: OPTIONS

You must answer One question from this section

### EITHER:

A4.9.  Write an essay on Religion and the Media.  In your essay you should:

(a) Describe and explain the range and purpose of religious programmes provided by either the BBC, ITV or Channel 4. (12 marks)

(b) Give your response to the view that:

"Television always presents religious people as out of touch with the modern world."

Give reasons for your answer showing that you have considered different points of view. (8 marks) (total 20 marks).

### OR

A4.10.  Write an essay on the subject of Religion, Wealth and Poverty. In your essay you should:

(a) Describe and explain how Muslim teachings on wealth and poverty could help relieve the problems of world development. (12 marks)

(b) Give your response to the view that:

"There should be no rich religious people as long as there is poverty in the world."

Give reasons for your answer showing that you have considered another point of view. (8 marks) (total 20 marks).

### OR

A 4.11  Write an essay on the subject of Religion and the Environment. In your essay you should:

(a) Describe and explain how Muslim teachings might affect attitudes to the environment. (12 marks)

(b) Give your response to the view that:

"Religious people are no different from anyone else when it comes to using up the world's resources."

Give reasons for your answer showing that you have considered different points of view. (8 marks) (total 20 marks).

## SPECIMEN PAPER FOR UNIT B6: ISLAM

### LONDON EXAMINATIONS GCSE
Religious Studies (1478)

Paper 2 (100% examination)

Time: 1 hour 45 minutes

These Instructions are given to Candidates

Answer Five questions, one question from each section, from the unit you have studied.

In the boxes on the Answer Book, write your centre number, candidate number, the syllabus title and number, paper number, your surname and initials, signature and date.

Answer All questions in the Answer Book.

Supplementary Answer Sheets may be used.

Information for Candidates

The marks for the various parts of questions are shown in round brackets: eg (4 marks).

## SECTION 1: THE BELIEFS OF ISLAM

You must answer One question from this section

### EITHER

B6.1 (a) Name Two Muslim prophets. (2 marks)

(b) Why is Muhammad called "the seal of the prophets"? (6 marks)

(c) Describe and explain Muslim beliefs about the nature of God. (8 marks)

(d) "If God really cared about us, he would send a prophet to tell us how to live in the twenty-first century."

Do you agree?

Give reasons for your answer showing you have considered another point of view. (4 marks) (Total 20 marks)

### OR

B6.2 (a) What will the angel Israfil do to bring in the Last Day? (2 marks)

(b) Explain, with examples, what Muslims mean by shirk (6 marks)

(c) Explain Muslim teaching about holy books. (8 marks)

(d) "People only believe in God because they are frightened of what will happen to them whey they die."

Do you agree?

Give reasons for your answer showing that you have considered another point of view. (4 marks) (Total 20 marks)

## SECTION 2: AUTHORITY AND VALUES

You must answer One question from this section

### EITHER

B.6.3 (a) What does "hadith" mean? (2 marks)

(b) What is the Shari'ah and on what is it based? (6 marks)

(c) Explain why Muslims regard hadith and sunnah as second in importance to the Qur'an (8 marks)

(d) "Religious laws should have nothing to do with the way we live today."

Do you agree?

Give reasons for your answer showing you have considered another point of view. (4 marks) (Total 20 marks)

### OR

B6.4 (a) What words begin every surah of the Qur'an except surah 9?

(b) Explain why the Qur'an is so important to Muslims. (6 marks)

(c) Why do Shi'ah Muslims believe religious leaders should be related to Muhammad? (8 marks)

(d) "You don't need holy books to tell you how to live your life."

Regents Park Mosque, London.

Do you agree? Give reasons for your answer showing you have considered another point of view. (4 marks) (Total 20 marks)

## SECTION 3 SERVING GOD

You must answer One question from this Section.

### EITHER

B6.5    (a) What does the word "wudu" refer to? (2 marks)

(b) What do Muslims mean by the word ibadah? (6 marks)

(c) Describe and explain how Ramadan makes a difference to a Muslim's daily life (8 marks)

(d) "If religious people were really generous, there would be no poverty."

Do you agree?

Give reasons for your answer showing you have considered another point of view. (4 marks) (Total 20 marks)

### OR

B6.6    (a) Name two things Muslims must do in Ramadan (2 marks)

(b) Explain how the Muslim prayer ritual (salah) demonstrates a Muslim's submission to God. (6 marks)

(c) Describe and explain how Hajj (pilgrimage) helps Muslims to understand that Islam is an ummah (community). (8 marks)

(d) "All places are holy places because they are made by God, so you don't need pilgrimages."

Do you agree?

Give reasons for your answer showing you have considered another point of view. (4 marks) (Total 20 marks)

## SECTION 4 BEING A MUSLIM IN GREAT BRITAIN

You must answer One question from this section

### EITHER

B6.7 (a) What is a madrassah? (2 marks)

(b) What difficulties might a Muslim family face in bringing up their children as Muslims in Great Britain? (6 marks)

(c) Outline Muslim teaching on riba (usury, interest) and explain how it might cause problems for Muslims living in Great Britain. (8 marks)

(d) "Modest dress and the separation of the sexes would remove the problems of abortion, single parents and AIDS from Great Britain."

Do you agree?

Give reasons for your answer showing you have considered another point of view. (4 marks)  (Total 20 marks)

### OR

B6.8 (a) What does the word halal mean? (2 marks)

(b) What problems may Muslim funeral rituals cause for Muslims living in Great Britain? (6 marks)

(c) Explain how the local mosque can make it easier for Muslims in Great Britain to keep their faith. (8 marks)

(d) "It is impossible for a Muslim living in Great Britain to avoid the haram (unlawful)."

Do you agree?

Give reasons for your answer showing you have considered another point of view. (4 marks) (Total 20 marks)

## SECTION 5 OPTIONS

You must answer One question from this Section

### EITHER

B6.9 Write an essay on the Mosque. In your answer you should:

(a) describe and explain the role and function of the mosque in the local Muslim community. (12 marks)

(b) give your response to the claim that:

"You don't need to go to the mosque to be a good Muslim."

Give reasons for your answer showing that you have considered different points of view. (8 marks) (Total 20 marks)

### OR

B6.10 Write an essay on jihad. In your essay you should:

(a) describe and explain the conditions necessary for a war fought by Muslims to be called a holy war and the religious beliefs on which these are based. (12 marks)

(b) give your own response to the view that "it is dangerous to believe that people can fight a war in the name of God."

Give reasons for your answer showing that you have considered another point of view. (8 marks) (Total 20 marks)

# *The Actual Paper One Set : June 1999*

## SECTION 1. BELIEVING IN ALLAH

You must answer ONE question from this Section: EITHER question 1(a), (b), (c), (d), OR question 2(a), (b), (c), (d)

## EITHER QUESTION 1

1.(a) Give TWO names of Allah in the Qur'an. (2 marks)

(b) Give TWO reasons why some people do NOT believe in God (6 marks)

(c) Explain how a Muslim upbringing may lead a person to believe in Allah. (8 marks)

(d) "There are signs of God all around us."

Do you agree? Give reasons for your opinion, showing that you have considered another point of view. (4 marks)

## OR QUESTION 2

2.(a) Name ONE feature of a religious upbringing in a Muslim family. (2 marks)

(b) What does Surah 1 say about the nature of Allah? (6 marks)

(c) Explain how Islam responds to the problem of evil and suffering.

(d) "Miracles don't happen today."

Do you agree? Give reasons for your opinion, showing that you have considered another point of view. (4 marks)

## SECTION 2. MATTERS OF LIFE AND DEATH

You must answer ONE question from this Section: EITHER questions 3(a), (b), (c), (d), OR question 4(a), (b), (c), (d)

## EITHER QUESTION 3

3(a) What is meant by the word euthanasia? (2) marks

(b) Outline Muslim attitudes to abortion. (6 marks)

(c) Explain why Muslims believe there is life after death. (8 marks)

(d) "everyone should treat life as a gift from God."

Do you agree? Give reasons for your opinion, showing that you have considered another point of view. (4 marks)

## OR QUESTION 4

4(a) What is meant by the word resurrection? (2 marks)

(b) Outline Muslim attitude to contraception. (6 marks)

(c) Explain why some people want euthanasia to be made legal. (8 marks)

(d) "When you're dead, you're dead: that's the end of you."

Do you agree? Give reasons for your opinion, showing that you have considered another point of view. (4 marks)

## SECTION 3 MARRIAGE AND FAMILY LIFE

You must answer ONE question from this section: EITHER question 5(a), (b), (c), (d), OR question 6(a), (b), (c), (d)

## EITHER QUESTION 5

5(a) What is meant by cohabitation? (2 marks)

(b) State the teaching of Islam on relationships between the sexes. (6 marks)

(c) Explain how changing attitudes to marriage have affected family life. (8 marks)

(d) "If everyone had an arranged marriage, there would be fewer divorces."

Do you agree? Give reasons for your opinion, showing that you have considered another point of view. (4 marks)

## OR QUESTION 6

6.(a) State ONE reason for marriage according to Islam. (2 marks)

(b) Outline the teaching of Islam on divorce. (6 marks)

(c) Explain how the mosque and madrassah may help parents to bring up their children. (8 marks)

(d) "Muslims should not mix with members of the opposite sex before marriage."

Do you agree? Give reasons for your opinion, showing that you have considered another point of view. (4 marks)

## SECTION 4 SOCIAL HARMONY

You must answer ONE question from this section: EITHER question 7(a), (b), (c), (d), OR question 8(a), (b), (c), (d)

## EITHER QUESTION 7

7.(a) What does the word discrimination mean? (2 marks)

(b) Outline the work of ONE modern Muslim person or organisation opposed to racism. (6 marks)

(c) Explain some advantages of living in a multi-faith society. (8 marks)

(d) "Religion should treat men and women equally."

Do you agree? Give reasons for your opinion, showing that you have considered another point of view. (4 marks)

## OR QUESTION 8

8(a) Islam is one religion practised in the United Kingdom. Name TWO others. (2 marks)

(b) Outline Muslim attitudes to the roles of men and women (6 marks)

(c) Explain Islamic teaching about relationships with other religions. (8 marks)

(d) "Living in a multi-faith society has more advantages than disadvantages.

Do you agree? Give reasons for your opinion, showing that you have considered another point of view. (4 marks)

## SECTION 5 OPTIONS - EXTENDED WRITING

You must answer ONE question from this section: EITHER question 9(a), (b), (c), OR question 10(a), (b), (c), OR question 11(a), (b), (c)

## EITHER QUESTION 9

9. Religion and the Media

(a) Describe how a religious theme of concern to Muslims has been presented in ONE film or television drama. (4 marks)

(b) Explain why this theme is important, and whether the presentation was fair to religious people. (8 marks)

(c) "Religious programmes on television are boring."

Do you agree? Give reasons for your opinion, showing that you have considered another point of view. (8 marks)

## OR QUESTION 10

**10 Religion and Wealth and Poverty**

(a) Describe how ONE Muslim person, community or organisation helps to relieve poverty and suffering in the United Kingdom. (4 marks)

(b) Explain, with reference to the teaching of Islam, why the person, community or organisation acts in this way. (8 marks)

(c) "Charging interest and not paying zakah are the main causes of world poverty."

Do you agree? Give reasons for your opinion, showing that you have considered another point of view. (8 marks)

## OR QUESTION 11

11. Religion and the Environment

(a) Describe how Muslims help to conserve the earth's resources.

(b) Explain, with reference to the teachings of Islam, why they act in this way. (8 marks)

(c) "Muslims should set an example in fighting pollution by giving up such things as cars and dishwashers."

Do you agree? Give reasons for your opinion, showing that you have considered another point of view. (8 marks)

# The Actual Paper Two Set : June 1999

## UNIT B6. ISLAM

### Section 1. The Beliefs of Islam

You must answer One question from this Section: EITHER question 1(a), (b), (c), (d), OR question 2(a), (b), (c), (d)

### EITHER QUESTION 1

1(a) What does the word Tawhid mean? (2 marks)

(b) What do Muslims believe will happen on the Last Day? (6 marks)

(c) Explain why, according to Islam, there cannot be any prophets after Muhammad (8 marks)

(d) "It doesn't matter what you believe as long as you help other people."

Do you agree? Give reasons for your opinion, showing that you have considered another point of view. (4 marks)

### OR QUESTION 2

2(a) Name TWO prophets other than Muhammad. (2 marks)

(b) Outline the teaching of Islam about al'Qad'r. (6 marks)

(c) Explain what it means for Muslims to submit their lives to the will of Allah. (8 marks)

(d) "Only people who follow the example of the Prophet can live a good life."

Do you agree? Give reasons for your opinion, showing that you have considered another point of view. (4 marks)

## SECTION 2 AUTHORITY AND VALUES

You must answer ONE question from this Section: EITHER questions 3(a), (b), (c), (d), OR question 4(a), (b), (c), (d)

### EITHER QUESTION 3

3(a) What does the word Shari'ah mean? (2 marks)

(b) Expain the main differences between Sunni and Shi'ah Muslims (6 marks)

(c) Explain why the umma is important in Islam. (8 marks)

(d) "All people need a holy book to guide their lives."

Do you agree? Give reasons for your opinion, showing that you have considered another point of view. (4 marks)

### OR QUESTION 4

4(a) What does the word Sunnah mean? (2 marks)

(b) Describe the sources on which the Shari'ah is based. (6 marks)

(c) Expain why Muslims regard Muhammad as the perfect exemplar. (8 marks)

(d)  "There shouldn't be any different beliefs among Muslims."

Do you agree? Give reasons for your opinion, showing that you have considred another point of view. (4 marks)

## SECTION 3 SERVING ALLAH

You must answer ONE question from this Section: EITHER questions 5(a), (b), (c), (d), OR question 6(a), (b), (c), (d)

## EITHER QUESTION 5

5(a)  State ONE belief contaned in the Shahadah. (2 marks)

(b)  Describe what Muslims do before performing salah. (6 marks)

(c)  Explain why Muslims observe Ramadan. (8 marks)

(d)  "Men and women should worship Allah separately."

Do you agree? Give reasons for your opinion, showing that you have considred another point of view. (4 marks)

## OR QUESTION 6

6(a)  Name TWO places visited on hajj (2 marks)

(b)  Outline Muslim law about food. (6 marks)

(c)  How and why do Muslims pay zakah? (8 marks)

(d)  "Worshipping Allah shouldn't interfere with your daily life."

Do you agree? Give reasons for your opinion, showing that you have considred another point of view. (4 marks)

## SECTION 4.  BEING A MUSLIM IN GREAT BRITIAN

You must answer ONE question from this section: EITHER question 7(a), (b), (c), (d), OR question 8(a), (b), (c), (d)

## EITHER QUESTION 7

7(a)  What is a madrassah? (2 marks)

(b)  What guidance does the Qur'an give about dress? (6 marks)

(c)  Explain why education in the United Kingdom may cause problems for Muslims (8 marks)

(d)  "Britain would be a better place without the National Lottery."

Do you agree? Give reasons for your opinion, showing that you have considered another point of view. (4 marks)

## OR QUESTION 8

8(a)  What does the word riba mean? (2 marks)

(b)  Describe what happens at a Muslim funeral. (6 marks)

(c)  Explain how the mosque helps Muslims living in the United Kingdom. (8 marks)

(d)  "A Muslim marriage is more likely to work than a non-Muslim one."

Do you agree? Give reasons for your opinion, showing that you have considered another point of view. (4 marks)

## SECTION 5. OPTIONS - EXTENDED WRITING

You must answer ONE question from this section: EITHER question 9(a), (b), (c), OR question 10(a), (b), (c)

## EITHER QUESTION 9

9    **The Mosque**

(a)    Describe the main features of a mosque (4 marks)

(b)    Explain why a mosque has these features. (8 marks)

(c)    "Only Arabic and English should be used in British mosques."

Do you agree? Give reasons for your opinion, showing that you have considered another point of view. (4 marks)

## OR QUESTION 10

10    **Jihad**

(a)    Give an outline of Muslim beliefs about jihad. (4 marks)

(b)    Explain how these beliefs may affect a Muslim's life. (8 marks)

(c)    "Religious people should never be involved in wars."

Do you agree? Give reasons for your opinion, showing that you have considered another point of view. (8 marks)

# *Appendix*

## CONTENTS

These specimen papers are included here, so that you can gain more awareness of the kind of questions examiners ask. Although these examinations were not set using your syllabus 1478, you can see how the topics asked for could easily be answered by students who have studied Syllabus 1478. In other words, although this work-book is specific to Syllabus 1478, students could have a go at other exams if they wished, and are not limited to Syllabus 1478.

It would be perfectly possible to put the NEAB syllabi A and D together, to get a full GCSE.

The reason for plugging Syllabus 1478 is that it is the only one, up to the present time, in which a student can gain a full GCSE in Islam alone, without being obliged to offer another world religion as well (eg. Christianity, Judaism, Hinduism, Buddhism).

## (i) SPECIMEN PRACTICE PAPERS CREATED BY SR. RUQAIYYAH

### PAPER ONE

*Belief in God. Answer one of these questions.*

### EITHER

A4.1. (a) Explain what is meant by taqwa. (2).

(b) How might the experience of taqwa alter a person's life? (6).

(c) What does the Qur'an teach on the nature of Allah as the Compassionate One? (8).

(d) 'Everything follows the laws of cause and effect, so there must be a God.'

Do you agree? Give reasons for your answer, showing you have considered another point of view. (4)  (Total 20 marks)

### OR

A4.2. (a) What is khitan (circumcision)? (2).

(b) Describe how non-Muslims might come to a belief in God by observing Muslim qualities of life and character. (6).

(d) 'Those who lie cannot be Muslims.'

Do you agree? Give reasons for your answer, showing you have considered another point of view. (4)  (Total 20 marks)

*Matters of life and death. Answer one of these questions.*

**EITHER**

A4.3. (a) What does capital punishment mean? (2)

(b) Describe two different Muslim attitudes towards it. (6).

(c) Explain what Muslims believe happens to sinners in the Life to Come. (8).

(e) 'No Muslim could ever kill another person.'

Do you agree? Give reasons for your answer, showing you have considered another point of view. (4) (Total 20 marks)

**OR**

A4.4. (a) What does contraception mean? (2).

(b) Describe two Muslim attitudes concerning contraception. (6).

(c) Explain Muslim beliefs about what happens to people between the time of their death, and their resurrection on the Last Day. (8).

(e) 'People are bodies, not souls.'

Do you agree? Give reasons for your answer, showing you have considered another point of view. (4) (Total 20 marks)

*Marriage and Family life. Answer one of these questions.*

**EITHER**

A4.5. (a) Describe what is meant by a nikah contract. (2).

(b) Why do Muslims disagree with sexual freedom outside marriage? (6)

(c) Explain Muslim teachings concerning (i) attitude towards and care of the elderly, and (ii) euthanasia. (8)

(d) 'Marriage' is only a piece of paper.

Do you agree? Give reasons for your answer, showing you have considered another point of view. (4) (Total 20 marks)

**OR**

A4.6. (a) What is talaq? (2)

(b) What are the grounds for divorce in Islam? (6).

(c) Explain ways in which Islamic divorce laws have sometimes been abused and caused hardship, especially for women. (8).

(e) 'Mothers should always have custody of their children.'

Do you agree? Give reasons for your answer, showing you have considered another point of view. (4) (Total 20 marks).

*Social harmony. Answer one of these questions.*

**EITHER**

A4.7. (a) What is sexual harassment? (2)

(b) Outline Muslim teachings on the duties of men towards women. (6).

(c) How might Muslim dress-code, morals and compassion bring advantages to women in non-Muslim society? (8).

(d) 'Muslim women should all wear complete cover-ups, as in Iran and Afghanistan.' Do you agree? Give reasons for your answer, showing you have considered another point of view. (4) (Total 20 marks).

**OR**

A4.8. (a) What is alcoholism? (2).

(b) Give an outline of Muslim teachings on alcohol and drugs. (6).

(c) Explain how far Muslim teachings are 'green' issues. (8).

(d) 'Allah will take care of the poor if they pray hard enough!'

Do you agree? Give reasons for your answer, showing you have considered another point of view. (4) (Total 20 marks).

## PAPER TWO

*Beliefs. Answer one of these questions.*

### EITHER

B6.1. (a) Name two Muslim angels and state their function. (2).

(b) Explain what Islam teaches about the involvement of angels with Muslims in their lifetimes. (6).

(c) Describe and explain Muslim beliefs about the Justice of Allah, and the role of prophets in this respect. (8).

'Allah should send us a new prophet.'

Do you agree? Give reasons for your answer, showing you have considered another point of view. (4) (Total 20 marks).

### OR

B6.2. (a) What is meant by tawhid? (2).

(b) Explain how superstition, idolatry and idolising such things as astrology or such people as pop stars of sport stars break tawhid. (6).

(c) Explain what is meant by extremism. What was the Prophet's attitude towards extremism? Why do you think extremism is so disapproved? (8).

(d) 'Only 100% Muslims are really Muslims.'

Do you agree? Give reasons for your answer, showing you have considered another point of view. (4) (Total 20 marks).

*Authority and values. Answer one of these questions.*

### EITHER

B6.3. (a) What does sunnah mean? (2).

(b) Explain the sunnah of the Prophet concerning personal cleanliness. (6).

(c) How should the Prophet's sunnah govern the way we treat refugees and prisoners of war? (8).

(e) 'Muslims should always eat with their hands.'

Do you agree? Give reasons for your answer, showing you have considered another point of view. (4) (Total 20 marks).

### OR

B6.4. (a) Explain what is meant by a surah. (2).

(b) Why are the surahs not in chronological order? (6).

(c) Why is the teaching of surah al-Fatihah (the Opener) regarded as so important that it is repeated so many times during Muslim prayers? (8).

(d) 'Learning surahs in Arabic is a waste of time.'

Do you agree? Give reasons for your answer, showing you have considered another point of view. (4) (Total 20 marks).

*Serving God. Answer one of these questions.*

### EITHER

B6.5. (a) Explain what is meant by salah. (2).

(b) What are the preparations a Muslim should make for salah?

(c) Explain how sawm makes a difference to a Muslim's daily life in Ramadan? (8).

(d) 'You can be religious without praying.'

Do you agree? Give reasons for your answer, showing you have considered another point of view. (4) (Total 20 marks).

**OR**

B6.6.  (a) Explain what is meant by zakah. (2).

(b) How is zakah intended to affect the use of money in a Muslim's life? (6).

(c) Explain the Muslim teaching concerning riba, and the general reasons for the Muslim attitude towards riba in banking, business and trade. (8).

(d) 'Zakat-ul-fitr is not necessary these days.'

Do you agree? Give reasons for your answer, showing you have considered another point of view. (4) (Total 20 marks).

### Being a Muslim in Great Britain. Answer one of these questions.

### EITHER

B6.7.  (a) Explain what is meant by jihad. (2).

(b) From the point of view of EITHER a school student OR a Muslim woman at work, how could a Muslim show jihad in everyday life in Great Britain? (6).

(c) Explain what problems are faced by Muslims as regards the National Health Service, burial facilities, and food facilities. (8).

(d) 'Muslims should keep to themselves and not mix with non-Muslims.'

Do you agree? Give reasons for your answer, showing you have considered another point of view. (4) (Total 20 marks).

### OR

B6.8.  (a) Explain what is meant by haram. (2).

(b) In what ways can what is shown on national TV channels and newspapers be haram? (6).

(c) What could a Muslim who has not gone on Hajj explain to non-Muslim friends about the state of ihram, the wuquf, and the connection of the sacrifice with the Prophet Ibrahim? (8).

(d) 'The culture of immigrant Muslims is not the same thing as Islam.'

Do you agree? Give reasons for your answer, showing you have considered another point of view. (4) (Total 20 marks).

## (ii) SPECIMEN PAPER FOR LONDON EXAMINATIONS GCSE SYLLABUS 1477

### Wednesday 10, June 1998 - Morning Religious Studies

## PAPER ONE

Time: 2 Hours

(The Units tested for Islam were called Units 13 and 16. The other units concerned other world faiths).

You must answer Two questions from this Unit, One from Part A and One from Part B.

*Part A: You must answer One question from this Part: Either 13.1 or 13.2.*

### EITHER

13.1 Beliefs and Practices

(a) Give an outline of Muslim rituals connected with either birth or death. (4)

(b) Explain why Muslims believe there can be no prophets after Muhammad. (4)

(c) Give an outline of two important events on Hajj (4)

(d) Explain why Muslims fast in the month of Ramadan (4)

(e) "Believing in God makes you a better person."

Do you agree? Give reasons for your answer, showing you have considered another point of view. (4) (Total 20 marks)

### OR

13.2 Authority and Organisation

(a) Give an account of Muhammad's call to be a prophet. (4)

(b) Why is the Qur'an important for Muslims? (4)

(c) What are the sources and purpose of Shari'ah? (4)

(d) Explain two differences between Shi'a and Sunni Muslims.(4)

(e) "There should be no divisions in the brotherhood of Islam."

Do you agree? Give reasons for your answer, showing you have considered another point of view (4) (Total 20 marks)

*Part B; You must answer One question from this Part: Either 13.3 or 13.4.*

### EITHER

13.3 Social Life

(a) Give an outline of Muslim teaching about alcohol and gambling. (4)

(b) Explain why Muslim teaching about riba (interest) may be difficult for British Muslims. (4)

(f) Muslims say that humans are God's vice-regents What do they mean by this? (4)

(g) How might being a Muslim affect a person's attitude to food? (4)

(e) "You should only speak good of others"

Do you agree? Give reasons for your answer, showing you have considered another point of view. (4) (total 20 marks)

### OR

13.4 Personal Relationships

(a) Outline Muslim teaching on family life. (4)

(b) Describe Muslim attitudes to abortion (4)

(c) How might being a Muslim affect a person's attitude to relations between the sexes? (4)

(d) Explain Muslim attitudes to non-Muslims. (4)

(e) "Arranged marriages work better than love marriages."

Do you agree? Give reasons for your answer, showing you have considered another point of view. (4) ( Total 20 marks)

## PAPER TWO

Time: 2 Hours

You must answer Two questions from this Unit, One from Part A and One from Part B.

*Part A: You must answer One question from this Part: Either 16.1 or 16.2*

### EITHER

16.1 Belief in Allah and the Prophets
   (a) What does Surah 1 teach about God? (4)
   (b) Explain why Yusuf is a good example for Muslims to follow.(4)
   (c) What do Muslims believe about Isa? (4)
   (d) Explain two ways in which Muslims regard Muhammad differently from other prophets. (4)
   (e) "We need modern prophets to tell us how to live today."

Do you agree? Give reasons for your answer, showing you have considered another point of view. (4) (Total 20 marks)

### OR

16.2 Authority and Practice
   (a) How might being a Muslim affect a person's attitude to money and possessions? (4)
   (b) Muslims say that life is a service to Allah. Explain what they mean by this. (4)
   (c) Outline Muslim teaching about destiny and freewill (4)
   (d) Explain Muslim attitudes to conflict within oneself. (4)
   (e) "Everyone needs the Qur'an to tell them how to live."

Do you agree? Give reasons for your answer, showing you have considered another point of view. (4) (Total 20 marks)

*Part B: You must answer One question from this Part: Either 16.3 or 16.4*

### EITHER

16.3. The Muslim way of life.
   (a) Describe, with examples, the differences between sin and crime. (4).
   (b) Explain how law and order should be organised in an Islamic state. (4)
   (c) State how being a Muslim might affect a person's attitude to work. (4).
   (d) Explain why Muslims should not fear death. (4).
   (e) 'No Muslim should ever commit a crime.'

Do you agree? Give reasons for your answer, showing you have considered another point of view. (4). (total 20 marks).

### OR

16.4. Poverty and Suffering.
   (a) Give an outline of the work of ONE Muslim organisation which helps to relieve poverty. (4)
   (b) How do Muslims explain the causes of poverty and suffering in the world? (4).
   (c) Describe Muslim attitudes to euthanasia. (4).
   (d) Explain why Muslims should care for sick and elderly people. (4)
   (e) 'If people followed Islam properly, there would be no poverty in the world.'

Do you agree? Give reasons for your answer, showing you have considered another point of view. (4) (total 20 marks).

## (iii) SPECIMEN PAPER FOR THE NEAB SHORT COURSE FOR 1/2 GCSE

### Syllabus A - Islam

*Part A: Answer all questions in this part.*

### A1. The Mosque

(a) Explain the purpose of the following features of the mosque.
Minbar (1)
Mihrab (1)
Minaret (1)

(b) How does the existence of a mosque benefit the Muslim community? (3)

### A2. Beliefs and Sources of Authority

(a) Explain what Muslims understand by the following:
Ummah (2)
Jihad (2)
Shari'ah (2)

(b) Outline Muslim teaching about wealth and poverty. (4)

### A3. Personal and Community Life

(a) Explain, with examples, the difference between halal and haram. (4)

(b) What does the Qur'an teach about drinking alcohol? (2)

(c) "The way religious people behave is much more important that what they eat or drink."

Do you agree? Give reasons for your answer, showing that you have thought about more than one point of view. (5).

### A4. Matters of Life and Death

(a) Explain Muslim teaching on the following:

Abortion (3)
Euthanasia (3)

(b) "We can't relive the past, so it's no use visiting holy places."

Do you agree? Give reasons for your answer, showing that you have thought about more than one point of view. (5)

*Part B: Answer all questions in this part.*

### B5. The Hajj

Figure 1 The Route taken by Haji Pilgrims is given

(a) Describe what happens and explain the importance of what happens during the Hajj at the points marked A and B on Figure 1.
A The Place Safa (4)
B The Place Mina (4)

## B6. Prayer

Look at Figure 3. These objects are used in connection with prayer.

(a) Explain the purpose of each object.
A The Prayer Mat (2)
B The Subha or Tasbih(2)

## B7. The Pillars

(a) Look at Figure 2, (a diagram naming the 5 Pillars in Arabic) and then explain why Shahadah is often said to be the most important pillar. (5)

(b) "Prayer is like talking to someone who does not answer."

Do you agree? Give reasons for your answer, showing that you have thought about more than one point of view. (5)

*Part C: Answer all questions in this part.*

## C8. Family Relationships

(a) What is the role and status of married women in Islam? (6)

(b) Explain how the rights of women are affected by Islamic teaching about:

(i) modesty.

(ii) polygamy,

(iii) divorce (9)

(c) "Having a strong religion within the family helps young Muslims to have high moral standards in their own life."

Do you agree? Give reasons for your answer, showing that you have thought about more than one point of view. (5)

## C9. Festivals

(a) Describe how Muslims celebrate either 'Id ul-Fitr or ' Id ul-Adha (8)

(b) Explain the religious origin and meaning of the activities that take place at the festival you have chosen. (7)

(c) "Festivals are for people to have a good time. The religious meaning is forgotten."

Do you agree? Give reasons for your answer, showing that you have thought about more than one point of view. (5)

## (iv) SPECIMEN PAPER FOR THE NEAB SHORT COURSE FOR 1/2 GCSE

*Syllabus D - Thinking about God and Morality*

(You could put this together with the previous paper, Syllabus A, and gain a full GCSE).

*Part A: Answer all the questions in this section.*

## A1. Ways of making moral decisions.

(a) 'Taking supermarkets' property isn't wrong,' says priest. An Anglican priest explained that he would have no conscience about taking things from supermarkets without paying for them. It is taking resources from the rich and giving them to the poor, something which is badly needed, he claimed.'

Explain whether a person who believes in absolute morality would agree with the Anglican priest. (2).

(b) (i) What is a person's 'conscience'? (2)
(ii) Besides 'conscience', state two other sources of moral superiority for a religious believer. (2).

(c) Show how the teachings of one religious tradition would help a believer to decide whether 'taking resources from the rich and giving them to the poor' is right or wrong. (4).

(f) 'It is never right to steal.' Do you agree? Give reasons for your answer..(3).

## A2. Sex, marriage and divorce.

(Pictures are shown of a Christian couple and a Muslim couple, both of mixed races)

(a) Choose one religious tradition that you have studied. Explain what responsibilities husbands and wives take on when they marry in this tradition. (6).

(b) Choose a different religion from that chosen in (a)
  (i) In this tradition, how are parents involved in the choice of their children's marriage partners? (2)
  (ii) What attitudes are taken by this tradition towards mixed race marriages? (2).

(c) 'For a marriage to be successful, the couple must share the same religious faith.'

Do you agree? Give reasons for your answer. (3).

## A3. Wealth and Poverty

(a) (A cartoon is shown with a rich person in a limousine saying 'What rubbish' about a man sleeping rough in a doorway).
  (i) What kind of inequality is referred to in the cartoon? (1).
  (ii) What point is the cartoonist making about wealth and poverty? (1).

(b) Outline the teachings of one religious tradition about the personal use of wealth. (4).

(c) How might religious believers put these teachings into practice? (4).

(d) 'It is wrong to be rich in a world where poverty exists.'

Do you agree? Give reasons for your answer. (2).
(Total altogether - 40 marks)

*Section B. Answer ONE question from this section.*

## EITHER

## B4. Abortion
A pregnant woman has been told that she will have a severely handicapped child. She is advised to consider an abortion.

(a) (i) Explain why believers in one religious tradition are against abortion in the situation outlined above. (5).
  (ii) Explain why believers in a different religious tradition think that abortion may be justified in the same situation. (4).

(b) State and explain two circumstances other than the example above, when abortion is regarded by some religious believers as acceptable. (6).

(c) 'If a baby is not wanted by its mother there are many people who would adopt it. It should not be killed.'

Do you agree? Give reasons for your answer, showing that you have thought about more than one point of view. (5) (total 20 marks).

## OR

## B5. Capital Punishment

(a)
  (i) Explain the reasons why some religious believers think that capital punishment is morally wrong. (5).
  (ii) Explain the reasons why some

religious believers think that capital punishment is morally justified. (4)

(b) How would the sacred texts of two different religious traditions help believers decide whether capital punishment was right or wrong? (6).

(c) 'Murderes can never change. They should be executed.'

Do you agree? Give reasons for your answer, showing that you have thought about more than one point of view. (5) (total 20 marks).

## OR

## B6. The Individual in Society

(a) Outline and explain the teachings about service to others is two religious traditions. (9).

(b) How does one of these religious traditions put its teachings into practice in the community? (6).

(c) 'People who spend their time doing things for others without deepening their spiritual lives will have nothing of real value to give to others.'

Do you agree? Give reasons for your answer, showing that you have thought about more than one point of view. (5) (total 20 marks).

## B7. Prejudice and Discrimination.

(a) Choose two different religious traditions and outline the teachings of each about prejudice and discrimination. (9).

(b) How do people in one religious tradition apply their beliefs about prejudice and discrimination in practical ways? (6)

(c) 'By sending their children to religious schools, some religious believers are encouraging them to be prejudiced against others.'

Do you agree? Give reasons for your answer, showing that you have thought about more than one point of view. (5) (total 20 marks).

*Answer to the Jesus Quiz in Unit 17*

The wrong statements were
numbers 2, 4, 5, 8 and 12.

**Tell Me About**
# HAJJ
What the Hajj Is, Why It's So Important
and What It Teaches Me

SANIYASNAIN KHAN

**Tell Me About**
THE PROPHET
# MUHAMMAD
What the Prophet's Message Is, Why His Life is So Important
and What He Teaches Me

SANIYASNAIN KHAN

**Tell Me About**
THE PROPHET
# MUSA

*The Blessings of*
# RAMADAN

Javed Ali

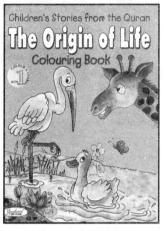

Children's Stories from the Quran
## The Origin of Life
Colouring Book

Children's Stories from the Quran
## The Ark of Nuh
and the Great Flood
Sticker Book

Children's Stories from the Quran
## The Two Sons of Adam
COLOURING BOOK

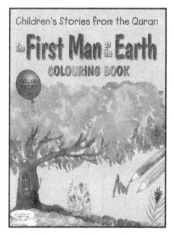

Children's Stories from the Quran
## The First Man on the Earth
COLOURING BOOK

Children's Stories from the Quran
## The Ark of Nuh and the Animals
COLOURING BOOK

# LIFE BEGINS
Quran Stories for Little Hearts

# THE FIRST MAN
Quran Stories for Little Hearts

# THE ARK OF NUH
Quran Stories for Little Hearts

# THE BRAVE BOY
Quran Stories for Little Hearts

# THE TWO BROTHERS
Quran Stories for Little Hearts

# ALLAH'S BEST FRIEND
Quran Stories for Little Hearts

# HONEYBEES
THAT BUILD PERFECT COMBS

HARUN YAHYA

# THE STORY OF THE PROPHET YUSUF

*The*
## Story of the
## Prophet Nuh
Quran Stories for Tiny Tots

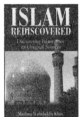
ISBN 81-87570-40-7

ISBN 81-87570-69-5

ISBN 81-87570-22-9

ISBN 81-87570-46-6

ISBN 81-87570-85-7

ISBN 81-87570-38-5

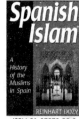
ISBN 81-87570-57-1

ISBN 81-87570-25-3

ISBN 81-87570-20-2

ISBN 81-87570-55-5

ISBN 81-87570-56-3

ISBN 81-87570-99-7

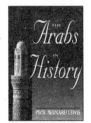
ISBN 81-87570-59-8

ISBN 81-87570-23-7

ISBN 81-87570-60-1

ISBN 81-87570-37-7

ISBN 81-87570-62-8

ISBN 81-87570-18-0

ISBN 81-87570-63-6

ISBN 81-87570-68-7

ISBN 81-87570-09-1

ISBN 81-87570-92-3

ISBN 81-87570-20-7

ISBN 81-87570-93-1

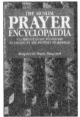
ISBN 81-85063-29-X

ISBN 81-85063-34-6

ISBN 81-85063-27-3

ISBN 81-85063-30-3

ISBN 81-85063-25-7

ISBN 81-85063-26-5

ISBN 81-87570-43-1

ISBN 81-85063-11-7

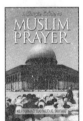
ISBN 81-87570-26-1

ISBN 81-87570-71-7

ISBN 81-87570-45-8

ISBN 81-87570-53-9

# BOOKS BY HARUN YAHYA

ISBN 81-87570-05-9

ISBN 81-87570-27-X

ISBN 81-87570-02-4

ISBN 81-87570-67-9

ISBN 81-87570-52-0

ISBN 81-87570-61-X

ISBN 81-87570-16-4

ISBN 81-87570-15-6

ISBN 81-87570-13-X

ISBN 81-87570-83-0

ISBN 81-87570-90-7

ISBN 81-87570-14-8

ISBN 0-7195-5143-9

ISBN 81-85063-38-9

ISBN 81-87570-21-0

ISBN 81-87570-17-2